Childhood Citizenship, Governance and Policy

Debates about children's rights not only concern those things that children have a right to have and to do but also our broader social and political community, and the moral and political status of the child within it.

This book examines children's rights and citizenship in the USA, UK and Australia and analyses the policy, law and sociology that govern the transition from childhood to adulthood. By examining existing debates on childhood citizenship, the author pursues the claim that childhood is the most heavily governed period of a liberal individual's life, and argues that childhood is an intensely monitored period that involves a 'politics of becoming adult'. Drawing upon case studies from the USA, the UK and Australia, this concept is used to critically analyse debates and policy concerning children's citizenship, criminality and sexuality. In doing so, the book seeks to uncover what informs and limits how we think about, talk about, and govern children's rights in liberal societies.

This book will be of interest to students and scholars of political science, governance, social policy, ethics, politics of childhood and public policy.

Sana Nakata is Lecturer in Political Science at the University of Melbourne, Australia.

Routledge studies in governance and public policy

Childhood Citizenship, Governance and Policy

The politics of becoming adult

Sana Nakata

Routledge
Taylor & Francis Group

LONDON AND NEW YORK

First published 2015
by Routledge
2 Park Square, Milton Park, Abingdon, Oxon OX14 4RN

and by Routledge
711 Third Avenue, New York, NY 10017

First issued in paperback 2017

Routledge is an imprint of the Taylor & Francis Group, an informa business

British Library Cataloguing in Publication Data
A catalogue record for this book is available from the British Library

Library of Congress Cataloging in Publication Data
Nakata, Sana.
Childhood citizenship, governance and policy: the politics of becoming adult / Sana Nakata.
    pages cm. – (Routledge studies in governance and public policy)
    Includes bibliographical references and index.
    1. Children's rights. 2. Citizenship. I. Title.
    HQ789.N34 2015
    323.3'52–dc23   2014041460

ISBN 13: 978-1-138-50491-2 (pbk)
ISBN 13: 978-0-415-74845-2 (hbk)

Typeset in Times New Roman
by Wearset Ltd, Boldon, Tyne and Wear

For Martin and Vicky,
who made everything possible

Contents

Acknowledgements

The research for this book was undertaken as part of the PhD programme at the School of Social and Political Sciences, The University of Melbourne. I am indebted to the many students and scholars in its halls and classrooms for their encouragement, friendship and good humour. I am especially grateful for the patience and trust of my supervisor, Professor Adrian Little, without whom it would have been too easy to retreat to the comfort and safety of my liberal disposition and the argument that follows in these pages would not exist.

I wish to acknowledge my father, Professor Martin Nakata, whose work as an Indigenous Australian scholar has had a profound impact on who I am, what I study and how I think. In 1997, he became the first Torres Strait Islander to receive a PhD. That thesis punctuates memories and experiences of my own childhood, in which his study of the Haddon Anthropological Expedition to the Torres Straits in the late 1800s and its lasting impact on Indigenous knowledge and education provided me with the political context and critical standpoint from which to make sense of my world as a young Islander girl in the classroom. I am grateful to him and my mother, to his mother, to his grandfather and his great-grandfather who together represent four generations who have negotiated and advocated for the education of Islanders since colonization. Their efforts have made everything possible.

I also wish to acknowledge Dr Daniel Bray, whose love, joy and pedantic attention to detail has helped to wrestle both this book and our son, Lucas, into existence.

Finally, I must thank the editorial staff at Routledge who have been patient and helpful at every stage, and to the anonymous reviewers who provided rigorous and helpful comment on crucial sections of this manuscript. Parts of the research in this book have been presented at the annual Australian Political Studies Association conference in 2010 and 2012, and at the sixth Global Conference on Pluralism, Inclusion and Citizenship in 2011.

Introduction

In 1957, Elizabeth Eckford, a 15-year-old African American high school student, attempted to enter the newly desegregated Little Rock High School in Arkansas. Flanked by state troopers, the National Armed Guard and shouting racists, she was eventually ushered into the school through a side entrance. Heated debate followed about whether it had been appropriate for a child to be placed in the middle of such a violent and explicitly political fight. In 1993, a two-year-old boy was abducted and beaten to death by two other young boys in England. The murder of James Bulger and subsequent trial of Jon Venables and Robert Thompson sparked public controversy driven by a deep moral outrage torn between two difficult realities: the child as victim and the child as murderer. In 2008, a photography exhibition of Australian artist Bill Henson included images of a naked girl on the cusp of adolescence. The exhibition was cancelled and the New South Wales police seized a number of photographs to assist with investigations into possible criminal acts. The subject of investigation concerned an adolescent girl's ability to consent to the photograph and the right, if any, of a parent to provide consent on her behalf. No charges were laid.

Each of these public controversies raise different questions: does a child have a right to a public education? Should young people be held fully responsible for criminal acts? Can a child provide consent? Can a parent on his or her behalf? These examples also elicit very different kinds of questions: what informs our discomfort with a child entering a public and political space? What makes children less culpable than adults for their crimes? What does consent have to do with the alleged sexual exploitation of a child? Directly, debates about "children's rights" are about those things that children have a right to have and to do. Indirectly, debates about children's rights are also about our broader social and political community, and the moral and political status of the child within it. These three public controversies produce two very different sets of questions. The first set poses children's rights problems. The second set poses problems with children's rights problems: a distinctly political problem about how we understand, discuss and debate childhood, children and their rights.

This book pursues the second set of questions, and argues that while children's political subjectivity may remain deeply contested, there does exist a form of children's politics that informs not only how we think, talk and argue about children's rights but how we think about the concept of the political itself. To do this, the book adopts a post-structuralist perspective as a critical position from which to re-read the children's rights discourse as a paternalistic paradigm bound to an unquestioned liberal rationality. The first part of this book begins by outlining this paradigm, this rationality, and then explaining the post-structuralist approach as a method for critical inquiry that is explicitly and unapologetically political in its purpose.

Claiming rights can be political in two respects: first, to be able to successfully claim rights suggests that you already have a political subjectivity that makes for the possibility of being a rights-holder; second, to claim rights in the first place requires the staging of a political act and not merely the exercise of a policy mechanism. In these two respects, children raise an interesting problematic: children are not generally regarded as having any political character, they do not often make rights claims for themselves, but rather other adults do so on their behalf;[1] for children to act politically is, for some, an injustice in itself. This is why Hannah Arendt declared that it was 'unfortunate and even unjust ... that the events at Little Rock should have had such an enormous echo in public opinion',[2] prompting her to ask:

> Have we now come to the point where it is the children who are being asked to change or improve the world? And do we intend to have our political battles fought out in the school yards?[3]

Viewed in this way, advocating rights that require the recognition of children as political subjects or even agents is regrettable.[4] And yet, a rights-holder without a recognized political subjectivity is also at risk of impotence: unable to claim the rights that they have at the very moments those rights are denied or breached. This book begins with the premise that we cannot fully understand the debate about children's rights, or the tensions within it, without an explicitly political perspective: one that studies not just the child, but the politics of being a child – a subject whose political status is characterized by its ambiguity, indeterminacy, inconclusiveness and vagueness.[5]

Who is the child?

The most comprehensive and coherent discourse that seeks to answer this question is the interdisciplinary field of 'childhood studies', comprised of knowledge about children across studies in sociology, psychology, medicine, education, cultural studies, history, law and criminology, philosophy and political science. And to the question of who is the child, each of these disciplines and studies within them provide a different perspective. Adult understandings of childhood and children simply do not belong to any one discipline. Understandings of what childhood is, and who children are, come to form part of a society's "common sense": informed as much by adults' own memories and experiences of being a child as anything learned from the formal disciplines of knowledge. We know that children are physically smaller than adults, less intellectually developed and emotionally immature; at birth they are dependents in the fullest sense. Childhood is revealed as a stage of life, during which most children will grow into physically, intellectually and emotionally independent persons. Childhood is the period in which children *become* adults. This characterization of childhood and children is far from controversial. However, this "common sense" of childhood is ruptured by examples of children who do not easily fit this simple characterization: child criminals, child soldiers, child geniuses, child carers and so on. Briefly, I offer two lenses through which we might see alternative understandings of childhood and children. First, an historical lens, in which it is possible to identify a pre-modern, modern and postmodern "child". Second, a political lens, in which it is possible to regard children as apolitical, pre-political, or political subjects. By exploring these, it will be evident that I am part of what sociologist Michael Wyness observes is now the main way of conceptualizing childhood: as a social construction, that is both historically and culturally contingent.[6]

What I term a "pre-modern" understanding of childhood might be regarded as an absence of any understanding of childhood whatsoever. In his seminal text, *Centuries of Childhood*, Philippe Ariès proclaims that; 'In medieval society, the idea of childhood did not exist.'[7] Ariès conclusions are based largely upon artistic representations of childhood. He claims that; 'Medieval art until about the twelfth century did not know childhood or did not attempt to portray it.'[8] He emphasizes that this lack of understanding of childhood is not to be equated with the neglect of, or disinterest in, children, but rather that children were not thought of in altogether different terms than adults. This is what Wyness describes as a 'lack of sentiment'.[9] Indeed, David Archard also identifies Ariès' French use of the term *sentiment*, rather than *concept*, emphasizing the absence of an "awareness" or "feeling" toward childhood, rather than the absence of a concept of childhood altogether.[10] This leads Archard to reject the possibility that there could ever be, in any historical moment or cultural space, no concept of childhood.[11] As a result, he goes on to distinguish between a concept of childhood, which identifies a difference between children and adults, and conceptions of childhood, which reflect alternative perspectives and feelings about how children are different from adults. However, it remains that a pre-modern concept of childhood, as is articulated in Ariès' thesis, suggests the absence of a concept of childhood altogether.

Second, and what Ariès' thesis is most highly regarded for, is a modern concept of childhood. The modern age, Ariès suggests on the opening page of his book, has seen our 'civic personality … more precisely expressed by the coordinates of our birth than by our surname'.[12] That is, our age is a greater statement of who we are in this life, than any other fact of our being. Again this conclusion is drawn from his analysis of European art: where children are represented as little more than miniature adults in medieval times, and only slowly begin to be represented as possessing distinctly child-like features. Further, the age of subjects in painting comes to be identified on the canvas itself, alongside the name of the subjects.[13] Ariès goes on to offer two distinct conceptions of childhood that emerge: that of the innocent, and that of a blank-slate.[14] Ariès suggests that in the modern age, it has come to be that 'not only the child's future but his presence and his very existence are of concern: the child has taken a central place in the family'.[15] I argue that whatever genuine concern exists for children as children, it does not displace or lessen the adjunct concern for children's future-adult lives. The child as a *future-adult subject* is evident across debates and discussions of children and childhood.[16] This newfound interest in a child's 'presence and very existence' makes the modern move toward "knowing" children in definitive terms possible. It is only once you have childhood as a distinct and separate period of life, that it is possible to make this the subject of knowledge: of science, of biology and psychology, of sociology, of politics and rights claims. With the Enlightenment, a conception of childhood and institutions of education for children emerged and age began to be employed as a mechanism for separating classes.[17] The weight of Ariès' work lies in its identification of the "invention" of childhood and how it came to be a central concept in the configuring of family and social life.[18]

In the twentieth century, this modern understanding of childhood developed not only in sociological terms, but biological and psychological terms. In 1923, Jean Piaget published *The Language and Thought of the Child*, establishing what is known as stage theory, which has become a key foundation of developmental psychology.[19] As Piaget writes on the opening page of his later book, *The Psychology of Intelligence*, 'Every psychological explanation comes sooner or later to lean on either biology or on logic (or on sociology, but this in turn leads to the same alternatives).'[20] And so it is that 'we must start from this dual nature of intelligence as something both biological and logical'.[21] A concept of childhood, as a distinct time of life, allows children to become the subject of these inquiries. The conclusions that Piaget draws establishes a science for knowing children as biological and psychological facts. The developmental model of understanding childhood positions children as "becomings" in fact, not just in theory. As a result, the discourse that emerged from this tradition allows foundational truth claims to be made about childhood.[22]

Leading children's rights scholar, David Archard criticizes the work of Piaget on two main grounds: first, its Western logic; second, its empirical basis. Piaget's study of children was limited to European children, and was largely undertaken in schoolrooms. Empirically, Archard counters that 'children arguably possess some crucial competencies long before Piaget says they do'.[23] Archard's evidence of this, however, is minor and incomplete when placed alongside the lifetime of Piaget's work and the discipline of developmental psychology it fathered. Archard's relatively undeveloped empirical basis makes it difficult to fully counter Piaget's claims. For this reason, Archard's criticism is persuasive not for its empirical challenge to Piaget, but its conceptual challenge. Piaget's stage theory is the articulation of an abstracted, "normal" child. It cannot speak to the experiences of any given individual child, and yet it remains as the dominant device for doing so. Indeed, stage theory, as originally articulated by Piaget, identifies very distinct stages of child development.[24] Michael Wyness summarises these as a "sensorimotor" stage (age 0–2); "pre-operational" stage (age 2–7); "concrete operations" stage (age 7–12); and, "formal operative" (age 12–14).[25] Today, these stages of childhood are reflected in the compulsory education system of Western nations. From zero to two years of age, many children remain in the care of a family member or day care; from two to seven, early childhood education begins at day care, Kindergarten, preschool and early primary school; from seven to 12, children are in primary school; with high school commencing at 12, and compulsory education ending at 15. This developmental theory was informed by, and reflected, the work of Charles Darwin in his *The Origin of Species*[26] and elsewhere.[27] That is, this child development theory was established at a time when the development of humanity as a whole was being studied.[28] The development of the child, it could be said, represented in a single lifespan the evolution of the whole of humankind.

If a modern understanding of childhood allows children to become the "subject" of knowledge and of study, then the postmodern understanding of childhood is one that seeks to reveal this knowledge of children as socially, historically and culturally contingent. It reveals childhood as social constructions. This postmodern perspective allows us to view Piaget's claim that 'these schoolrooms [in which he conducted his research for *The Language and Thought of the Child*] supply a first-class field of observation for everything connected with the study of the social life and of the language of childhood' as deeply problematic.[29] It is problematic because Piaget regards the schoolroom as the natural social environment for the child, and the concept of childhood as a given. This is despite the lengths he goes to in the preface to the first edition of the book not to succumb to 'preconceived ideas' or to 'unwittingly subscribe' to existing logics and epistemologies of psychology and intelligence.[30] By the time Piaget undertakes his research, childhood is not an idea, but a natural state of being that could be "known". A postmodern perspective, which views childhood as socially constructed, offers this further critique of Piaget's highly influential work.

Wyness identifies some important limits to the socially constructed perspective upon childhood. Rather than just problematizing the social, historical and cultural meanings that are attached to childhood, he argues that social constructivism in childhood sociology prioritizes social meanings over biological meanings of childhood.[31] In this sense, reducing childhood to a set of contingent meanings risks overlooking the biological differences between children and adults altogether, not simply questioning the meaning attributed to those physical differences. Adopting a postmodern or socially constructivist perspective of childhood risks 'interpret[ing] all differences between adults and children as works of imagination'.[32] However, rather than reject outright that children are different from adults, it is possible to be mindful of what meanings are employed and attached to this difference; for example, by acknowledging that children are defined, in part, by their smaller physicality than adults, at least until puberty. What is important is that we do not attach to this difference the social meaning of "vulnerability" as a natural condition of childhood: smaller physicality is not necessarily analogous to vulnerability. Further, to attach a physical vulnerability that exists due to a size differential is not the same as attaching physical vulnerability to the arbitrary category of age. Put simply, a postmodern perspective takes as a primary task the avoidance of conflating physicality and age as the natural condition of vulnerability. Children may also be viewed as vulnerable from an emotional and rational standpoint, on the basis of their lesser experience and intellectual immaturity. This suggests that children cannot, in their own ways, exercise control and influence. A tantrum-throwing child in the lolly aisle has thwarted many a parent in the supermarket. Is the child really the vulnerable person in this picture? On the one hand, no, it is the position of the adult that is compromised by the child's behaviour; on the other hand, a child might throw a tantrum in this context because they are more vulnerable to the advertising strategies of lolly manufacturers than adults: bright colours, toys and recognizable cartoon characters placed at child-height. Yet again, does this vulnerability exist because children are less able to process these strategies? Or, are adults vulnerable to exactly the same strategy, in exactly the same place, at exactly the same time, only at a different height? There are no definitive answers to these sorts of questions, whether in the context of lollies or more serious debates affecting children. This book is much attuned to the real ways in which children are different from adults, but maintains a postmodern reluctance to attach any fixed and natural meanings to this difference.[33]

David Archard also grapples with the desire to address the "real" differences of children, without being overly definitive about what children are. Michael Wyness describes Archard's approach as a "synthesis", but in fact, it is less a synthesis than a re-description of terms.[34] Archard distinguishes between a "concept" of childhood, which he intends to capture an *idea* of childhood (as different from adulthood) and "conceptions" of childhood, which captures the *sentiment* of childhood (meanings of childhood).[35] This, he argues, is a more accurate interpretation of Ariès' thesis.[36] I follow in Archard's approach, by discussing throughout this book conceptions of childhood to reflect alternative ways of understanding what childhood is, and who children are. However, I do so without the explicit focus on the child as the subject of my analysis. Instead, I take the knowledge produced about and around childhood as the key site for analysis.

Just as we can think about childhood and children through pre-modern, modern and postmodern lenses, so too can we think about children as apolitical, pre-political or political beings. To regard children as apolitical is to view them as having no political subjectivity. In this sense, children are not the subject of politics, but may remain a subject of policy. Insofar as they may be the subject of policy, they are usually only so within the frame of the family unit rather than as independent subjects. Further, the concept of children understood as existing only in the family unit, speaks to the privatized life of children: they do not belong to the public realm in which politics takes place. A pre-political perspective of children, regards them as "citizens-in-making"; that is, as people who will one day have a political subjectivity and may be required to act in political ways. This perspective emphasizes childhood as a time for civic education and for practicing the skills required for politics in age-appropriate contexts. A political perspective of children suggests that children already are political subjects and even, perhaps, political agents.[37] This perspective informs especially the thinking of child liberationists, who argue that children should have the full gamut of civil and political rights available to adults.[38]

The distinction between a pre-political and political view of the child may also be described as the distinction between a becoming and a "being". This language is used across discussions of children's rights, and was the subject of particular criticism by Barbara Arneil, who considers becoming a function of liberal political theory more broadly.[39] The distinction between viewing the child as a becoming or a being is illuminated by the following example provided by David Archard:

> If, for instance, there is a right to healthcare the child might be said to have this because it is good for the child to be healthy and flourishing, sound of mind and body. But you might also think that a healthy child will develop, all being well, into a healthy adult. It is the future-adult who has the right when a child to be healthy. I [Archard] am thus glad that I was properly cared for as a child so that I could grow up into the hale and healthy person I now am. We could of course think that the child has the right to both in her own right as a child and in the person of her future self. However, these are two very different ways to think of the same right.[40]

Indeed, they are two very different ways of thinking about the subject of children's rights: one as a "becoming", the other as a being; one as a future-adult, one as a present-child. In this book, I argue that it is the child as a future-adult subject that is the central focus of children's rights debates. Further, I argue that any politics around childhood is necessarily oriented toward this future-adult subject. This is what I characterize in the Conclusion of this book, as a politics of becoming adult.

The Western, liberal lens of this project

It is necessary to acknowledge that this project is firmly situated within a Western knowledge system. As a result, the children and childhoods to which it speaks, are confined to the Western, developed world. More specifically, I only draw on debates from Australia, the United Kingdom and the United States of America. This orientation means that when I speak of children and childhood, it is not as an absolute or universal category that can speak of a Sudanese child in a Kenyan refugee camp and an Australian child in an expensive, exclusive private school as the same. Like adults, children's experiences are determined by much more than their age: sexuality, sex and gender, race and ethnicity, religion, class, geography, language and physical (dis)abilities are just some of the many factors (natural and constructed) that determine our subjectivity. This book is interested in age and in childhood as the conceptual opposite (in Western thought) of adulthood. In order to attend to this interest, I leave other characteristics to the side.

Throughout this book, I will refer to liberal rights, liberal political philosophy and liberalism. It is important to acknowledge that liberal thought represents diverse, varied and sometimes conflicting ideas. In exploring children's rights, this book identifies a particular tension between two competing sets of rights claims: a protectionist mode and autonomy mode. These rights claims emerge from a Western literature of children's rights that is grounded in the liberal international human rights regime. The choice to explore Kantian liberalism in this project is an explicit attempt to connect the tension between protection and autonomy (discussed in Chapter 1) to the broader liberal political philosophy (discussed in Chapter 2) that makes this tension possible. Further, when I refer specifically to a future-adult subject, and sometimes more specifically a future-adult citizen, I am referring to a Kantian liberal ideal: one that views autonomy, premised upon reason and maturity, as the source of individual Enlightenment and society's Enlightenment.[41] I understand this ideal as a problematic, and later draw on Barry Hindess' notion of liberal *unfreedom* to capture how this ideal problematizes liberal citizenship: it is an ideal that requires citizens to be free to realize liberty as a key characteristic of liberal societies, but also governed sufficiently enough that they do not undermine the liberal state.[42] The liberal future-adult citizen of this book is a consenting citizen, both free and limited. In this sense, I am employing the liberal future-adult citizen as a heuristic device to explore how reason, maturity and autonomy limit how we think not only about children, but also about citizenship and the concept of the political itself.

Rights and children

In 1973, Hillary Rodham (now Clinton) argued that the 'phrase "children's rights" is a slogan in search of a definition'.[43] In 1989, this phrase was given a defining framework in the United Nations Convention on the Rights of the Child (CRC).[44] Today, it is the most ratified international treaty in history. Children are also the subjects of human rights detailed in other international treaties. However, the CRC attends to rights that are specific to children. The Preamble to the CRC explains that this is necessary because:

> the child, by reason of his physical and mental immaturity, needs special safeguards and care, including appropriate legal protection, before as well as after birth.[45]

The international human rights regime suggests there is little doubt that children are the bearers of rights. It is the case that all children possess the same human rights as adults, and also possess particular rights as children due to the immaturity this status assumes. However, while children have been ascribed rights by the international human rights regime, it is much more difficult to establish whether children possess these rights in any meaningful sense. As Jacqueline Bhabha argues in her analysis of the rights of stateless children, the international human rights regime presents an "enforcement gap" when it comes to children.[46] The widespread commitment to the CRC might be explained by Bhabha's observation that:

> states knowingly sign on to human rights instruments without any serious political commitment to changing their practices, precisely because they realise that there is so little accountability and that the diplomatic kudos of signing is not offset by any corresponding costs for non-enforcement.[47]

In short, children may possess a broad range of human rights, not in spite of a lack of enforceable protections for those rights but because of a lack of enforceable protections. Children, in this sense, have rights because they cannot enforce or protect the rights that they have. The lack of enforceability of international human rights regimes is, of course, not limited to children. The lack of enforceability of human rights is what prompted Hannah Arendt to describe them as the rights of the rightless,[48] a notion that Jacques Rancière extends in his thinking around the 'rights of those who have not the rights that they have'.[49] Despite the premise that children possess all human rights within the liberal rights discourse, a number of scholars have articulated a distinction between children and adult rights. In the case of Arendt and Rancière, children present as rightless: unable to be seen and heard in their own right within the political sphere.[50] For children's rights advocates there is still scope for, and a language with which to articulate, children's rights as a coherent and enforceable concept.

Joel Feinberg identifies three classes of rights that help inform how we might think about children as the bearers of rights. First, liberty rights (what I describe as autonomy rights) belong only to adults. These rights are based on the capacity to make decisions. As such, they are near impossible for children to claim. Even if children could claim rights, it is important to be mindful that rights do not always achieve better outcomes. A right to vote does not immediately alleviate systemic and intergenerational poverty, for example. Yet, for many marginalized and oppressed social groups, such a right has been utilized to create further social and political pressure for justice. Second, welfare rights belong with both adults and children. These rights provide social goods that are necessary for the overall welfare of society: an accessible health care system, education and so on. And, third, protection rights belong only to children.[51] These are rights that secure children access to goods they are unable to secure for themselves. While adults may also be entitled to these goods, they are expected to secure them for themselves.

Arguably, children do not require liberty (or what I describe as autonomy) rights, as children have parents and guardians who act and make decisions on their behalf, in their "best interests". Unfortunately, children's rights debates are premised upon the many examples in which children's best interests[52] are often not being thought about, much less acted upon. If all children had parents, guardians and other adults always acting in their own best interests, they would never need rights, and we could all rest easy in the knowledge that children everywhere are going to bed each night, clothed, fed, sheltered, loved[53] and unharmed. We know this is not the case. The purpose of human rights is to ensure that when we are not being afforded respect and dignity, we are able to argue that we have suffered a moral (if not legal) wrong deserving of redress.[54] For children, this is very difficult. David Archard claims that children, as human beings, have a certain moral status. On the basis of this moral status, he argues that it must be possible for there to be some conception of children's rights. From this perspective the question becomes, 'what kind of rights can be claimed for children on the basis of their moral status alone?' Human rights are an obvious candidate. Yet, as mentioned, children's human rights are difficult to enforce.[55]

One of the central questions of the children's rights discourse is whether or not children can be rights-holders. David Archard considers this question and, ultimately, argues that children can have rights, but that these rights need to be mediated according to the actual capacities of children and the specific problems children face in which the need for rights emerge.[56] Martin Guggenheim argues that rights are not at all helpful for children.[57] While Michael Freeman argues that children's rights are not taken seriously enough.[58] Onora O'Neill calls for a theory of obligations as a more useful way of conceptualizing questions and problems of children's lives.[59] For O'Neill, children have a unique remedy available to them that no other social group does: they can grow up.[60] Children have been extended formal rights through international human rights regimes, and in various protections that exist in domestic legal regimes. I accept that these rights are, in the main, unenforceable rights and this opens the question as to whether or not children can seriously be regarded as rights-holders. However, I also accept that children can be deemed to have rights, whether they are written down or not, on the basis of a moral imperative. That is, I would agree that children have human rights by the fact of their existence as human beings. The fact that children find themselves unable to exercise legal and moral rights presents a political problem, rather than a legal, sociological or biological problem. It is for this reason that this project on children's rights pursues an explicitly political line of inquiry rather than adopting a normative rights-based approach.

Chapter outline

In this Introduction, I have cast my interest in children's rights as explicitly political. The need to politicize children's rights is explained in Chapters 1 and 2 of this book, by arguing that children's rights as a discourse is informed by (1) a paternalistic paradigm that reflects an imperfect analogy to the political movements of women and Indigenous Australians, and (2) a liberal rationality that reveals the exclusion of children as a key component in how liberal political philosophers since the Enlightenment have constructed their ideal political communities. Both these chapters argue that children's rights is a discourse that is premised upon the child as an apolitical or prepolitical subject, which may or may not seek to extend to children a recognized political status. This occurs as a result of reason, maturity and autonomy in liberal political thought operating as key conditions of a person's political status, as subjects or citizens in a community.

To argue this, Chapter 2 situates children's rights within the broader liberal rights discourse. I reveal a paternalistic paradigm that explains the autonomy rights claims of women and Indigenous Australians. This paradigm reveals how the metaphor of parent/child relationships was employed to justify paternalistic practices that marginalized women and Indigenous Australians from public and political life. Further, I suggest that these practices included an emphasis on the importance of "protecting" these groups from the burdens of society that they were ill-equipped to handle. In order to operate against these paternalistic practices, I argue that autonomy rights claims were required to displace the emphasis on protection. In this sense, autonomy operates against paternalism. Children's rights discourse is similarly shaped by two opposing claims: protection and autonomy. I argue that this tension is a product of the paternalistic paradigm of liberal rights. However, unlike for women and Indigenous peoples, this tension produces an irresolvable problem for children. Children are not simply childlike, as women and Indigenous Australians were characterized. Children are defined against autonomy, and defined against the reason and maturity it demands. To claim autonomy rights for children is to claim that children have the requisite capacities for reason, maturity and autonomy. In this sense, advocating autonomy rights for children may be, in itself, a form of injustice: one that casts children prematurely out into the world as autonomous individuals unable to protect themselves and their own interests.

I explore this tension further by making sense of the broader liberal political philosophy from which these rights claims emerge. I do this as an attempt to identify and explore knowledge around childhood, not just knowledge of childhood. I offer three conceptions of childhood that can be identified in Western thought: the blank-slate, innocence and sinfulness. I argue that for all the differences in how children are conceived in Western thought, it remains true that children are thought of in terms of their future, rather than their present, selves. This is what I call the future-adult subject.

In Chapter 3, having established the political status of children as a key problem for how we think, talk and argue about children's rights, I lay out a post-structural form of critical analysis that informs the research conducted in Chapters 4, 5 and 6 of the book and foreshadows the line of argumentation it produces in Chapters 7 and 8.

In Chapters 4, 5 and 6, I explore three children's rights debates in turn: criminality, sexuality and citizenship. In each of these debates, I argue that the future-adult subject emerges as the key site of concern. This is quite a distinct concern from the present-child. Further, in these debates, I seek to identify the rupturing of key conceptions of childhood that challenges how we think of the political subjectivity of children. In debates about criminality, child criminal behaviour is a direct rupture of an innocent conception of childhood, and it presents a contemporary example of a sinful conception of childhood. Again, debates about children's rights are forced into establishing whether or not children are "good" or "bad". The real risk in these debates is tied to the future of a good, liberal society rather than the experiences of children. Debates about childhood sexuality again present a direct rupture of an innocent conception of childhood. In debates about citizenship, attempts to account for children's autonomy (and reason and maturity) in order to claim greater political rights emerge as a site in which children need to be re-conceptualized as adult-like. However, I argue that to do so risks the political realm itself. The risks these debates are preoccupied with are, once again, of the future-adult subject and the integrity of the liberal political realm.

It is for all these reasons that I argue in Chapter 7, that childhood is a process of governing, not of growing and "natural" development. Given that the subject of children's rights debates is that of a future-adult subject, it is not surprising that the child is a governed being. What is crucial for children's rights debates is an understanding that a child must be governed toward their future-adulthood, to serve the interests of the political community in which they will be citizens, not just the best interests of the child herself. It is in this way that my critique of children's rights speaks not only to our understandings of children, their lives and their rights, but also to our understanding of the concept of the political itself. Despite the apparent conceptual impossibility of characterizing children as political citizens, it remains that children and childhood are a key delimiting aspect of the political realm. It is in their exclusion, justified by the importance of their future-role as citizens of a liberal political community, that the politics of childhood emerges. In the concluding chapter, I argue that this is the politics of becoming adult.

Notes

1 Martin Guggenheim is also uncomfortable with children's rights being used to further adult political agendas. He argues that one of the key problems of children's rights is that it

> can be useful for masking selfishness by invoking a language of altruism ... [t]ime and again we will see the frequency with which the concept of children's rights is used by adults to gain some advantage in their struggles with other adults.
>
> (Guggenheim 2005: xiii)

2 Arendt (1959: 46).
3 Ibid., 50. I have discussed this previously in Nakata (2008).
4 In similar sentiment to Arendt's argument, Guggenheim rejects that children 'like other minorities, are an oppressed group' and argues that children's rights claims premised upon 'a sense of oppression or subordination ... are highly problematic'. He argues that they are problematic because these claims are posed in terms of children's right to equal protection and that. as a matter of fact, children are *not* equal to adults. Therefore, he regards positioning children's rights claims as political risks displacing children's interests for adult interests and implies an injustice Guggenheim (2005: 9).
5 Freeden (2005).
6 Wyness (2006: 26). Also see Oswell (2013: 38–42).
7 Ariès (1962: 128).

8 Ibid., 33.
9 Wyness (2006: 12).
10 Archard (2004: 21).
11 Ibid., 22.
12 Ariès (1962: 15).
13 Ibid., 17.
14 Ibid., 132–3. Ariès' terms are different from mine: he describes the first concept as 'coddling', and the second as 'eager to ensure disciplined, rational manners'.
15 Ibid., 133.
16 Here, I use *future-adult subject* to refer to the idea that children are thought about in terms of who they *become* rather than who they *are*. It is not a normative account of this future-adult subject. Later, when I refer to a *liberal future-adult subject* or *future liberal citizen,* I am employing an account of political subjectivity or citizenship that has a normative content which values the liberal qualities of reason, maturity and autonomy.
17 Ibid., 170–240.
18 Archard (2004: 23).
19 Piaget (2002).
20 Piaget (2001: 3).
21 Ibid., 4.
22 This has been the subject of extensive criticism by John Morss (1995).
23 Archard (2004: 94).
24 Piaget (2001).
25 Wyness (2006: 124–5).
26 Morss (1995: 40–1).
27 Oswell (2013: 163–9) also provides an account of Darwin's 1877 essay 'A Biographical Sketch of an Infant' and the analysis it informed.
28 Archard (2004: 41).
29 Piaget (2002: 6).
30 Ibid., xvii–xviii.
31 Wyness (2006: 20).
32 Lee (2001: 1).
33 Chapter 3 will explain how this postmodern reluctance informs the method for analysis adopted in subsequent chapters.
34 Wyness (2006: 23).
35 Ibid., 23–5; Oswell (2013: 12–14).
36 Ariès (1962: 27–9).
37 For example: Cohen (2005); Lister (2007).
38 Farson (1974); Cohen (1980).
39 Arneil (2002).
40 Archard (2004: 56).
41 Kant [1784] (2004).
42 Hindess (2001).
43 Rodham (1973: 487).
44 'Convention on the Rights of the Child', (United Nations General Assembly 1989).
45 Ibid.
46 Bhabha (2009: 425–6). This enforcement gap affects all international human rights regimes, not just children's rights.
47 Ibid., 425–26. This argument is informed by the work of Oona Hathaway (2002).
48 Arendt (1951: 290–302).
49 Rancière [2004] (2010: 62–75).
50 Arendt (1951); Rancière (2004).
51 Joel Feinberg (1980).
52 "Best interests" is a key term central to the practice of Australian family law. In this book, I employ the term in the context of children's rights literature, and specifically

with reference to Article 3 of the United Nations Convention on the Rights of the Child, which states that 'In all actions concerning children, whether undertaken by public or private social welfare institutions, courts of law, administrative authorities or legislative bodies, the best interests of the child shall be a primary consideration.' David Archard and Marit Skivenes discuss the tension between the principle of best interests and the principle of a child's right to be heard (Article 12 of the UNCRC) in legal decision-making: Archard Skivenes (2009). John Eekelaar (1986, 1994) has discussed the transformation of interests into rights.

53 For emerging literature on a child's right to be loved see: Liao (2006). For a criticism of a child's right to love see Cowden (2011).

54 This description of human rights is an attempt to bring together both the moral and legal traditions of human rights, with principles of respect and dignity emerging from liberal moral philosophy and also articulated in the Universal Declaration of Human Rights (1948).

55 It is generally difficult to enforce human rights, not just children's human rights. As Costas Douzinas has argued, the rise of human rights in the twentieth century paradoxically coincided with its greatest breaches: 'The twentieth century is the century of massacre, genocide, ethnic cleansing, the age of the Holocaust.' See: Douzinas (2000: 2).

56 Archard (2004: 53–55). Archard has a particular interest in the rights to vote, and to sexual consent, but also in the tension that exists between children's rights and parental rights.

57 Guggenheim (2005).

58 Michael (1997a). His original idea is developed into a book of the same title.

59 Onora O'Neill (1988, 1992). Also see Manson and O'Neill (2007).

60 O'Neill (1998: 39).

1 The paternalistic paradigm of children's rights

Introduction

As adults, we have been educated to know the world through particular frames, employing modes of reason that allow us to be recognized by others as equal and legitimate members of our liberal political community. We learn that childhood is a stage in this process: we will grow up and our childhood will be placed into such perspective that our concerns and grievances during that time will appear insignificant. We come to accept that our way of knowing the world as children is incomplete and inadequate. We reflect on our former perspective as naïveté, ignorance or innocence. Such reflections are nostalgic, and rarely political. Consequently, debates about what rights children should or should not have often come to rely on moral claims rather than political claims. There are significant hurdles to making political claims on behalf of children. This chapter will explore why and argue that these hurdles arise from the paternalistic paradigm of children's rights. To do this, it explores how the paternalistic paradigm operates in relation to sex and race by embedding debates about women and Indigenous Australian's capacity for autonomy in accounts of their reason and maturity. These accounts draw upon the child–parent relationship as a metaphor for the lesser autonomy of women and Indigenous Australians.

I argue that the metaphorical child–parent relationship that served to justify paternalistic practices against women and Indigenous peoples is now being projected back onto the actual child–parent relationship in children's rights debates. That is, a metaphor is being projected back onto its original, literal form. This distorts how we understand the paternalistic paradigm as a metaphorical device in liberal rights debates, and how we understand the literal parental–paternal relationship between children, their parents and other adults. This chapter explores this distortion, arguing that the latter paradigm informs, shapes and limits how we think and argue about children's rights debates. It is in this way that the paternalistic paradigm which brings together reason, maturity and autonomy as key characteristics that separate the included from the excluded in political life, and operates discursively to delimit the possibilities for children's rights.

Reason, maturity and autonomy in liberal thought

Individual autonomy has been defined by democratic theorist, David Held, as the 'capacity of humans to reason self-consciously, be self-reflective and to be self-determining',[1] In these ways, autonomy operates as a political device against paternalistic practices that involve:

> the interference of a state or an individual with another person, against their will and justified by a claim that the person interfered with will be better off or protected from harm.[2]

In this way, autonomy and paternalism are defined against each other. This explains, in part, the tension between autonomy and protectionist modes of thinking about children's rights. It also helps explain how both are tied to a paternalistic paradigm: the latter relies on a paternalistic sentiment, while the former is its critical reflex and antidote. For David Archard, in children's rights debates, autonomy is a "rational autonomy", comprised of 'rationality, maturity and independence', which are the very qualities that children are defined against.[3] In this light, it is worth considering whether the autonomy claims that have countered paternalistic claims in the past, are useful for children. To do this, I consider autonomy in liberal societies and draw on the work of liberal philosopher, Immanuel Kant.

In 1784, Immanuel Kant wrote that:

> Enlightenment is man's emergence from his self-incurred immaturity. Immaturity is the inability to use one's own understanding without the guidance of another. This immaturity is self-incurred if its cause is not lack of understanding but lack of resolution and courage to use it without the guidance of another.[4]

In this case, immaturity is the absence of reason. As described by Andrews Reath, 'Kant's conception of autonomy is that rational agents are sovereign over the employment of their rational capacities.'[5] Similarly, Mika Lavaque-Manty describes it as 'to act on reason you give yourself, as opposed to being the vehicle for some other force', whether it is another person, a drug, or something else.[6] All these descriptions tie autonomy to the exercise of reason. These rational capacities are developed through maturation: physical and intellectual, natural and learned. It is not possible for autonomy to be ascribed to any given individual by another. Instead, it is the responsibility of individuals to realize it for themselves. Nonetheless, liberal societies recognize a general level of autonomy at an arbitrary age, most symbolically when a right to vote is conferred. In Australia, this age is 18. By this time, young people have been able to work and earn money, pay taxes and are subject to the full obligations and sanctions of the law. Autonomy, in this way, operates to include rational and mature individuals in our liberal political community: they are able to vote, to stand for Parliament;

they are also able to speak for themselves in a range of contexts, and if they adhere to social and political norms, are generally heard.

Immanuel Kant would reject the premise than any person is fully rational.[7] For Kant, autonomy is achieved not in the realization of some measurable level of reason or maturity, but in the ongoing commitment to reach toward full rationality. Kant refers to immaturity as the antithesis of autonomous action. For him, maturity, understood as the realization and exercise of an individual's capacity to reason, is developed through education, whether formal (schooling) or informal (experience). In this respect, it is within the capacity of each individual to realize their own enlightenment. In a social contract theory of the liberal state, the rational capacity of the adult is that which facilitates the individual citizen's consent to political authority. Thus, it is through the development of reason and maturity that 'the subject child, becomes the adult citizen' in liberal societies.[8] Reason allows the child to cast off parental authority in favour of consenting to political authority. In the next chapter, this argument will be further developed in the broader context of liberal rationality, particularly the legitimate political authority of the liberal state. What is relevant here is that by tying reason and maturity to autonomy, Kantian liberalism sets the boundaries between those who are legitimate members of a social and political community and those who are not. Children, defined against reason and maturity, are both necessarily and naturally excluded.

To grapple with a more complex view of children's potential autonomy, one that refuses this simplicity and the "naturalization" of children's lack of autonomy, it is helpful to think more critically about autonomy itself. Philosopher Onora O'Neill offers a reductive view of traditional Kantian ideas of autonomy. While her analysis informs a theory of obligations in relation to children, I will not follow her analysis to this end. Instead, her analysis offers a framework for alternative readings of Kantian autonomy. Rather than viewing Kantian autonomy as oriented toward a fixed, definitive measure of reason and maturity, she instead considers his idea of autonomy as "radical reflexivity".[9] It is the critique of reason, rather than the application of a fixed, logical form of reason that characterizes Kantian autonomy. Kant makes this argument himself in his *Critique of Pure Reason*:

> Reason must in all its undertakings subject itself to criticism; should it limit freedom of criticism by any prohibitions, it must harm itself, drawing upon itself a damaging suspicion. Nothing is so important through its usefulness, nothing so sacred, that it may be exempted from this searching examination, which knows no respect for persons. Reason depends on this freedom for its very existence. For reason has no dictatorial authority; its verdict is always simply the agreement of free citizens, of whom each one must be permitted to express, without let or hindrance, his objection or even his veto.[10]

For Kant, it is impossible to vindicate reason altogether; the only way to undermine or reject reason is through rational argument. It seems equally impossible to vindicate reason from autonomy. As O'Neill observes, 'If the vindication was reasoned, it would be circular; if it was not, it would not vindicate ... no vindication of reason could meet reason's own standards.'[11] Therefore, to aspire to a conception of autonomy for children, which is free of reason altogether and, therefore, might escape the constraints of the paternalistic paradigm, presents an enormous philosophical challenge. Yet, to continue to subscribe to a concept of autonomy tied to reason makes autonomy claims for children, including citizenship rights, near impossible. What O'Neill questions is why Kantian autonomy is taken for 'conformity to reason' rather than critique of reason.[12] In this way, Kant, and particularly O'Neill's interpretation of Kant, offers scope to use reason against itself in how we think about autonomy. This scope is not one that vindicates reason altogether, but it allows a conceptual shift away from empirical questions about whether or not children are rational beings, and should be recognized as having individual autonomy and therefore entitled to autonomy rights, toward more critical and political questions such as why reason and maturity come to be tied to children's rights claims in the first place. To understand this, I look at how reason, maturity and autonomy have been related to one another through sex and race.

Paternalism, sex and race

During the 1960s a number of social movements challenged the subjugated status of politically marginalized and excluded groups: women, African Americans, colonized Indigenous peoples, gays and lesbians. With hindsight, it is possible to understand these movements not as those concerned with "minority" groups, who together constituted a majority of the world's population, but rather as those concerned with the political authority of a European, male elite that ruled so powerfully for so long.

As discussed above, the paternalistic paradigm is one that employs the child–parent relationship as a metaphor for disparities in power. In this section, I consider how the paternalistic paradigm operated in respect to debates about women's rights and Indigenous Australians' rights, and the role autonomy claims played in rejecting this paternalism. I argue that in these debates reason, maturity and autonomy operate as key discursive terms that inform, shape and limit the terms of children's rights debates. These brief examples cannot fully explain the social, historical and political arguments and complexities of these two significant rights movements. Nonetheless, they demonstrate how claims to reason and maturity came to be tied to assertions of autonomy and equality. Indeed, the claim to autonomy directly undermined the paternalistic attitudes and practices that shaped the lives of women and Indigenous peoples. I conclude this chapter by showing how this paternalistic paradigm comes to be projected back onto children in a distorted manner. This paradigm reinforces reason, maturity and autonomy as the discursive limits of children's rights debates and presents children's autonomy as a paradox.

Continuing to draw on the liberal Kantian account of autonomy, it is important to recognize that in the mind of Kant:

A woman needs a man to take care of her, both economically and intellectually.... As an economic dependent, she is not entitled to full or 'active' citizenship, any more than *children* or servants.[13]

I use Arnulf Zweig's account of Kant's misogyny here, as it neatly captures three key criticisms that are relevant to my analysis of autonomy, women and children. Kant implies that dependence renders a lesser political status via a reduced form of citizenship. This suggests that human beings who exist in relations of dependency and interdependency lack the requisite qualities of full citizenship. First, this overlooks the fact that all human beings, irrespective of their gender, exist in interdependent relationships at some point in their lives (universally, as infants). A second criticism is that Kant assumes that a woman's dependence, if and where it exists, can be attributed to a natural inferiority. Third, Kant's position also reveals an unquestioned, natural claim that children are not citizens. To justify the exclusion of women from full citizenship, they are deemed "child-like". This proves deeply problematic for thinking and debating children's rights.

Zweig suggests that Kant's understanding of women is informed by his Lutheran religious background and is 'merely incidental' to his broader liberal philosophy.[14] Yet, to meet Kant's own account of reason, as a critical reason,[15] we may question how such sexist assumptions are able to persist as 'merely incidental'. It is as much the incidental and invisible, as the deliberate and visible, which determines the scope of discourse. I am not suggesting that we ought to dismiss Kant's work entirely due to these assumptions. On the contrary, his thinking around autonomy remains central to this project. However, it is also important to be alive to the knowledge that these assumptions about women's rational capacities and proper place in society were a part of Kant's thinking in developing his idea of autonomy. Indeed, in the act of claiming autonomy by relying on demonstrations of "masculine" qualities, such as reason and maturity, women risk being characterized as less feminine. That is, reason and autonomy come to represent male attributes and women who claim them risk the charge that they are not being true to their natural feminine qualities.

Another sexist foundation that characterizes women against autonomy is evident in the work of Jean-Jacques Rousseau and his conception of the nuclear family unit. Susan Moller Okin argues that in distinguishing three states of nature, Rousseau refers to the ideal "golden" age as that which sees the first examples of cohabitation 'in the form of the monogamous nuclear family'.[16] This is quite different from the original state of nature, in which Rousseau describes the perfect equality and freedom of all.[17] For Susan Moller Okin, the shift from perfect equality to a patriarchal order appears out of nowhere. She argues that women – originally conceived as independent and equal in Rousseau's original state of nature – are suddenly the subject of a sharp division of labour between the sexes. When Rousseau describes the shift, he fails to describe the moment of change and instead describes a distinction between men and women that is consistent with his contemporary world:

> Women became more sedentary and grew accustomed to tend the hut and the children, while the man went to seek their common subsistence.[18]

As for Kant, social roles as they existed in seventeenth-century Europe appear in Rousseau's work as natural. And so, Moller Okin points out that the "nuclear family" emerges as a 'natural and God-given institution' in a manner wholly inconsistent with his original state of nature.[19] The consequence of this naturalization of patriarchy is the conclusion that a 'woman's education and entire socialisation must be founded on the principles that "woman is made to please and to be subjected to man" and "it is according to nature for the woman to obey the man." '[20] Jean-Jacques Rousseau and Immanuel Kant are not alone responsible for the naturalization of patriarchy in Western philosophy. Nonetheless, they remain foundational thinkers in liberal political philosophy and in accounting for the reason, maturity and autonomy required of citizens.

As a result of relating reason, maturity and autonomy in a way that necessarily and naturally excluded women, Andrea Baumeister explains that the first wave of feminism had to appeal to evidence of women's equal rational capacities with men.[21] Thus, Mary Wollstonecraft, writing in 1792, argued that:

> If, due to their capacity for rational thought, all human beings deserve equal rights and respect, then women, as beings capable of reason, are surely entitled to the same rights as men.[22]

And in Australia in 1901, shortly after the colonies had federated, the Commonwealth Parliament debated whether to extend the right to vote to women in federal elections. During this debate, Sir Edward Braddon from Tasmania argued that his 'objection is that women are apt to decide on instinct rather than reason'.[23] This is the position from which feminists argued for equal education, since:

> education would enable women to realise their rational faculties and would provide them with a foundation for autonomous action. Once women had attained rationality and autonomy they could not reasonably be denied the right to vote.[24]

As such, this was not a rejection of the claim that these faculties of reason were necessary to be recognised as a citizen with voting rights in a liberal society. Instead, it accepted that claim, while using it as the foundation for calling for girls to be educated in a manner similar to boys. This is to ensure that both women and men in adulthood are in possession of the reason necessary for civil and political life. However, the realization of women's political autonomy has presented challenges as well as rights. In some ways, rendering paternalistic practices less visible makes advocating some feminist agendas more difficult. Women, as equal, competent, rational adults now face much greater difficulty in identifying and explaining ongoing patriarchal power dynamics that shape much of a woman's experience in the twenty-first century. It is possible today to look back upon the wearing of corsets in Europe and tiny shoes in China as explicitly oppressive practices imposed upon women via a web of power and discursive practices that fashion women painfully, as smaller, less mobile and less physically independent than their male counterparts and recognize the parallel between the containment of the female body and the constraint imposed on women's autonomy.[25] However, today, in an age of apparent female equality, the wearing of high heels and the surgical augmentation of women's bodies are claimed as choice, and even as empowerment.[26] When claimed as an autonomous choice, rationalized on the grounds that certain beauty practices further one's position in the workplace or society more broadly, these practices may come to be understood as a free and rational choice. This is not to say that there are not differences between the relative oppression and autonomy of the eighteenth and twenty-first century woman. What I am emphasizing here is that the complexities of gendered power relations continue to control dominant paradigms of knowledge and that external coercive forms of power may disappear with the recognition of an equal, rational autonomy.[27]

Where autonomy serves to include citizens, the absence of autonomy equally serves to exclude by legitimizing and maintaining the conditions for paternalistic practices. In Australia, alongside debates for the enfranchisement of women, Aboriginal and Torres Strait Islanders were agitating, negotiating and resisting their subjugated political status at the hands of their colonial masters. In the Torres Straits, it was claimed that:

> The islanders have not yet reached the state where they are competent to think and provide for themselves; they are really overgrown children, and can be best managed, for their own welfare, as a prudent parent would discipline his family.[28]

Torres Strait Islander scholar, Martin Nakata, observes that conceptualizing Torres Strait Islanders as overgrown children rationalized the need for a range of paternalistic practices in relation to the management of Islanders during the colonial period.[29] These practices prevented Islanders from freely exercising the autonomy they had prior to colonization and served to legitimize the colonial presence in the Torres Strait. In this way, the paternalistic paradigm was underpinned by, and attached to, a theory of human evolutionary development.[30] For example, the work undertaken in 1898 by a Cambridge anthropological expedition led by A. C. Haddon to the Torres Strait illustrates how theories of evolutionary development both reflected, and upheld, the colonial project.[31] This anthropological research comprised studies of linguistics, psychology, physiology and other indicators of cognitive and physical maturity. It allowed for such conclusions as, 'the inferiority of the black races is due to the cessation of the growth of the brain at an earlier age than in white races'.[32] In this sense, science was able to characterize all those "primitive natives" and "noble savages" across Europe's empires as children: undeveloped, immature and irrational; inferior races who were identified as physically and psychologically immature. The difference between these inferior races and children was that the inferior races were deemed unable to develop into fully rational, adult beings – unlike children of superior races.

Just as women's social roles were redescribed in terms of a natural order, here science is used to naturalize the paternalistic treatment of Islanders. This is the operation of a paternalistic paradigm. It employs the metaphor of child/adult to explain and justify practices between Indigenous peoples and colonial authorities. It takes the "fact" of childhood, as a less-developed, incomplete state of becoming; as the state in which certain groups are to be held in their own best interests. This process relies upon the European colonial gaze discovering Other as the subject of knowledge in science, history, literature, art and politics. This has been a central site of analysis for postcolonial discourse. These Western discourses assisted the reinforcement of power relations between the colonizers and the colonized.[33] The rise of this framework since the 1970s developed cogent and compelling arguments regarding the political autonomy of Indigenous people, both as individuals and as sovereign groups entitled to self-determination. During this time, the New South Wales Department of Education offered a radically new position regarding the rational capacity of Indigenous people:

> Research has indicated that the pupils are of average intelligence, and that social deprivation and depressed environment are the reasons for initial retardation rather than low intelligence.[34]

Western knowledge characterized Indigenous people as children in such a way that there was no reason to provide education equal to those of non-Indigenous Australians, let alone autonomy or self-determination. However, in a different political climate this knowledge of Indigenous intellectual capacity was then used to include them as equal, autonomous beings. The paternalistic paradigm is one that reinforces reason, maturity and autonomy as requisite characteristics for political status and inclusion.

I argue that this tension extends from the broader liberal rights movement that gave rise to children's rights. There are connections between the claims of women and Indigenous peoples, and the later claims made on behalf of children. Shulamith Firestone has argued that the relationships between women and children are 'intertwined and mutually reinforcing'.[35] For Firestone, women and children are similarly oppressed.[36] Indigenous Australians were similarly characterized as childlike, reflecting a natural lesser status.[37] Indeed, David Archard and John Morss have each taken time to consider how children's naturally lesser status, demonstrated in psychology, was supported by ideas that emerged in theories of social Darwinism.[38] The convergence of social Darwinism with psychological claims about childhood gave rise to the idea that 'the development of the child into an adult mirrors, without literally reproducing, the progress of humanity as a whole'.[39] This psychology was premised upon the view of non-Europeans as primitives and savages.[40]

Erica Burman also observed that during these early expressions of child psychology, it was an explicitly "scientific" gaze that was being cast upon the bodies of children. In constructing knowledge about children and their development into adults, particular forms and sources of knowledge were explicitly excluded. Specifically, the perspectives and information of mothers and women were excluded from scientific exploration, due to their lack of objectivity.[41] This, Burman argues, reproduced the 'division between rationality and emotion' in the scientific study of human development, and gave rise to a split between the domains of psychology and psychoanalysis.[42]

In the domain of psychology, John Morss offers a social constructivist critique of developmental psychology literature, which claimed that 'the mental development of all mankind [came to be] ... found in the child in an abbreviated form'.[43] For example, he quotes from an 1895 text, which states: 'as we all know, the lowest races of mankind stand in close proximity to the animal world. The same is true of the infants of civilized races'.[44] This mapping of evolutionary theory onto developmental theory cast an image of the child as a "savage", with observations by some that, 'the expression of pain in the infant resembled that of a monkey or Negro';[45] or, 'the three-year old presented "the picture of a savage".'[46] For G. Stanley Hall, the eight- to 12-year-old of the late nineteenth century represented the adult of the ancestor.[47] Thus, in an Enlightened age, in a civilized world, the development of the young person reflected civilization's own development. The Age of Reason becomes a moment of historical achievement as well as individual achievement.

This sort of analysis was possible following an interpretation of what was known as "recapitulation" theory, following the evolutionary work by Charles Darwin. John Morss describes it in the following way: 'Recapitulation theory demands that adult features come to be located in the young and embryo of descendants. Thus, the embryo *changes* with evolution. For Darwin ... the embryo remains unchanged.'[48] That is, the modern embryo is not all that different from the ancient embryo. Ergo, we all begin at the beginning, in evolutionary terms. Darwin's work emerged at the same time as a rise in interest in children, particularly working-class children.[49]

By the time Jean Piaget began his work in the 1950s, these ideas of recapitulation were well entrenched. While his work departed significantly from the Darwinian ideas of the earlier century, Piaget regarded prehistoric humans as an 'ideal subject from the investigation of the genesis of knowledge' and noted that the 'child is in a sense a poor substitute'.[50] Jean Piaget is most famous for his stage theory, which views the development of an individual in a number of distinct, sequential stages. The first stage must be fully realized in order for the second to be possible, and so on. Piaget's studies also helped to connect these stages to age. That is, most individuals fully realize specific "developmental stages" at specific ages. This has been highly influential in educational pedagogies in the West, and in school systems that see children demonstrating particular skill levels in order to progress to the next grade. It has also been influential in early childhood markers of normal development, such as walking, talking, imagining and so on.

The paternalistic paradigm in this book does not describe a paradigm of oppression, but rather a paradigm that inscribes relationships that have been constructed between women, Indigenous peoples and children. In each of these domains, their lesser intellectual and moral status has rationalized their lesser rights. Further, this lesser status has been rationalized on claims about their rational and intellectual capacities. These claims, in turn, were successfully naturalized with the help of scientific observations and study. Women and Indigenous peoples have, for the most part, successfully debunked claims about their lesser intellectual capacities. For children, however, natural incapacities remain a key part of how their lesser status and rights are rationalized. Further, overcoming claims about children's incapacities is not easily achieved. The rest of this book seeks to understand why, and to what effect on debates about children's rights.

Paternalism and children's rights

There are two main ways in which we may characterize children's rights claims: a protectionist mode and an autonomy mode. I argue that individual autonomy plays a constitutive role in civil and political rights in liberal societies, in ways that are problematic for children's rights claims. Children are defined against autonomy, understood as immature, dependent and lacking in reason. Further, children are understood as part of the private domain of family, and so they have no individual status in broader political and social life. If individual autonomy is a key element of liberal rights, then claiming those rights for subjects who lack individual autonomy presents a problematic: not just a problem of children's rights, but a problem with how we understand children's rights problems. I offer brief examples that demonstrate how the paternalistic paradigm operated in respect to the liberal rights claims of women and Indigenous Australians. I do this to argue that the protectionist and autonomy modes of children's rights, which characterize the discourse, are bound to this paternalistic paradigm in a deeply problematic way: producing children's autonomy as a paradox, where autonomy is a key, defining feature of a rights-holder in liberal societies and a characteristic that defines childhood by its very absence.

The protectionist mode of children's rights regards the child as weak, vulnerable and innocent.[51] This child needs protection from exploitation, as well as their own immaturity, and this mode emphasizes welfare and protection rights. The autonomy mode regards the protectionist mode as inadequate for realizing better outcomes for children.[52] This inadequacy arises from the assumption that protection rights, largely enforced by adults, can prevent all "harms" against children.[53] Where harm does occur, protection rights leave little to no scope available for children to seek redress without an adult to advocate for them. This mode emphasizes civil and political rights, and grounds these in a normative position that children, as human beings, have an equal, moral status to adults, or empirical claims about children's reason and maturity. These two positions characterize contemporary debates about children's rights. On the one hand, there are those who seek to protect children on the basis of their inherent vulnerability. On the other, there are those who seek to provide children with greater autonomy in order to better protect themselves. Michael Freeman describes this debate as a choice between 'either salvation or liberation', 'either nurturance or self-determination' and that 'one protects children, the other their rights'.[54] The alternatives highlighted by this choice are informed by different conceptions of what childhood is, and empirical claims about who children are. Judging which the better approach is, therefore, turns on our understandings and knowledge of what childhood is and who children are.

During the nineteenth century, children's rights presented as a matter of concern in Western societies in areas of education, juvenile delinquency, social work, housing and child labour. It coincided more generally with the rise in concern by domestic states for social welfare and for the mitigation of the risks presented by the lower working classes.[55] In the United States and Britain, and across Europe, a number of welfare agencies were operating with a focus upon working-class children. With the Industrial Revolution came a rise in widespread child labour among the working classes. The late nineteenth and twentieth centuries saw a rejection of child labour, which in turn saw large numbers of working-class children becoming idle on the streets; these children were out of work and came from families that did not have the means to provide care and education.[56] Out of concern for how these children would occupy their time, a compulsory education system emerged, which was designed to keep children busy but also to socialize and educate them toward a future-adult citizenship.

Internationally, Dominique Marshall has argued that it was the 1924 Declaration on Children's Rights by the Council of the League of Nations that marked the transformation of children into an object of international relations.[57] This document stated that: 'the child, by reason of his *physical and mental immaturity*, needs special safeguards and care, including legal *protection*'.[58] This text remains in the Preamble of today's United Nations Convention on the Rights of the Child.[59] Today, this Convention is the most ratified treaty in United Nations history. Consequently, the children's rights discourse is largely an international discourse, with some of the organizations involved in the original drafting of the 1924 Declaration, such as "Save The Children", remaining key organizations in children's rights advocacy today.[60]

The international nature of children's rights largely results from the context in which the 1924 Declaration was produced. Following the events of the First World War, the international community recognized that children were disproportionately and unfairly affected by war. Children had nothing to do with the decision to go to war, but nonetheless were dramatically affected by the loss of parents, trauma and economic hardship. Marshall observes that 'saving the children of Europe' was one of the few objects of international cooperation in the immediate aftermath of the War.[61] At the very first session of the General Assembly of the League of Nations, it was decided that 'child welfare for victims of war' would be one of its primary concerns.[62] Marshall argues that these documents did not establish anything distinctly new about how children were thought of, only that, for the first time, it should be written down. Hence, it was written that 'all Mankind owes to the child the best it has to give' and that the 'child must be the first to receive relief in times of distress'.[63] Due to this document, it became possible to articulate concerns for children explicitly in terms of rights that extended beyond the domestic state onto an international stage. In doing so, the Declaration largely employed a protectionist mode of rights that sought to emphasize state and adult responsibilities to prevent harms to children. As Andrew Rehfeld has observed, this protectionist mode remains in the language of the modern day Convention.[64]

Judith Ennew offers a more critical perspective on the historical moment that created an international discourse of children's rights. She argues that while the United Nations has always recognized children's rights to protection, its much lesser emphasis on citizenship rights is conspicuous.[65] Where Marshall recognizes an important moment in including children within an international discourse of human rights, Ennew finds an opportunity to question how meaningful this inclusion is. She identifies two problems: first, that the initial practical expressions of human rights were national, rather than international. This meant that a tradition of human rights has arisen in complicity with nation-states and constitutions governing both citizens and denizens.[66] Second, and a consequence of this, is that a set of rights that does not emphasize citizenship is not particularly helpful. She argues that the 'UN lays down the human rights conditions for *citizen* membership of a state' but says nothing of those people who are not fully-fledged citizens of their state, such as children.[67] For Ennew, this is unjustified because '[a]ll categories of persons can and do take citizenship actions, for example shouldering responsibilities or defending their own interests'.[68] This is a sentiment shared by Ruth Lister, who argues that children's citizenship practices demonstrate their de facto status as citizens of nation- states.[69] As discussed further in Chapter 6, the basis for these claims is not elaborated upon with strong empirical evidence. As a result, it is easy to refute them by arguing that the responsibilities Ennew refers to are responsibilities to the state, which are not necessarily the same responsibilities that children fulfil, which are more likely directed to their role in the family home. As discussed in Chapter 4, in many Western countries, children aged under ten years are subject to the doctrine of *doli incapax* and, therefore, cannot be charged with criminal offences. This example would suggest that not all categories of persons do, indeed, shoulder the responsibilities of full citizens. If shouldering personal responsibilities, say within a family unit, is constitutive of citizenship, then a more elaborate argument that reconceptualizes citizenship and the conditions that make it possible is necessary. For example, it might be possible to link family responsibilities that children owe their parents to the stability of the state, and thereby establish a form of social contract. However, Ennew does not draw this conceptual link in her argument for children's citizenship rights.

Such an argument has potential, but would be undermined by claims that children do not have any responsibilities even within the family unit, and accounts of children who do (such as carers) would likely not establish the empirical basis to claim that children, on the whole, undertake citizenship actions. The claim that children, as a group, defend their own interests also rests on uncertain ground. After all, at law, children for the most part do not defend their own interests, instead requiring adult proxies to bring claims on their behalf. In criminal law, they appear either as victims of crimes, or perpetrators with a lesser culpability for those actions than their adult counterparts.[70] More broadly, the defence of children's interests is largely undertaken by child advocacy organizations, managed and staffed by adults. Nonetheless, what is helpful in Ennew's argument is the rejection of the usefulness of an exclusively protectionist mode of children's rights.

This is the tension that emerges between protectionist and autonomy modes of children's rights. The autonomy mode, unlike the protectionist mode, draws on the tradition of child liberationists. The arguments of child liberationists emerged in the 1970s and heavily emphasized children's equal moral, if not rational, status as the basis for full and equal rights. Richard Farson's *Birthrights* and John Holt's *Escape from Childhood* together present as the height of this children's liberation movement, comprising the strongest arguments that have been made for the extension of all adult rights to children.[71] At this time, liberationist claims were consistent with contemporary broader social movements. They called for children to be given the full gamut of rights and freedoms that adults have. This extends to civil and political rights, such as the right to vote, but also to the right of young people not to attend school or, perhaps most controversially, to choose their guardian and type of upbringing.[72] In making these sorts of claims, one must abandon the notion that age carries any significance, and instead recognize it is only an arbitrary measure that facilitates exclusion and oppression. However, as David Archard argues, even Farson and Holt cannot escape age, and the capacities or incapacities it implies, as a relevant factor in deciding what children should or should not have a right to do.[73] Since the 1970s, the child liberationist movement has ebbed away. Hence, my choice to use the term "autonomy" to describe the tradition that has been informed by the extensive rights claims of Farson and Holt, but not bound to it. Instead, the autonomy rights this book refers to are those claimed for children based upon some articulation of their emerging capacities.

In order to escape age and its assumed corresponding capacities, as Farson and Cohen attempted to do, it is necessary to lay claim to rights on the basis of a moral status. To argue that children are equal, moral beings and that this moral status is the only condition for being the full bearer of rights and freedoms circumvents the need for any discussion of reason, maturity or autonomy. However, this emphasis on equality is also problematic. It collapses any distinction between the concept of childhood and adulthood. It compels one to view children as the *same* as adults. In doing so, this prevents making rights claims on the basis that children are *different* from adults, and so should be included in political communities to ensure that these differences are better accounted for in policy making.[74] David Archard observes that sometimes child liberationists make both these claims: that children require greater rights than they have because they are the same as adults; and, also, that they require greater rights than they have because they are unique, and different from adults.[75]

Thus, liberationist arguments are now largely discounted as a serious area of children's rights. When I describe Lister and Ennew's recent claims for children's citizenship rights, however, the legacy of these liberationist arguments is evident. Autonomy claims are far less radical than those of the 1970s liberationists, but they are still informed by a rejection that protectionist rights alone are useful to children. The liberationist mode of children's rights is a critical reaction to the dominant protectionist mode of children's rights, and works towards countering conceptions of children as innocent, weak and vulnerable. Both Lister and Ennew, and others like them, seek to demonstrate instances when children do act with reason and maturity in order to argue that they are autonomous beings, with interests of their own, distinct and apart from their parents and adults more generally. They present children as more like adults than they are generally viewed to be, whilst also maintaining that there are differences between children and adults that make it ever more important for children's rights to be taken seriously.

Part of what distinguishes protectionist and autonomy rights is the basis upon which these rights are claimed. Protectionist rights are claimed on the basis that children require protection. Autonomy rights are claimed on the basis that children are, like adults, autonomous moral beings. It should be pointed out that human rights, as laid out in international treaties, apply to children as much as adults. Children are the subjects of *all* human rights, not just those children's rights laid out in the Convention. However, it is evident that children are not in the same position to enforce their rights as adults. Indeed, even adults find it difficult to enforce human rights.[76] As an individual, you must first exhaust your human rights avenues within your state, before seeking the attention of international arbiters, and even where those international arbiters might find in your favour, they can offer no enforceable mechanism for requiring a member state to protect your rights. This all happens within the domain of law. At the domestic level, no child could bring such a claim on their own. Like an adult, they will require lawyers. But unlike an adult, they will also require a proxy to stand in their place. And unlike an adult, they would be less likely to have the financial independence to fund their representation. This, all before we even ask whether a child could identify their human rights, whether these human rights had been breached, and whether they could articulate their argument well enough to gain the serious attention of an adult to act on their behalf. The question of what a rights claim is founded upon is important for children, as it determines whether or not it is possible for children to possess rights. If it can be shown that children do, in fact, possess rights (such as human rights), then there is a much stronger basis upon which to argue for better ways of facilitating children's enforcement of those rights.

Today, protectionist and autonomy modes of thinking about children's rights continue to inform, shape and limit debates. On the one hand, the 'particularly modern and arguably Western view of the child as a vulnerable, weak and dependent creature, bereft of those capacities that entitle adults to be regarded as full members of society' suggests that children are in need of protection from exploitation and their own immaturity.[77] On the other hand, there is an interest in dispensing with this socially constructed notion of the child as less than a full member of society; to recognize the child as an individual equally affected by the world around them, with the same moral status as any adult. Barbara Arneil recognizes that autonomy rights, 'embraces a conception of children focused upon their rational capacity'.[78] Such a conception is a double-edged sword. On the one hand, it facilitates autonomy rights and answers Ennew and Lister's concerns about the absence of citizenship rights for children. However, Michael Freeman is less eager to abandon a protectionist mode of rights in favour of thinking about children's autonomy. For Freeman, the call to take children's rights more seriously demands consideration of their 'actual and potential' autonomy, but with a care to confine 'paternalism ... without entirely eliminating it'.[79] Here, he distinguishes between the exploitation that is necessarily implied by "paternalism" in its metaphorical use, and the realities of a parental relationship between children and their carers, which is not necessarily exploitative. Indeed, for Freeman, maintaining a degree of paternalism is necessary to ensure that children can 'mature to rationally autonomous adulthood'.[80] To ignore protectionist rights, premised as they are on a paternalistic metaphor, is to fail to take children's rights seriously. To do so risks throwing children out into the world as equal to adults, in all senses, thus responsible for their own care and protection.

In this way, paternalism and autonomy are defined against each other. In Kantian terms, it is unjust for an autonomous individual to be subject to paternalistic practices because autonomy and paternalism are defined against each other. Paternalism is premised upon immaturity and a need for protection, while autonomy is realized when an individual is delivered from this immaturity into enlightenment. Therefore, paternalism can only be justified where an individual can be said *not* to be autonomous. This tension is reflected in children's rights debates through the tension between protectionist and autonomy modes of rights claims. In subsequent chapters, this tension will be analysed in debates regarding children's sexuality, criminality and citizenship. In the next chapter, I discuss individual autonomy as a key component of how we understand rights in liberal societies.

Conclusion

An analysis of children's rights debates about citizenship, criminality and sexuality will similarly reveal reason, maturity and autonomy as key terms that inform, shape and limit how we think and talk about children and their rights. The important point here is that despite the parallels and connections between the children's rights and other liberal rights movements, they cannot be understood in the same way. As philosopher Onora O'Neill has explained, while for other groups the paternalistic paradigm is employed as a metaphor for the power relationships at play, it is 'no mere analogy when we speak of mothers and fathers as parents, and children are not just metaphorically childlike'.[81] As a result, the paternalistic paradigm is projected back onto children's rights debates in a distorted manner. That is, the relationship between children and parents comes to operate, metaphorically, to justify paternalistic practices. These paternalistic practices are evident in children's rights debates that emphasize protecting children's best interests, over extending to children autonomy political rights. However, to describe "paternalistic practices" in respect to children's actual relationship with their parents is imperfect. A child's relationship to its parents is not necessarily unjust, if one views children as dependent, vulnerable and unequal rather than autonomous.

Debates about children's rights must either value parent–child relationships, as is the case for protectionist approaches, or consider these relationships potentially harmful, as is the case for autonomy approaches. Children's relationships with adults, including their parents, are at once crucial to their well-being as well as inherently risky, due to their vulnerability. The paternalistic paradigm makes it difficult to account for these simultaneous possibilities: one as paternalistic and harmful, the other as parental and supportive. David Archard makes this distinction by choosing to reject the language of paternalism to describe a relationship between children and parents, instead referring simply to "parental" relationships. For Archard, following O'Neill, paternalism only operates as a metaphor. It cannot speak to the literal relationship between parents and children. So it is against this metaphor of paternalism that those struggling with the complexities of children's lives must operate. Yet, the protectionist and autonomy perspectives establish the terms and discursive limits of children's rights debates, which remain tied to this paternalistic paradigm. That is, the projection of this metaphor back onto debates about children's rights in a distorted manner is most problematic because it cannot be escaped.

In this chapter, I have set the broad parameters of the analysis that follows in this book. The discourse of children's rights is an attempt to account for children's lives and their experiences, whatever they may be. The two main modes of children's rights fall into somewhat contradictory claims about their protection and their autonomy. These two modes of rights claims, I argue, extend in part from a narrative that emerges from the broader liberal rights discourse. This broader discourse is one that has seen greater rights extended to marginalized, adult, groups. In discussing only two of these groups: women and Indigenous peoples, I have attempted to demonstrate the parallels that exist in liberal rights claims, despite the diverse populations they are made by. It is the paternalistic paradigm that captures this parallel: a shared narrative that pitches autonomy rights against paternalistic practices. Historically, these paternalistic practices have underpinned "protection-based" claims. That is, that women and Indigenous peoples were only given limited rights in their own best interests, in order to protect them from their own incapacities and others' exploitation. Today, such a claim is met with the criticism of being highly patronising, and, with similarly critical tone, paternalistic.

Indeed, grappling and negotiating the tensions between protectionist and auto-nomy rights claims, disrupts how we understand this paternalistic paradigm. We cannot look to the paternalistic practices that surround children and automati-cally view them as inherently unjust. Children, and their subordinate position to their parents and adults, represent not a metaphorical power relationship but a lived one. Perhaps, depending on your regard of psychology and other biological sciences, it is also a natural one. If this is your view, then claims about children's greater rights, premised upon notions of their rational capacities or equal moral status, must appear deeply problematic. If it is not your view, then claims about children's protection rights, at the exclusion of all others, may smack of an injus-tice constructed for the perpetuation of a patriarchal order. In short, thinking about children, forces us to think differently about how we understand rights claims. It forces us to think more critically about the foundations for different rights claims. It forces us to think more seriously about reason, maturity and autonomy as inescapable terms in arguing about who should have what rights. Children complicate matters of politics: the political subjectivity of rights-holders, but also of our conceptions of childhood and the rights-claims that these conceptions inform.

In the next chapter, I undertake an analysis of the liberal rationality of chil-dren's rights. To pursue further discussion of developmental psychology would be unwarranted, given that others have already pursued this line of analysis and research. It would also belong to an altogether different domain of study. Just as John Morss problematized what we know about children through a critical ana-lysis of developmental psychology, I wish to do so through a critical analysis of liberal political philosophy. The next chapter identifies three alternative accounts of childhood. Each conceptualization returns to claims about reason, maturity and autonomy as the basis for rationalizing what individuals have a right to have and to do. Second, in making these claims, all are preoccupied not necessarily with the child as a child, but with the child as a future-adult subject; more specif-ically, as a future-adult citizen, worthy of political recognition and participation in a liberal state. Together these two factors set the discursive limits that inform and shape debates about children and their rights.

Notes

1 David Held (1987: 270). Also quoted in Kulynych (2001: 255).
2 Dworkin (2005).
3 Archard (2004: 93).
4 Immanuel Kant [1684] (1966):17); In more recent translations the term "tutelage" has displaced "immaturity". See: Kant [1784: 29].
5 Reath (2006: 173).
6 Lavaque-Manty (2006: 365).
7 Zweig (1998: 122).
8 Arneil (2002: 70).
9 O'Neill (1989).
10 Ibid., 15 and 57.
11 Kant (1990: 187)

12 Ibid., 53.
13 Zweig (1998: 123).
14 Ibid., 123.
15 Kant [1784] (2004).
16 Okin (1979: 398).
17 Rousseau (1986).
18 Okin (1979: 399).
19 Ibid.
20 As quoted by Okin, ibid., 401. Rousseau (1993: 385 and 443, respectively). Note that Barbara Foxley translates the second quote differently: 'Moreover, the law of nature bids the woman obey the man.'
21 Baumeister (2000: 18).
22 Mary Wollstonecraft and Ulrich H. Hardt (1982: 58).
23 House of Represenatatives Parliament of Australia, "Hansard," (Canberra: Government Printer, 1902), 11937.
24 Baumeister (2000: 19).
25 Jeffreys (2005).
26 Ibid.
27 For Foucault, of course, power never disappears. What has been described in this paragraph is a shift from external practices of power that are more easily recognized as power that is exercised over another's body, to less easily recognized embodied practices of power that an individuals exercise upon themselves.
28 Queensland State Government Protector's Report quoted in Nakata, *Disciplining the Savages, Savaging the Disciplines*: 129. Original unavailable in Victoria.
29 Ibid.
30 Morss (1995).
31 Nakata (2007: 26–31).
32 Ibid., 201.
33 Said (1978).
34 Quoted by Nakata (2007: 155).
35 Firestone (1970: 81).
36 For a critical discussion of Firestone's particular interest in children see: Purdy (1998).
37 Nakata (2007).
38 Archard (2004: 40–4); Morss (1995).
39 Archard (2004: 41).
40 Morss (1995).
41 Burman (1994: 12).
42 Ibid., 10–12.
43 Morss (1995: 21).
44 Ibid., 22.
45 Ibid., 24.
46 Ibid., 23.
47 Ibid., 35.
48 Ibid., 10.
49 The late nineteenth century in Western Europe and America saw movements against child labour, the establishment of compulsory public education, and the rise of social work to manage the risks of children who were idle on the streets. See Hawes (1991); Rose (1989).
50 As discussed by Morss (1995: 66).
51 Archard (2002, 2006: 6).
52 This argument was made most strongly in the 1970s by child liberationists. See Richard Farson (1974); Cohen (1980).

53 I use the term "harm" here to broadly capture the full breadth of concerns that children's rights literature addresses. This accounts for those who deal with harms in a physical and immediate sense (generally, these are the protectionists), as well as those who view political exclusion and unequal rights as a harm (such as child liberationists like Howard Cohen and Richard Farson).
54 Freeman (1992: 66).
55 Nikolas Rose (1999); Hindess (2001).
56 Ennew (2008); Hawes (1991).
57 Marshall (1999: 103–4).
58 Ibid., 104.
59 'Convention on the Rights of the Child', (United Nations General Assembly 1989).
60 See, 'The construction of Children as an Object of International Relations: The Declaration of Children's Rights and the Child Welfare Committee of the League of Nations'.
61 Ibid., 108.
62 Ibid., 106.
63 Ibid., 129 and 33 respectively.
64 Rehfeld (2011).
65 Ennew (2008: 66).
66 Ibid.
67 Ibid., 67.
68 Ibid.
69 Lister (2007: 717).
70 This is discussed further in Chapter 4.
71 Farson (1974); Cohen (1980).
72 Archard (2004: 72).
73 Ibid., 70–7.
74 Iris Marion Young grapples with the difficulty of sameness and difference in liberal political communities: see Young (1990).
75 Archard (2004: 74).
76 See generally: Douzinas (2000).
77 Archard (2006: 6).
78 Arneil (2002: 80).
79 Freeman (1997a: 66–7).
80 Ibid., 67.
81 Onora O'Neill (1988: 40).

2 The liberal rationality of children's rights

Introduction

In this chapter, I argue that ideas of reason, maturity and autonomy inform, shape and limit how we are able to think and talk about children and their rights. I do this by considering how a number of Western, liberal philosophers talk about childhood. Across a diversity of perspectives, I argue that children do not necessarily appear in the work of these philosophers as a distinct subject, but as images of potential implicit in their broader vision of liberal political society; as images of the future-adults they ought to grow into. This presents two implications: one, different conceptions of childhood offer different narratives of development into adulthood informing what is valued in childhood as a precursor to a full and adult life; and two, these alternative conceptions of childhood are premised upon the normative ideals of different philosophical traditions. This, in turn, produces claims about what children's rights should be that are premised upon different normative ideals about the adults they ought to become.

First, I identify three main conceptions of childhood that philosophers subscribe to: the sinner, the innocent and the blank-slate. Each of these conceptions establishes a different narrative of children and the adults they ought to grow into. Blank-slates must be educated toward an autonomous moral reasoning so that they can navigate the world on their own terms. Innocents have an innate goodness that must be preserved as much as possible into adulthood. Sinners must be disciplined into appropriate behaviour before they are cast out into the world as autonomous, risky beings. In turn, these narratives of childhood inform different perspectives on children's rights. The innocent is the subject of a protectionist mode of rights, while the blank-slate informs an autonomy mode of rights. Meanwhile, the sinner appears most clearly in contemporary rights debates. This sinful conception of childhood does not emerge directly from Western liberal philosophy. Rather, the sinner presents as the failure of childhood innocence or of an improperly educated blank-slate. As such, the development of this conception is less extensive than that of the innocent and blank-slate. However, as will be evident in subsequent chapters, particularly Chapters 4 and 5 on criminality and sexuality, the sinner emerges as a strong conception of childhood in these debates.

The second implication this chapter attends to is the role these conceptions of childhood play in the normative objectives of Western philosophers. I argue that, across a number of texts, philosophers are preoccupied with the future-adult and how that adult serves their broader political project. John Locke's notion of the child as a blank-slate especially reflects our contemporary understanding of childhood in the West. This blank-slate must be educated into a rationality that allows that subject to become a citizen that is able to consent to the political authority of the liberal state. John Dewey shares in Locke's understanding of children as blank-slates, but attempts to regard children as a more embedded (rather than hypothetical) subject. This embedded perspective is able to recognize children as members of society already, as "beings" rather than becomings. Jean-Jacques Rousseau's hypothetical students, Emilé and Sophie, represent a sentimental and Romantic conception of childhood as innocent. This is an innocence that is lost upon entering a modern, civilized world. Christian puritanical literature portrays children as innately sinful. As mentioned, this conception is less influential in conceptions of childhood. However, I argue that this sinner is still evident as the innocent's opposite, and the blank-slate's failure. In subsequent chapters I will argue that the sinner emerges in children's rights debates as the risk that arises in the failure of innocence and education of the blank-slate. It is against this risk and failure the future-adult subject must be "governed" and, in Chapter 7, a governmentality analysis demonstrates that the child, at least as a *potential* sinner, continues to pervade liberal understandings of children.

These three alternative conceptions of childhood are offered as a heuristic device to facilitate the analysis of the subsequent chapters. I endeavour not to adopt any of these conceptions as my own. As discussed in the Introduction, it is possible to have no conception of childhood whatsoever (what I termed a pre-modern perspective), a conception of the child as natural (a "modern" perspective), or a conception of childhood as entirely socially constructed (what I termed a "postmodern" perspective). My analysis of childhood as a blank-slate, innocent or sinner is informed by a view of childhood as socially constructed. Further, these constructions of childhood serve an explicitly political purpose: to occupy the place of the ideal future citizen in an ideal liberal political community. The philosophers and texts that are deliberately selected are intended to highlight this argument and illuminate how these conceptions inform, shape and limit debates about citizenship, criminality and sexuality rather than as an analysis of the full canon of Western liberal political thought.

Sin and the non-innocent child

When Frank Musgrove asserted that the 'adolescent was invented at the same time as the steam engine', he was referring to the idea that previously most thought of children simply as "small adults".[1] Writing in 1964, Musgrove reiterates the argument made two years earlier in Phillipe Ariès', *Centuries of Childhood*. As discussed in the Introduction, Ariès distinguished between infants (as younger than three or four years) that tended to be markedly different due to their significant physical dependence on others; and older children, who were not viewed as all that different from their "adult" counterparts. Ariès comments that this 'is why, as soon as the child could live without the constant solicitude of his mother, his nanny or his cradle-rocker, he belonged to adult society'.[2] That is, prior to the Enlightenment, there was no concept of childhood, only of infancy and adulthood.

In some ways, the conception of the child as a sinner relies upon this lesser distinction between childhood and adulthood. The sinful child is one that possesses the same responsibilities and obligations as an adult, or at least is subject to the same punishments as any adult would be for sinful behaviour. This is evident in accounts of puritanical America, where children were a crucial part of household and agricultural labour, and subject to severe punishment.[3] It can also be argued that the child as a sinner appears in contemporary debates as characteristic of adolescence, rather than childhood. That is, broadly speaking, it is teenagers who can be characterized as "sinners" and teenagers are *not* children. This distinction relies upon an acceptance of developmental theories of childhood, which is not one that I share. In the following chapters on sexuality and criminality, while teenager behaviour can be tied to a "sinner" characterization, I also attempt to demonstrate how it is also tied to younger children.

Historian Joseph Hawes offers a conception of children as sinners that was present in early colonial America. In this historically, geographically and culturally specific moment, he argues that the child was viewed as being born in original sin; innocence was merely a façade. The purpose of childhood, then, was to seek redemption for this sin.[4] Children faced the risk of never outgrowing this original sin. Lack of discipline and punishment would only serve to increase this risk. This view of children, Hawes argues, was supported by the sense of children as small adults, rather than individuals at a distinct stage of life. This allowed children to be held to the same standards as adults: working, contributing to the household and being accountable to the regulations and punishments of their society. Duties to the family extended to the point that to curse or smite a parent was punishable by death in some American colonies.[5] Nonetheless, this puritanical view of children as the embodiment of original sin justified severe punishment as a means of facilitating redemption for that sin. The purpose of education, therefore, was primarily aimed at moral development.[6] In this way, it is possible to conceptualize the child as neither an innocent nor a blank-slate, but rather as a person capable of morally wrong acts.

The above account presents sin as a polar opposite to innocence. However, there is also an alternative theological account of Original Sin that presents the counter to innocence as a more neutral form of "non-innocence", rather than inexplicable and innate evil. This interpretation arises from the theology of St Augustine. However, it is also a very contemporary narrative that plays out especially in debates about children's criminality. The term "sinful" is used throughout this text to distinguish it sharply from innocence, but it has been persuasively argued that an Augustinian account of childhood is not one of wilful sin but instead of non-innocence produced by the inheritance of Adam's sin: 'For Augustine all creatures stood in the shadow of Adam, and the goodness of creation had been vitiated for all who follow him, including those newly born.'[7] As a result, Augustine's theology examines children's behaviour that today would be understood in developmental terms, 'for evidence of the burden of a sin that had infected all of Adam's progeny'.[8] Distinguishing sin from non-innocence in Augustine's analysis, pivots on the distinction between wilful wrongdoing that requires a capacity to decide and to act on those decisions, and a wrong that is inherited from Adam despite absence of will. For theologians, such as Augustine, this presents problems for thinking not just about children's characters and developing maturity (which he regarded as coinciding with increasing levels of responsibility), but also for thinking about unbaptized children who have not yet received forgiveness for their original sin and thus are either damned to hell or to limbo. The relevance to this book is not to provide a theological account of childhood, but to consider its social and political implications in our contemporary age.

Paul Weithman considers how Augustine and Thomas Aquinas treat political authority in relation to their understanding of Original Sin. For Augustine, political authority is 'exercised only to coerce or restrain the vicious' and 'since there would be no vice if there were no sin', it suggests that there is no need for political authority in the innocent state of nature. Adam's original transgression, resulting in the Fall from innocence, produces the need for political authority. By contrast, for Aquinas, political authority can contribute more positively to a life of virtue and would have existed even in a state of innocence.[9] Staying with the Augustinian interpretation of sin as non-innocence, and the necessity (and legitimacy) of political authority as arising from Original Sin, Weithman claims that the

> authority [that] would have been exercised in a state of innocence, would ... have been paternal authority like that the Old Testament patriarch or Roman *paterfamilias* exercised over his wife and children. *It would not have been the political authority a king exercises over his subjects.*[10]

What this suggests is that the only form of authority in a state of nature, also being the state of innocence, is a paternalistic rather than political form. The authority exercised by a patriarch over his wife and children is presented as a natural authority, which requires no justification or rationale. Political authority, by contrast, exists to regulate the sins of humanity after the Fall. What this analysis suggests is that children's subjugation to parental authority is both natural and without need for justification, in the same way that other (political) forms of authority are.

In contemporary society, these narratives of sin and non-innocence are at work. Australian philosopher, Joanne Faulkner, offers a characterization of the child as sinner as innocent's counterpoint, which directly reflects the Christian narrative of original sin. She writes:

This loss of innocence is our original sin, an indelible strain of guilt inherited from Adam and Eve as part of the human condition. Innocence had been a state of blissful oneness with God's will. But it is also an unsustainable condition, yielded once one lives in a world rife with harm and compromise. To be agents of one's own life one must cast off innocence. Living a mortal life involves getting one's hands dirty. Or so the story goes.[11]

In this way, innocence cannot be separated from sin. In Augustinian terms, innocence and non-innocence are related and imbedded in one another. For example, Janet Dolgin, in her discussion of childhood and autonomy, identifies the twentieth century as one in which the child as an innocent emerged as the dominant conception. However, she argues that by the end of that century, children had begun to re-emerge as inherently risky, though not necessarily sinful.[12] Nikolas Rose's discussion of the rise of social policies around young people in the late nineteenth century produced early examples of what we today call children's rights,[13] and operated twofold. As child labour laws were introduced to protect vulnerable and poor children, a new population of working-class children were left idle on the streets of Western, industrialized, cities. Government responded with three institutions: the Kindergarten, the orphanage and the juvenile courts.[14] Education for working-class children was designed to mitigate the risk they posed to society; education for middle-class children was designed to maximize their potential for society.[15] As Harry Hendrick has argued, the institutional shift from child labour to childcare and education sought 'to reclaim the factory child for civilisation'.[16] Orphanages minimized the potential risk of unloved and uncared for children, while the courts responded to the criminal behaviour of young people, which arose from the failure of schools and orphanages. The institutionalization of childhood served the explicit purpose of governing childhood: one designed to minimize the risk of working-class children, and one to maximize the potential of middle-class children. In doing so, it reflected the relationship between innocent and non-innocent accounts of the child.

Conceptions of the child as non-innocents and sinners appear prevalently in contemporary debates in opposition to the ideal of children as innocents and blank-slates. For example, in the discussion of child citizenship in Chapter 6, the risk of a child that is not educated toward liberal citizenship is that they will enter adult life ill-equipped to responsibly manage their freedom. This again is highlighted in the discussion of governmentality in Chapter 7, which provides an analysis of the need for liberal citizens to self-govern their own freedom so that the state does not need to. In Chapter 4's discussion of criminality, the child emerges far more explicitly as a possible sinner. Indeed, I raise a number of examples in which the criminal wrongs of children are explained as a kind of evil that is only possible *because* of their childishness. In Chapter 5's discussion of sexuality, the child as sinner emerges as the sexually promiscuous child. Indeed, in this chapter I also raise Michel Foucault's discussion of sexuality that highlights how sex came to be viewed as a source of great personal risk, a source of anxiety and increased need for personal vigilance and self-care. Again, this raises an aspect of self-government that is addressed in Chapter 7's discussion of governmentality. While the conception of sinner does not arise directly from liberal thought, as the other two conceptions do, it remains a key conception that informs, shapes and limits debates about children's rights.

In the chapters on citizenship, criminality and sexuality it will be evident that this conception of the child as sinner emerges when liberal conceptions of childhood are disrupted. Either in the corruption of innocence, or the failure of the blank-slate, a conception of sinfulness reflects the limits of our liberal understandings of childhood. An analysis of sinfulness in these debates allows us a perspective of individuals beyond the neutrality or good that liberalism emphasizes. Further, it allows us to highlight what is at stake in emotive and passionate claims made on behalf of children and their rights.

Preserving innocence: Jean-Jacques Rousseau's *Émile*

Jean-Jacques Rousseau's educational treatise, *Émile*, famously begins by stating that, 'God makes all things good; man meddles with them and they become evil.'[17] His Romantic regard of the state of nature and of youth leaves him fearful of how the modern, civilized world might corrupt such innocence. In this opening statement, Rousseau offers a conception of childhood that is Romantic and innocent, but also potentially evil (a potential sinner). This reflects his broader perspective on the state of nature.[18] In contrast to Locke, Rousseau regards the modern, civilized age, including its preoccupation with private property, as an unfortunate development in the history of mankind. He writes that:

> so long as they undertook only what a single person could accomplish, and confined themselves to such arts as did not require the joint labour of several hands, they lived free, healthy, honest and happy lives.... But from the moment one man had to have enough provisions for two, equality disappeared, property was introduced, work became indispensable, and vast forest became smiling fields which man had to water with the sweat of his brow, and where slavery and misery were soon sent to germinate and grow up with the crops.[19]

For Rousseau, property coincides with man's emergence from an uncivilized state, where people are nonetheless happy and free.[20] With the dawn of civilization arrives a mandate to work and the necessity of material belongings gives rise to the basis of inequality.[21]

It is against this backdrop that Rousseau formulates his philosophy of education:

> We are born weak, we need strength; helpless, we need aid; foolish, we need reason. All that we lack at birth, all that we need when we come to man's estate is the gift of education.[22]

In *Émile*, Rousseau advocates an education that focuses upon the natural development of the child, driven by the latter's own curiosities rather than an adult view tainted by a corrupt modern age. Rousseau argues that an education by men is misguided because it can only fail in teaching what Nature herself is better placed to do.[23] The purpose of allowing Nature to instruct children is not only about the desire for children to be free to direct their own learning, but also about his own notion of what a more meaningful, educated, adult life would be: a life that preserves the closeness of the child to Nature for as long as possible. That is, 'the more nearly a man's condition approximates to this state of nature the less difference there is between his desires and his powers, and happiness is therefore less remote'.[24] In a modern society where natural freedom is seemingly impossible, bound as it is to material wants that no one person can achieve alone, Rousseau develops a philosophy of education that attempts to realize an adult who is not just happy, but also free:

> There is only one man who gets his own way – he who can get it single handed; therefore freedom, not power is the greatest good. That man is truly free who desires what he is able to perform, and does what he desires.... Apply it to childhood, and all the rules of education spring from it.[25]

Here, Rousseau equates freedom with an individual existence, unencumbered by obligations to others: a conception of autonomy. As discussed in the first chapter, for Immanuel Kant, autonomy or individual freedom extends from the attainment of a superior intellectual reason. By contrast, Rousseau claims that: 'With the age of reason the child becomes the slave of the community.'[26] While Rousseau seems resigned to the fact that efforts preserving the state of nature are futile, it is nonetheless this enslaved future that Rousseau hopes to educate out of existence by holding children as close to the state of nature as possible: a possibility that Rousseau believes only exists in childhood.

Indeed, in contrast to Locke, Rousseau considers it a mistake to make children 'reason about things they cannot understand'.[27] The purpose of education is less about vocational training, or the transmission of knowledge. Instead, it is about developing a sense of self and interpersonal relations that are grounded in moral, ethical and virtuous principles that extend from our place in Nature, rather than our place in modern society. These moral, ethical and virtuous principles that are grounded in a Romantic state of nature should guide one in modern society in ways that avoid the corruption Rousseau recognizes around him. So, for Locke, who regards modern liberal society as necessary to overcome the injustices likely to arise from a perfect equality in the state of nature, children must be reasoned with. To demonstrate the kind of reason that makes this possible, it is necessary to draw upon a form of reason only possible in modern society; a deliberate departure from our natural state. For Rousseau, with his alternative ontological foundation, to reason with children is to employ a mode of thinking that arises from a corrupt modern age. Instead, one should aim to derive principles that existed in the state of nature, and have since been departed from. Only on this basis is it possible to raise a generation of citizens who might do better than the last. This is an innocent conception of childhood. It is a conception that regards children on the one hand as "our" (society's) hope for the future, and on the other hand views children's growing up as a loss.

Rousseau pursues a philosophy of education that follows natural tendencies, in the hope that it will direct the child toward a happier and a freer, more autonomous, adult life. This reflects, on the one hand, a sincere concern for the well-being of the child as a child. However, it also reflects an equal concern for the well-being of the adult version of this child. In hoping that the right form of education will provide an antidote to the "yoke" of civilized society,[28] Rousseau's educational pedagogy outlines not only how a child ought to be educated, but also how society can be improved, and how happiness, freedom and equality can be preserved in a civilized age. This conflates the well-being of children with the well-being of adulthood and society. In attempting to protect the child from the burden of modern, adult life, Rousseau nonetheless ties children to his political narrative: the most important role for children is the future-adult he thinks they ought to become.

Sophie, and Rousseau's gendered innocence

Jean-Jacques Rousseau distinguishes between an education for boys and for girls. This has been the subject of analysis by Susan Moller Okin.[29] Rousseau hopes to educate Sophie, Émile's future wife, so she remains as close to her natural state as possible. He tells her that, '[t]he essential thing is to be what nature has made you; women are only too ready to be what men would have them'.[30] However, despite the shared philosophical foundation, he produces two distinct forms of education for boys and girls. For Susan Moller Okin, this presents an opportunity to consider 'what reasoning is employed to discover the natural man, and how this reasoning differs from that used to discover the natural woman'.[31] Her analysis pivots on two methods employed by Rousseau: one, the state of nature as a social concept; and two, his attempts to determine which characteristics are innate to an individual, and which are learned.[32] Thus, Moller Okin allows us to read Rousseau in two ways: one, for what he says about reason; and two, for what reason he employs to say it. I argue with Moller Okin that what he understands as reason is a direct result of his understanding of the state of nature. Further, this understanding of the state of nature more closely reflects relationships between men and women in his contemporary age, rather than the hypothetical past he imagines. The result is the production of a mode of reason specific to the Enlightenment and one that continues to dominate intellectual and public debates today, including those about children's rights.

Moller Okin begins with one of Rousseau's many statements about the equality present in the state of nature:

> there is, in the state of nature, in fact, a real and indestructible equality, since it is impossible in that state for the bare difference between one man and another to be sufficient to make one dependent on the other.[33]

Rousseau's understanding of equality in the original state of nature reflects the lack of familial relationships he envisaged between men and women. This equality, Moller Okin observes, is demonstrated in part by the fact that in Rousseau's imaginings there is 'no marriage, family or any other sign of dependence of one sex on the other'.[34] However, she argues that this understanding shifts somewhere in Rousseau's work, as he does not continue to view women or girls as the equal counterpart of men and boys in producing a completely different pedagogy for the education of Sophie, who must serve the role of wife, not future-citizen.[35] The shift, Moller Okin argues, is produced by Rousseau's historical distinctions between three different ages in the state of nature. The first age of the state of nature is one that produces perfect equality. It is the loss of this state of nature that Rousseau laments so heavily in his *Discourses*. In the second age of the state of nature, the "golden age", a 'patriarchal nuclear family' emerges.[36] As mentioned, for Moller Okin, this is a sudden and unjustified shift from equality to patriarchy.[37] The third state depicts a rise of organized labour in agriculture and metallurgy, and material want; Rousseau's "corrupt age" and the height of social inequality.[38]

Like Locke, Rousseau requires a social contract to legitimate the transformation of free and equal men in the state of nature, into consenting subjects of the liberal state. This is a greater trade-off for Rousseau than for Locke, whose subjects consent to the social contract because it protects their freedoms and liberties. For Rousseau, the trade-off is a reluctant but necessary one: given a new modern, corrupt age man must find the best means to protect his limited, remaining freedom and preserve any remaining equality.[39] Moller Okin observes that for Rousseau it was important to have a reason for this trade-off, yet 'he did not feel at all compelled to explain why proud and unconquerable women should have done that same unreasonable thing'[40] in their submission to a patriarchal order. For Moller Okin, this offers illuminating areas of discussion for feminist understandings and the critique of Rousseau's work and Western political philosophy more broadly.[41] It reveals that reason is a key concept that distinguishes those who are relevant and included in public and political discourse: men, who have it; and women, who apparently do not.

As discussed in Chapter 1, with respect to the paternalistic paradigm, Rousseau's construction of a patriarchal family unit informs understandings of relations of power, not only between men and women, but also between other subjects like the poor and uncivilized, and those who assert authority over them. The full weight of *Émile* – and the distinct educations of this young boy and his future wife, Sophie – is that it necessarily maintains not only a division of labour, but also a division of knowledge, reinforcing a patriarchal set of power relations at the heart of a liberal social order, public and private. In the division of knowledge, reason is presented as a masculine quality while females are defined by its absence. Indeed, it is to this aspect of Rousseau's work that Mary Wollstonecraft retorted:

> In fact, it is farce to call any being virtuous whose virtues do not result from the exercise of its own reason. This was Rousseau's opinion respective of

men: I extend it to women and confidently assert that they have been drawn out of their sphere by false refinement and not by an endeavour to acquire masculine qualities.[42]

That is to say, the lack of women's reason is by no means natural, but rather the direct result of the control of women by men, and their unjust relegation to a private sphere. In this, Moller Okin challenges Rousseau's own exercise of reason: 'He is using the concept of the natural and the law of nature very selectively, in order to justify what he, the philosopher, deems to be good and useful for mankind.'[43] With respect to childhood, this could be said of most philosophers who frame children in terms of their future-adult role in their ideal political society. Any position of childhood, children's education and any conception of their rights are necessarily theorized within a broader philosophical project. The understanding and treatment of children is always, necessarily, consistent with broader social and political objectives.

Susan Moller Okin argues that in Rousseau's attempt to distinguish man's innate characteristics from those that are learned, he constructs the female as the complete opposite of the male.[44] In taking the position that women, by nature, are so amiable as to submit to authority over them without any exercise of their own reason, she argues that Rousseau reverses the reason he uses elsewhere to reject Aristotle's argument for slavery.[45] Rousseau contradicts his own theory of natural freedom by refusing to attend to women's subjugated position in modern society with a rational analysis that he applies to their male counterparts. Moller Okin argues that:

> Rousseau suggests in a teleological fashion that such characteristics as duplicity and tolerance of injustice are innate in women because of the subordinate position in life for which they are naturally destined.[46]

Thus, for Rousseau, women's subjugated position is not the result of an illegitimate exercise of power by men over women in the home, society, politics and the broader public realm.

What Moller Okin does so convincingly is take apart the purported reason demonstrated by Rousseau. She argues that his understanding of the golden age of the state of nature fails to explain the emergence of a faithful wife and mother as the woman's natural place within a natural, nuclear family. As a result, he draws 'conclusions about what her intellectual and other capacities *should* be like'.[47] So, Sophie's education is distinguished from Émile's in the following way:

> The search for abstract and speculative truths, for principles, for axioms in science, everything that involves the generalization of ideas, is not within a woman's province: their studies should concern practical things; it is their task to apply the principles discovered by man, and it is up to them to make the observations that lead man to discover these principles.[48]

There is no reasoning here about what a woman is. Instead, there is only a reason employed with respect to Rousseau's broader political project that regards the ills of the world as a direct result of man's emergence from his state of nature. As Moller Okin argues, it is this preoccupation with man and his experience of the world that results in such a deficient political philosophy, failing as it does to meaningfully account for women. The educational pedagogy that Moller Okin's analysis unmasks is highly problematic as a result. She quotes Rousseau, who argues that:

> the entire education of women must be relative to men. To please them, to be useful to them, to be loved and honoured by them, to rear them when they are young, to care for them when they are grown up, to counsel and console, to make their lives pleasant and charming, these are the duties of women at all times, and they should be taught them in their childhood. To the extent that we refuse to go back to this principle, we will stray from our goal, and all the precepts women are given will not result in their happiness or our own.[49]

In this sense, the goal of a girl's education is not necessarily related to women's happiness, or even men's, but rather to redemption from our own corruption; a corruption that has resulted from our having grown too far from our natural state. This has little to do with Sophie's childhood, yet it informs her education dramatically. Indeed, it also has little do with Émile's life and education. Instead, Rousseau's treatise offers us his understanding of what men and women should be in his ideal political society, and the education that boys and girls must receive to realize that goal.

This conception of innocent childhood plays out in a range of children's rights debates. As I will show in the following chapters, it tends to emphasize protection: protecting children from the burden of public and political life, thereby rationalizing their exclusion from citizenship rights; protecting children from facing the full weight of the criminal law, by emphasizing the lack of capacity children have for knowingly committing grave moral wrongs; protecting children not only from sexual exploitation and abuse, but also from sexual imagery that is claimed to be inherently exploitative or dangerous. All these uses of innocence will be unpacked in the following chapters.

The blank-slate and legitimate political authority

For John Locke, the state of nature is characterized by a perfect freedom and a realm of equals, 'wherein all power and jurisdiction is reciprocal, no one having more than another'.[50] In this state, there is no superior person or being that might claim greater authority than another. Yet, we are not born into this state of nature as equals, not as men or even as women. We are born into this state of nature as children; notwithstanding our potential, the weakest and most unequal of the lot. Indeed, John Locke, without any sense of contradiction, discloses this directly:

'Children, I confess, are not born in this full state of equality, though they are born to it.'[51] So, on the one hand John Locke's *Second Treatise of Government* emphasizes man's equality (a more contemporary reading appropriately extends this principle of equality to both men and women) in the state of nature,[52] but on the other hand accepts that 'age or virtue may give men a just precedency'.[53] As a result, there are two legitimate grounds for different and unequal treatment in Locke's just society: the first is age, an arbitrary but natural indicator of reason and maturity; the second is virtue, or merit, premised upon actual and demonstrated capacities that make one person more deserving than another.

For John Locke, the idea that age is a natural basis for differential treatment coincides with the dependency of the young on their parents:

> Their parents have a sort of rule and jurisdiction over them when they come into the world, and for some time after, but 'tis a temporary one. The bonds of subjection are like swaddling clothes they are wrapped up in, and supported by in the weakness of their infancy. Age and reason as they grow up, loosen them till at length they drop quite off, and leave a man at his own free disposal.[54]

Children are not the equals of the adult members of Western, liberal, political communities. Rather, and somewhat paradoxically, age and reason are conditions of equality. Yet, John Locke seems to regard individuals in the state of nature as beings that already possess these two characteristics. If they do not, it would not be possible for the state of nature to be a realm of perfect equals. Leaving aside how this view of children within Locke's philosophy complicates his understanding of the state of nature, it remains that a realm of perfect equals presents a problem for John Locke. In Locke's state of nature, the equality of all individuals carries the great risk that they might act in ways that inhibit each other's exercise of freedom. His treatises on government, therefore, are an attempt to remedy what he regards as the limitations of the state of nature: civil society is an improvement on the state of nature. Locke's principles of legitimate political authority are governed by a responsibility of government to only act insofar as individuals have consented, and to protect a man's (and woman's) natural rights (rights that existed in a state of nature; namely, freedom, equality and private property). The challenge for Locke is not how to remain as closely connected to a natural order as possible, but how to best establish a social and political order that supports natural rights.

These rights are problematically built around structures of private property.[55] Indeed, Locke's free, equal and independent men refer to a very small class of people: European, property-owning, males. However, these broader weaknesses of Locke's philosophy are not the subject of inquiry here. Rather, the focus is how his view of the state of nature (and the imperative of a modern, civilized social and political order it demands) influences our understanding of the rights of children today.

The legitimate political authority of Locke's liberal state

According to Locke, the legitimate political authority of the liberal state is premised upon a social contract between the governed and those that govern.[56] Shaped by the historical events of the Enlightenment, the rejection of monarchs' claims to divine authority required an alternative conception of how a state could legitimately exercise power over those it governed, lest there be anarchy.[57] The notion that the King was sovereign had been superseded by a notion that each and every individual was sovereign over himself or herself. Social contract theories share, across various iterations, an account that sees this sovereign individual consent to limits of some of his or her freedoms in exchange for the favours of care, protection and certain (citizenship) rights from the state. This weaves together three key ideas that are central to my argument.

First, in order for sovereign power to be legitimate the "people"[58] must consent to its exercise, or it will be regarded as totalitarian, despotic or oppressive for its citizens. In order for this to be so, those who are subject to power must consent to the exercise of that power over them. Consent is required because each individual is a sovereign being. Unless that individual consents to the trespass of that sovereignty, any trespass upon that sovereignty is a wrong and is unjustifiable. There are some trespasses that cannot be consented to, such as slavery.[59] However, this relationship between the sovereign self (as citizen) and those that govern (the state) is taken to be a hypothetical act of consent: each individual is not given the opportunity to offer up this consent; there is no individual contract between a citizen and a state; and opportunities to exit from the state of citizenship – out of objection to the liberal social contract – do not exist. Yet, despite being a hypothetical scenario, this social contract is still fundamental to how the liberal state conceives of the sovereignty of both individual citizens and itself.

Second, within this hypothetical scenario, the consent that must be provided is quite literal consent: a rational being must make it and it must be freely given. A subject, then, must be willing and able to trade some freedom in exchange for some benefit. Quite literally, people must exchange government for a right to vote and for political participation, taxes for public services and physical restraint for public safety. However, once sovereignty is transferred to the state, you cannot take it back. If you find yourself unable to make any of these bargains, you are not excised from your responsibilities to the liberal state but instead remain subject to it, as its prisoner or as its outcast. This is the liberal bargain.

Third, what this hypothetical scenario produces are quite real consequences: not only for those who attempt to reject the social contract, or live outside its terms, but for liberalism itself. What this social contract theory demands is a free and consenting participant. Without this person, social contract theory finds itself without the individual needed to legitimate the political authority of the state. It is presumed that a rational individual person would always choose to surrender some of his individual sovereignty to the sovereignty of the state. There is no possibility that this bargain could not be struck: if it could not be struck, it must be because it is not a rational person contemplating the hypothetical act of consent, in which case that person is not part of the social contract (children are an example of this). The rationality of liberalism is such that the only rational thing to do is accept the bargain. Thus, what this social contract theory demands is an individual who is free to consent, but not beyond the rationality of the liberal state. This is what Barry Hindess regards as liberalism's "unfreedom".[60] When Michel Foucault calls for us to 'cut off the king's head',[61] he is highlighting how the ongoing commitment to sovereignty in the liberal state (irrespective of the demise of divinely determined Kings) maintains the problems of law and prohibition, which are forces that undermine individual freedom and autonomy. In this sense, sovereign power is challenged by the Enlightenment with the rejection of a sovereign King ordained by God, but also reinforced by a political liberalism that maintains the sovereign power of the state: a power that requires free citizens, but reinscribes laws and prohibitions that limits those freedoms. While this power no longer concerns choosing who dies or lives – and instead regulates life, while allowing others to die – the power of the sovereign over life is one that remains a problem for Foucault's vision of autonomy.[62] While the Enlightenment saw the individual appear as the first sovereign that provides the legitimacy of the state, the state remains a legitimate sovereign power and a possible impediment to individual freedom. This remains a pervasive and problematic aspect of liberal political thought.[63] In this way, liberalism produces its own rationality. In turn, this liberal rationality becomes the condition of liberalism's consenting subject: a rational, autonomous, adult citizen that is free to consent to the sovereignty of the state over himself, but not free to reject it.

John Locke's social contract is informed by his particular understanding of humankind in the state of nature and the need it creates for civil society and a legitimate political authority.[64] There is no natural authority that rightly places one individual above another; no divine authority that justifiably places a King above his subjects. In monarchies and autocracies there is no legitimate exercise of political authority, because there is no consent. The conditions of individuals providing that consent are, in turn, age and reason. For Locke, it is the lack of these very qualities that distinguishes children from adults.[65] Children are thus excluded from the social contract. As indicated above, the legitimacy of authority exercised over children, by their parents, is a natural one. Further, in the absence of parents, the doctrine of *parens patriae* requires the state to substitute for parents without the requirement of consent.

Political freedom appears in John Locke's work, not as a natural right, but as a right conditional upon reason and maturity. In reply to his own questions about what makes individuals free from the law of nature and the holder of property rights, he answers:

> a state of maturity wherein he might be supposed capable to know that law, that so he might keep his actions within the bounds of it. When he has acquired that state, he is presumed to know how far that law is to be his guide, and how fare he may make use of his freedom.[66]

And:

> Is a man under the law of England? What made him free of that law?... A
> capacity for knowing that law. Which is supposed by that law, at the age of
> one and twenty years and in some cases sooner. If that made his father free,
> it shall make his son free too.[67]

In these passages, Locke's freedom is not innate to mankind but contingent upon
the following: a state of maturity, capacity to know and an acquisition of knowledge. In these statements is also the sentiment that together these provide the
basis upon which an individual can make the judgement of what is a justified
exercise of sovereign power over them, and what is a justified exercise of sovereign power by themselves over others. This foreshadows a form of Kantian autonomy: an ability to reason and decide for oneself what is fair, good and right.
This maturity, capacity for, and acquisition of, knowledge is tied to an arbitrary
age: 21 years, perhaps earlier. In all, children cannot be born into this world free,
but only with the potential to be free. This potential may or may not be realized.
The realization of this potential is only demonstrated by maturity and knowledge. In order to be an individual who is free to and capable of consenting to
the legitimate exercise of political authority over him or her, it is necessary for
that individual to demonstrate reason and maturity. Indeed, this is where we find
John Locke's child: a blank, neutral slate ready to be written upon by all the
experiences and knowledges of the world. We are able to identify in his work a
developmental understanding of the child that establishes their status as a future-
adult citizen as the holy grail of social and political inclusion.

Consent and liberal political authority

That consent provides political legitimacy is fundamental to the liberal state. It is
the basis for legitimate political authority and action. Theoretically, the power of
one person to rule over a state and all its citizens is legitimate in liberal states
only because those who are subject to that sovereign power consent to it via a
social contract. There are two aspects to this: consent to the very structure and
system of political power, and consent to those who hold power within it. The
first aspect refers, of course, to the authority of a liberal democratic state and the
willingness of citizens to be governed. While the second refers to a democratic
process in which citizens express their choice about who they wish to be governed by. With respect to the first aspect, as Albert Weale points out, the act of
consent is a hypothetical act in a contemporary context: as citizens we do not
have an immediate opportunity to offer our actual consent to the system of government, only a democratic act to choose the leader within it.[68] However, there is
tacit consent implicit in the absence of any revolutionary agenda. For a population to express its lack of consent to the political system, force is likely to be
required: it would take more than a referendum; it would require a revolution.
The absence of significant attempts within the political community to undermine

and overhaul a political system suggests a tacit consent, but it is hardly a direct and immediate expression of consent.

It remains to be noted that according to this social contract theory, political authority can only be legitimate if those that exercise control have the consent of those subject to its commands. For John Locke, each person has a natural right to freedom, implying that at the age of maturity no one may be subordinated to anyone else's commands by nature.[69] This notion is one of individual autonomy. Autonomy may be a ground for democratic decision-making.[70] Democracy is the collective self-government of individuals. This conception of democracy relies upon alternative views of autonomy. A republican view focuses more strongly on moral autonomy, which combines freedom and responsibility as the right and obligation of the autonomous individual. This connects individuals to their capacity for autonomy and establishes democracy as the appropriate form of collective decision-making. The more liberal view is that the individual is the best judge of his or her own interests, which in its own way relies upon the capacity (and maturity) of the individual to do so.

However, there are some critiques of the consent theory of political authority. Briefly, the instrumentalist critique argues that political authority is necessary to protect each person's equal freedom.[71] Thus, each person has certain duties to comply with political authority in order to realize justice: 'one protects the liberty of each and every person better by instituting political authority and by treating its commands as authoritative'.[72] However, in a social contract model the duty to comply only exists where you have consented to the governing authority, rather than where you are a member of its polity by force or coercion.[73] However, to be born into a particular polity or social community has no voluntariness or autonomy involved.[74] At the age of maturity, upon which you are deemed to be a citizen of your state, you are taken to have the requisite autonomy to give consent to both the political system (even if it is only tacit consent, evidenced by your failure to reject the system) and its leader, through the exercise of the right to vote. In these ways, consent has become a concept central to liberal democracy and it relies heavily upon the capacity of individuals to give that consent. This is so, notwithstanding that there are few mechanisms that ensure meaningful and informed consent. One of the key tasks of society then, is to educate children toward the form of reason and level of maturity necessary for consent.

Educating John Locke's blank-slates

John Locke's essay *Some Thoughts Concerning Education* (1963) was written for a father friend of his. It begins most enthusiastically with details for an appropriate diet, sleep patterns and pedagogies for the instruction of disciplines such as French, Latin and geometry. Indeed, it is not altogether different from a modern-day parenting manual. John Locke's essay is an explicit statement on how to educate a child to ensure they grow into a good, liberal, adult citizen; a citizen that will be able to provide the necessary consent to the liberal political state, without diminishing that individual's own rights and freedoms.

In Locke's *Thoughts*, we can identify a developmental approach to understanding childhood and the lifespan into adulthood. Children are presented as imperfect, incomplete versions of their adult selves. For Locke, children do not yet have reason but will acquire it if they are *reasoned with*:

> It will perhaps be wondered that I mention *reasoning* with children: and yet I cannot but think that the true way of dealing with them. They understand it as early as they do language; and, if I misobserve not, they love to be treated as rational creatures sooner than is imagined.... But when I talk of *reasoning* I do not intend any other but such is suited to the child's capacity and apprehension. Nobody can think a boy of three or seven years old should be argued with as a grown man.[75]

It is through education, based upon reason itself, that children are brought into reason. One educates children through the demonstration of adult qualities. This reason serves as the discipline to overcome irrational inclinations of will and passion, which are the natural disposition. As well as serving a necessary political purpose for realizing his ideal form of government, this education of reason also serves a moral purpose. David Archard asserts that an 'education in virtue' is necessary for John Locke 'because children must become adult citizens by the law of nature'.[76] This education in virtue is far more difficult to achieve than an education in reason. John Locke argues that this is because an education in virtue requires a taming of "Wills", rather than just the demonstration of reason. It is this virtue, like reason, that must be demonstrated – and not simply taught – by parents for the benefit of children. Children must witness their parents not only exercise reason, but also exercise self-restraint and good moral judgement. It is only through education by example that Locke can be certain that children will grow into good adult citizens. In articulating his political project in his *Two Treatises* (1960) and outlining his ideal education of the child in *Some Thoughts Concerning Education*, John Locke constructs a relationship between reason, maturity and liberal citizenship that serves his liberal vision of government. In doing so, Locke plays a role in setting the terms of debates about children's rights that continue today; one that positions the need for children's protection against the need for children's greater autonomy.

Locke emphasizes the importance of children being reasoned with, in order to ensure that they develop into rational citizens themselves. By instructing parents to engage with children with a level of reason appropriate to their capacity, Locke acknowledges children's emerging capacities. By suggesting that children may have capacity for certain levels of reason, it seems possible that children may also be able to demonstrate certain degrees of autonomy. Indeed, this is what David Archard relies upon when he calls for a theory of children's rights that accounts for emerging rational capacities of children and respects their emerging autonomy. However, at the same time, identifying children as being in a state of development highlights the importance of that development not being disrupted or hindered by inappropriate treatment. This emphasizes, not the rational capacities of children themselves, but the importance of their protection while they become fully rational beings.

Contemporary discussions of childhood

So far I have offered three alternative conceptions of childhood: the sinner or non-innocent, the innocent and the blank-slate. I will refer to each of these conceptions in subsequent discussions of criminality, sexuality and citizenship. I will argue that each of these conceptions informs alternative children's rights claims, whether protection or autonomy based. These conceptions are grounded historically and culturally in ways that are not easily argued around. The debate between protectionist and autonomy claims about children's rights cannot be won on rational and logical debate alone. They each emerge from distinct onto-logical claims about the nature of childhood and who children are. The purpose of this book is to understand how these different ontological claims, these dif-ferent conceptions of childhood, these different claims for rights, inform, shape and limit how we think and talk about children and their rights. Before moving on to an analysis of how this occurs in debates about criminality, sexuality and citizenship I will spend a little more time considering how contemporary liberal philosophers John Dewey and John Rawls considered childhood. In doing so, I will reinforce my argument that conceptions of childhood are oriented toward a future-adult liberal subject.

John Dewey

The pragmatic philosophy that John Dewey's broader work on democracy is grounded in frequently and explicitly references children.[77] He is certainly inter-ested in the real, lived worlds of children and ensuring an education appropriate to that world and respectful of children's place in it. However, his interest just as equally focuses upon educating young people into a responsible citizenry that best realizes his vision of a democratic society.

Initially, there are some recognizable concepts that Dewey shares with Rous-seau. Like Rousseau, he is interested in humans as natural beings.[78] Dewey rejected the idea of purely objective knowledge-bearers, as the 'spectator looking at some object from a vantage point outside it'.[79] In a similar way to Rousseau, he argues that '[t]he child's own instincts and powers furnish the material and give the starting point for all education',[80] Dewey recognizes human beings as embedded, with knowledge arising from their experience in a particular environ-ment. For children, that environment is the home and school.

According to his "Pedagogic Creed", Dewey believes that 'the school is prim-arily a social institution'.[81] Flowing from this, he emphasizes education as a 'process of living and not a preparation for future living'.[82] Here, Dewey does not appear overly focused upon the future-adult and works hard to maintain the child at the centre of his educational pedagogy. In this way, he considers chil-dren to be properly part of society. Nonetheless, Dewey does not regard school as the same as the broader social world, though it sits within it. Rather, the school, he says, 'should simplify existing social life; should reduce it, as it were, to an embryonic form'[83] in order to allow children to properly and meaningfully participate. Were the school as complex as the broader social world, the child would be, he suggests, confused or distracted, resulting in a poor education.[84] However, the importance of recognizing the school as part of the social world, and students as properly part of society, supports his broader philosophical project. For Dewey, '[t]here cannot be two sets of ethical principles, one for life in the school, and the other for life outside of the school'.[85] That is, the purpose of recognizing children and students as part of the social world, and schools as a social institution within that world, serves to ensure that they develop the skills, knowledge and practices that allow them to navigate the world, now as well as in the future. He writes that:

> The social work of the school is often limited to training for citizenship, and citizenship is then interpreted in a narrow sense as meaning capacity to vote intelligently, disposition to obey laws etc. But it is futile to contract and cramp the ethical responsibility of the school in this way. The child is one, and he must either live his social life as an integral unified being, or suffer loss and create friction.... We must take the child as a member of society in the broadest sense and demand for and from the schools whatever is necessary to enable the child intelligently to recognise all his social relations and take his part in sustaining them.[86]

Here, Dewey rejects an education that is only oriented toward the future. The failure of this approach, he argues, results from the limitations that arise when you educate a person for only one end: that of citizen, worker, family member or neighbour, as these are all discreet, separate aspect of one's existence. He continues:

> It is an absolute impossibility to educate the child for any fixed station in life. So far as education is conducted unconsciously or consciously on this basis, it results in fitting the future citizen for no station in life, but makes him a drone, a hanger-on, or an actual retarding influence in the onward movement.[87]

In this statement, Dewey begins to reveal what is at stake for his ideal society. An education oriented toward some abstracted and specific future role fails to prepare a person for the complexities of social life. Education and the school have a crucial role to play in preparing people, not for a future life, but for unanticipated and unimagined encounters that may occur in the future. He writes that:

> In directing the activities of the young, society determines its own future in determining that of the young. Since the young at a given time will at some later date compose the society of that period, the latter's nature will largely

turn upon the direction children's activities were given at an earlier period. This cumulative movement of action toward a later result is what is meant by growth.[88]

Here we see that despite Dewey's sincere efforts to address children and students as being properly part of society, he nonetheless becomes oriented toward a future-adult subject. Thus, when Dewey states that the 'primary condition of growth is immaturity',[89] he refers not only to the growth of the individual but also to the growth of the collective body: the growth of a society toward some better and greater end, ever toward Enlightenment. This teleological sense reflects Kant's view of critical reason as an ever-unaccomplished goal.[90] As discussed in the previous chapter, Kantian reason is that which is always worked toward, but can never be fully realized because it must always be questioned. Of course, Dewey did not refer to critical reason but to critical intelligence.[91] There are, nonetheless, parallels in the commitment of each to the pursuit of reason and intelligence as a lifelong aim and practice. Crucially, this is not a definitive goal accomplished upon the acquirement of a certain age or educational status.

John Rawls and justice for future generations

John Rawls recognized that his theory of justice would have difficulties in accounting for future generations. In Rawls' theory, to realize justice as fairness, measured by our willingness to accept the position of the least advantaged in society, Rawls places us behind a "veil of ignorance". Behind this veil, we stand in the "original position", a hypothetical site from which we can deliberate upon the principles of justice that we would be prepared to accept in a social contract between the liberal state and ourselves.[92] This veil precludes us from any knowledge of what our position in society might be, or our particular, individual characteristics. The idea is that if we do not know whether we will be wealthy or poor, white or black, marginalized or privileged, powerful or not, then the principles we select are principles we must be prepared to accept, even as the worst-off in society. John Rawls' theory of justice, and his hypothetical original position, has been the subject of great analysis, both supportive and critical. Despite being placed behind a hypothetical veil of ignorance, an individual is nonetheless aware that they belong to a generation already living in society.[93] In this original position, it is possible to a person of any age so long as they are a member of the current generation. Rawls recognizes that in this hypothetical little motivation exists to make decisions that also serve the interests of future generations.[94] Further, by being required to employ a method of reason, it is an adult, rather than a child, that must occupy this original position.

To overcome this difficulty, Rawls introduces the "heads of families" assumption in his theory of justice to address the absence of benevolence between generations that would otherwise result from the original position.[95] This assumption clarifies that it is always an adult standing in this position. For Rawls, it is possible to assume that parents are interested in the welfare of their children. By creating the assumption that the individual who stands in the original position is the head of a family, it is possible for Rawls to expect that the interests of the next generation (at the very least) would be accounted for. This is possible through a savings principle, in which a head of family would be prepared to make certain sacrifices in their own lifetime to ensure that the next generation is provided for in a just manner.[96] Despite the sincere attempt to provide a more comprehensive theory of justice, this assumption became the subject of much criticism from feminists and, indeed, Rawls would later dispense with this assumption altogether.

Jane English argued that the heads of families assumption operates on the basis that the private sphere of the family is already just. By operating on this basis, she argues that 'Rawls makes the family opaque to claims of justice.'[97] Indeed, if the purpose of Rawls' theory of justice as fairness is to realize principles that can serve the interests of the least advantaged in society, it is inconsistent to have an adult patriarch – the traditional head of family and a position of privilege (rather than disadvantage) – standing in the original position. The heads of families assumption is inadequate for theorizing justice on Rawls' own terms. Rather than have a veil of ignorance cloaking our identity in this hypothetical assumption, we now know that we are likely to be a male (the traditional head of a family), who is the main breadwinner (the traditional role of the male head of family) and in a heterosexual relationship. Further, if we are attempting to theorize principles that serve the least advantaged in society, then the contexts that the least advantaged in the world live in are relevant and these contexts cannot be assumed to include just family environments.[98]

Jane English disagrees with the need for the assumption in the first place. By establishing a present-time entry principle, then behind the veil of ignorance you would not know which current living generation you belonged to. On this basis, she claims that it is possible to belong to any one of three or four generations: you are as likely to be a grandparent as an infant.[99] This alone, she argues, should be able to establish the benevolence to motivate savings between generations. However, as mentioned above, it would be difficult for an infant to deliberate in a rational manner from the original position. English's criticisms came in 1977, shortly after Rawls *A Theory of Justice* was published. By 1993, Rawls had dispensed with the heads of families assumption.[100] However, as Susan Moller Okin would argue, even in his revised work fundamental problems with Rawls' assumption of families as just institutions remained.[101]

In *Political Liberalism*, Rawls acknowledged that he had 'assume[d] that in some form the family is just' and thus omitted 'justice of and in the family' from his earlier text.[102] He deliberately stopped referring explicitly to men, and also specifically stated that in the original position, one would not know their sex. He also emphasized that the family, as an institution at the core of society, is central to what his theory of justice as fairness concerns itself with. However, within this hypothetical scenario, he was aware that the person standing in the original position belonged to the present time. There was no way to know that the principles of justice selected would ensure a just society for future generations. He also placed a caveat on the full reach of his revised theory, pitching it as a political conception of justice concerned with key institutions of political and social life, rather than for lived experiences as a whole. Despite these efforts, Moller Okin criticises Rawls for offering an incomplete explanation of how we might assume families to be just, or how we might theorize justice to ensure that families, as the basic structure of society, are just institutions.[103]

As mentioned, and contrary to English, the person who stands in the original position, whether male or female, whether a head of family or not, most certainly cannot be a child. For Rawls, the individual in the original position must be a mutually disinterested and rational being. This necessarily excludes a child conceptualized as a dependent and pre-rational being. Moller Okin maintains that a Rawlsian account of justice still has potential, notwithstanding her concerns regarding the absence or assumed subordination of women in his theories.[104] Accepting criticisms that Rawls' theory is 'excessively rationalistic, individualistic, and abstracted from real human beings', she maintains that at the centre of Rawls' work 'is a voice of responsibility and concern for others'.[105] For Moller Okin, the problem for feminists in Rawls' work is a commitment to the perspective (which she identifies in his Kantian heritage) that women are people who sense rather than reason, and that this sense is an inadequate and inappropriate way of knowing the world.[106] The legacy of this distinction, that separates reason from other ways of knowing, is especially problematic for children.

One aspect of the feminist movement has been to challenge this process of discounting women's ways of knowing the world. On the one hand, as we saw in Chapter 1, women have been able to appeal to evidence that their rational capacity is not different significantly (or at all) from men; that women are perfectly rational and reasonable. On the other hand, Susan Moller Okin has also demonstrated how the prioritization of a particular kind of rationality (a male rationality) as the only way of knowing the world in the first place offers an incomplete perspective of justice.[107] The argument follows that women should not necessarily have to establish their "equal" rationality to men, in order to demand recognition of their own rationality. This second perspective risks falling to essentialist claims about women's and men's rationalities, by relying on assertions of men's and women's differences.[108] Nonetheless, what is useful about this kind of argument is the space it opens up to begin to identify and value multiple rationalities. That is, there are different ways of knowing the world and that there is more than one way of thinking. Whether children, as a matter of fact, know the world in quite distinct ways from the adults around them is not the subject of inquiry here. Nonetheless, in the West, we construct the world of children in different terms from the adult world: regulated by different rules, subject to different institutions, physically and biologically separate. So, without making an empirical claim that children know in different ways, I argue here that different ways of knowing the world are possible, and that a child (like any individual) embodies this possibility for reasons that may be natural or constructed. However, as Dewey holds at the centre of his philosophy, these children and the world they live in are nonetheless also our own.[109] As adults engaging in debates about children's rights, the tension remains: do we recognize the differences between children and adults, at the expense of recognizing their experiences in a *shared* social world, in order to best protect them from harm? Or, do we go to lengths to recognize the kinds of rationality that children may very well employ in negotiating their world, and extend to them a greater level of autonomy to better serve their interests? The protectionist and autonomy modes of children's rights appear once again.

Conclusion

In the first part of this chapter, I outlined three conceptions of childhood that inform, shape and limit how we think and talk about children and their experiences: the sinner or non-innocent, the innocent and the blank-slate. The blank-slate is perhaps the most benign of these conceptions, appealing to contemporary understandings of childhood as a biological and psychological precursor to a mature and rational adulthood. This conception of childhood best serves the goals of a compulsory education system, oriented toward life as a citizen and worker in liberal society. The sinner and innocent are two sides of the same coin, though emerging from distinct traditions. Rousseau's Romantic conception persists in protectionist arguments about children's rights. This will be explored further in the chapters on sexuality and criminality. By contrast, the conception of the child as a sinner, which extends from a less cohesive and influential literature, nonetheless plays heavily into these debates. The second part of this chapter considered two later philosophers' perspectives of children: John Dewey, who wrote explicitly about children, their education and democratic society; and John Rawls, who wrote very little about children, education and, by comparison to Dewey, democracy. Dewey sought to theorize children into society properly, as a present and relevant population. Rawls viewed children as explicitly future-subjects, rather than individuals who may already be experiencing forms of injustice within a presumably just institution – the family. Nonetheless, Rawls' attempt to include future generations speaks to his belief that a properly just society must be just now and in the future. For John Dewey, his discussion of children and education speaks little of principles of justice and not at all about future generations. The education of children is fundamental to his realization of an ideal democratic society. Children are, for Dewey, not just adults in the making, but also society in the making.

Across all these varied accounts of childhood and political communities, the child presents as a future-adult subject. This future-adult subject is one that necessarily serves the goals of broader political ideologies. While these conceptions of childhood may possibly continue to serve the best interests of the child, such interests now appear only as a secondary and incidental concern. Together, these conceptions of childhood, informed as they are by these broader political concerns, position the future-adult citizen as the subject of children's rights debates. In the following chapters, I explore how this occurs in contemporary debates about children's social and political status. Before doing so, I explain how these conceptualizations – and the contemporary debates that they come to inform – are an explicitly political problem of children's rights. Adopting a post-structuralist approach allows us to identify the political nature of our claims about childhood, children and their rights, without being compelled toward either empirical or normative claim-making, but nonetheless produces valuable and critical insight.

Notes

1 Musgrove (1964: 33).
2 Ariès (1962).
3 Hawes (1991).
4 Ibid., 4.
5 Ibid., 4–5. It should be noted that Hawes also argues that there is no evidence that such a punishment was ever enforced.
6 Ibid., 3.
7 Stortz (2001: 88).
8 Ibid., 100.
9 Weithman (1992: 354).
10 Weithman (1992: 356).
11 Faulkner (2011: 8).
12 Dolgin (1999: 421).
13 Nikolas Rose (1999).
14 Hawes (1991: 36–41); Rose (1999)
15 Ibid., 128–39.
16 Harry Hendrick quoted in Oswell (2013: 220).
17 Rousseau (1993: 5).
18 Rousseau (1986).
19 Ibid., 91–2.
20 In discussion of Rousseau the term "man" is used to reflect Rousseau's distinction between how he views boys and girls and their education, and other gendered distinctions that Rousseau makes across his work. In contemporary interpretations, charitable readings of Rousseau extend many of his ideals to both men and women, but I do not do this here. In part, to address the feminist critique of Rousseau by Mary Wollstonecraft and Susan Moller Okin that follows.
21 Ibid., 83.
22 Rousseau (1993: 6).
23 Ibid., 6, here Rousseau refers to Nature as a teacher; at 56–61, Rousseau develops his argument of the benefits of an education by Nature and the problems attached to an education by men.
24 Ibid., 52.
25 Ibid., 56.
26 Ibid., 62.
27 Ibid., 85–6.
28 As discussed in Rousseau (1986: 90–3).
29 Okin (1979).
30 Rousseau (1993: 418); Okin uses a different translation (1979: 396).
31 Ibid.
32 Ibid., 403.
33 Ibid., 397.
34 Ibid.
35 Rousseau's discussion of the education of Sophie (in Foxley's translation, 'Sophy') forms 'Book V' of Rousseau (1993: 384–533). The gendered aspect of Rousseau's work is also discussed by Schaeffer (1998) and Weiss (1990).

36 Okin (1979: 398).
37 Ibid.
38 Rousseau (1986: 83–4).
39 Ibid.
40 Okin (1979: 402).
41 Ibid; Okin (1989, 1994).
42 Mary Wollstonecraft and Ulrich H. Hardt (1982: 58).
43 Okin (1979: 401).
44 Ibid., 405.
45 Ibid.
46 Ibid., 405.
47 Ibid., 406.
48 Ibid., 406.
49 Quoted in ibid., 407; Again Barbara Foxley's translation is slightly different, see Rousseau (1993: 393).
50 Locke (1993: §4, 116).
51 Ibid., §55, 141.
52 Ibid., §4, 116.
53 Ibid., §54, 141.
54 Ibid., §55, 141.
55 Ibid., Chapter V, 'Of Property', 127–40.
56 Ibid.
57 John Locke defines his understanding of political power in the following manner: 'the right of making laws with penalties of death, and consequently all less penalties, for the regulating and preserving of property, and of employing the force of the community, in the execution of such laws, and in the defence of the commonwealth from foreign injury, and all this only for the public good' (ibid., §3, 116). Foucault would describe this as sovereign power.
58 Those people recognized as having political status, such as citizens.
59 Locke (1993: §23, 126). The reason for this is because the one thing that man does not have sovereignty over, in respect to himself, is his life itself:

> The freedom from absolute, arbitrary power is so necessary to, and closely joined with a man's preservation, that he cannot part with it, but by what forfeits his preservation and life together. For a man, not having the power of his own life, cannot, by compact, or his own consent, enslave himself to anyone, nor put himself under the absolute, arbitrary power of another, to take away his life, when he pleases.

For Foucault, slavery presents as the absence of power (which he understands in relational terms) rather than the abuse of power.
60 Hindness (2001: 26).
61 Michel Foucault (1994d: 122).
62 Michel Focault (1984).
63 For a sophisticated analysis of the role of sovereignty in political authority, see Shaw (2008). It is written in the context of Indigenous peoples and international relations, but her discussion of Thomas Hobbes and liberalism is just as relevant in the present context.
64 Locke (1993: §95, 163).
65 Locke's understanding of equality in the state of nature excludes the unequal state in which each and every person enters it, while also asserting the naturalness of reason, which infants lack: 'The state of nature has a law of nature to govern it, which obliges everyone: and reason, which is that law, teaches all mankind ...' ibid., §6, 117.
66 Ibid., §59, 143.

67 Ibid., §59, 141.
68 Weale (1999).
69 This is discussed in Chapter II of the Second Treatise in John Locke, *Two Treatises of Government* (1993: 116–22).
70 Weale (1999: 64).
71 Christiano (2004).
72 Ibid.
73 Ibid.
74 Ibid.
75 Locke (1996: §81, 58).
76 David Archard, (1998b: 89).
77 Dewey (1966,); Dewey [1897] (1998a, 1998, 2011).
78 Cooney (1993: 134).
79 Ibid., 134–5.
80 Dewey [1897: 229].
81 Ibid., 230. Hannah Arendt also locates the school in the social realm: see Arendt (1998, 2006, 1959).
82 Dewey [1897: 230].
83 Ibid., 231.
84 Ibid. For Dewey, a poor education is one that inadequately prepares a person for navigating social, political and private realms.
85 Dewey [1909: 246].
86 Ibid., 46.
87 Dewey (1966).
88 Ibid., 41.
89 Ibid.
90 Kant [1784] (2004).
91 Dewey [1917] (1998b: 67).
92 Rawls (1971: 17–21).
93 Ibid., 137–40. For a critique of John Rawls' theory of justice and the heads of families assumption see: Brennan and Noggle (1998: 205–10); English (1977: 91–104).
94 Rawls later revises his theory of justice to account for the justice of future generations: see Rawls (1993, 2005).
95 Rawls (1971: 148).
96 John Rawls revises his just savings principle in *Political liberalism* (1993) acknowledging criticisms following his *Theory of Justice* (1971) and *Political liberalism* (2005: fn 20, xlvi, 273–4).
97 English (1977: 95).
98 Susan Moller Okin writes that Rawls 'neglects the issue of the justice or injustice of the gendered family itself. The result is a central tension within the theory, which can be resolved only by opening up the question of justice within the family'. See Okin (1989: 231).
99 English (1977: 92).
100 Rawls (1993).
101 Okin (1989)
102 Rawls (1993: xxix).
103 Okin (1989).
104 Ibid.
105 Ibid., 230.
106 Ibid.
107 Ibid.
108 Ibid., 233–4.
109 Dewey (2011).

3 The political problem of children's rights

Introduction

The political problem of children's rights lies in the distortion of the child subject at the heart of its debates. As argued in the previous two chapters, the child who appears in children's rights debates is a future-adult citizen that serves the goals of political ideology. Reframing the discourse of children's rights in this explicitly political manner is possible through a post-structuralist approach that produces a critique and alternative analysis of debates about children's rights. The following chapter explains this approach and defends the need for an analysis that reveals children's rights as a deeply political problem, beyond a liberal account of individual rights and freedom. It does so by nonetheless accepting that this liberal account is essential and provides the theoretical foundation and historical context from which children's rights emerges. Consequently, the critique presented in this book is not to argue against liberal accounts of children's rights but is an argument designed to reveals its *limits*. By doing so, the purpose of the critique is not to abandon liberal human rights agendas nor children's rights agendas, but rather to push these agendas into a space that engages with the theoretical and teleological limits of its own foundations rather than ignore or circumvent those limits.

A post-structuralist approach develops an explicitly political account of children's rights by positioning the child subject in rights debates as a deeply contested and ideological figure. The value of such an approach is increasingly recognized in the field. This is particularly informed by the late twentieth-century shifts in sociology that have reoriented how "we" as a society come to "know" and make claims about who children are and what childhood is. David Oswell argues at the conclusion of his book, *The Agency of Children*, that the task of thinking about children beyond rights and claims to capacity 'is not a call to abnegate responsibility to care for the child; it is, on the contrary, to demand a reframing of children's human rights in the context of *the political*'.[1] It is to this end that a post-structural approach, constrained by some limitations of its own, directs the researcher. As Oswell earlier acknowledges, the enduring lament against post-structural analysis is the collapse and disappearance of a tangible human subject into paradigms of power and knowledge that claim the subject as little more than an ideological construct. The disappearing subject, however, is a fallacy. Post-structuralism insists that we retain our grasp of the subject, while also recognizing the many, dispersed threads of power and knowledge that come together not only to constitute the subject itself, but also the social and political meanings that coincide with its subjectivity. In doing so, a post-structural approach delivers a very different perspective from the more common liberal approach to children's rights. It analyses the child as a subject, of politics and of rights, differently. It does so by presenting different questions about knowledge and power than liberal approaches ask, and as a result provides an insightful and critical departure.

To achieve this, the book resists presenting empirical and normative claims as the basis for its argument. A Foucauldian methodology provides an approach that does not seek to redescribe the empirical reality of children's lives or to develop new normative goals for the children's rights discourse. Instead, its purpose is to reveal how ideas and concepts grounded in liberal political thought serve to inform, shape and limit how we speak of particular problems, debates and controversies about children in politics. This approach provides an orientation that allows an examination of these empirically grounded problems as a foundation for critical theorizing. It is what provides scope to identify a politics of becoming adult that informs and is maintained by the children's rights discourse. This politics radicalizes our understanding of children's rights as being a project oriented toward ideal future political subjects rather than a project exclusively for children during childhood.

A Foucauldian critique

In the Introduction, I detailed my reluctance to attach definitive meanings to childhood, and my interest in the political subjectivity of children. The work of Michel Foucault informs both this reluctance and interest.[2] According to Eric Paras, Foucault identifies in his studies across the social sciences a subject that holds a natural, autonomous and neutral position.[3] What Foucault's work does is reveal the relations of power and knowledge that discursively constitute the subject, thus revealing it as constructed rather than natural, constrained rather than autonomous and political rather than neutral. Despite the constructed nature of the subject, it remains the case that the subject is always a living human being grounded in a social and political community and not just an abstracted idea of a human being. In his studies of sexuality, madness and criminality, Foucault seeks to focus not on the abstracted subject, but on the human body itself. It is not this individual subject that is at the centre of Foucault's study, but rather the rules and relations of power and knowledge that construct the subject in the first place. It is in this sense that the "archive" is his subject of study in his archaeologies, and discursive formations are his subject in his genealogies. In this project, de-centring the child subject is designed to look past questions of "who" children are, "what" childhood is, and "which" rights children ought to have, to broader discourses of political theory and liberal rights that make children's rights possible, as well as impossible. My interest in the political subjectivity of the child is conducted through my interest in the archive and discursive formations surrounding this subjectivity.

As a discourse, children's rights is constituted by a number of concerns and questions relating to childhood, children, their rights and (for those who do not favour children's rights) broader justice claims.[4] Internationally, children's rights captures questions and debates about child poverty and labour, health and education, child trafficking and war. It largely captures children's rights "problems" in the developing world. In this sense, children's rights advocacy in the developing world is not just about lifting children, but entire nations out of poverty. In the West, children's rights addresses these issues, but also the sorts of debates that will be the focus of this book: the right to vote, children in the criminal justice system, and children's right to make decisions about their sexual lives. In choosing to explore these debates, rather than (arguably) more urgent debates about children who are, sometimes literally, fighting for their lives around the world, I am directing my interest in children's rights toward an explicitly political project. This is not a normative project, but rather a critical and theoretical one.

Michel Foucault raised a number of methodological approaches across his life's work, which are relevant to this project. He claimed that 'Discourse in general ... is so complex a reality that we not only can, but should, approach it at different levels and with different methods.'[5] Common across these approaches was his effort to reject the consciousness of the individual as the central subject of knowledge.[6] Instead, he seeks to reveal the rules and practices that occur around the subject of knowledge, and it is in these otherwise "peripheral" movements that Foucault attempts to locate his study. Foucault takes as his object of study, not a subject but an archive. In *The Order of Things*,[7] the *Birth of the Clinic*[8] and *History of Madness*,[9] Foucault developed his archaeology. He then sought to develop this methodology fully in his book, *The Archaeology of Knowledge*.[10] In the second phase of his work, Foucault's *Discipline and Punish*,[11] followed by his three volumes on *The History of Sexuality*,[12] produced his genealogical methodology.[13] Finally, toward the end of his life, Foucault began to raise the method of "problematization", a 'history of problematics'.[14] These three methodological approaches each inquire into a different aspect of knowledge.

His archaeology, broadly speaking, was an effort to identify and compare different discursive formations around a body of knowledge. They were an effort to establish "discourse" as a site for analysis itself, rather than as a site within which we uncritically operate. He later presented genealogy as an attempt to explain the discursive formations that his archaeology reveals. His method of problematization speaks more broadly to his critical style, which seeks to operate at the limits of discourse rather than within it. I discuss each of these approaches in turn.[15]

Archaeology does not focus upon the subjects and objects of knowledge, but upon the ruptures and discontinuities that challenge cohesive narratives in domains of knowledge. This is in keeping with Foucault's efforts to depart from historical studies of continuities.[16] It is in this sense that his work can be described as post-structuralist, despite his own protest against such descriptions.[17] His archaeologies of madness, medicine and other disciplines sought to study a set of discourses that 'conditions what counts as knowledge in a particular period'.[18] Thomas Flynn observes that the proper objects of Foucault's archaeology are the discursive and non-discursive practices of discourse, where these practices are the 'preconceptual, anonymous, socially sanctioned body of rules that govern one's manner of perceiving, judging, imagining and acting'.[19] Further, these 'practices establish and apply norms, controls and exclusions ... they render true/false discourse possible'.[20] This methodology lends itself clearly to the study of the sciences, which are premised upon the search for definitive true/false conclusions. With the Enlightenment, this desire for truth as a tangible and definitive outcome of research and inquiry (rather than religious faith and dogma) shaped discourses of knowledge in the natural and social sciences. Indeed, much of Foucault's work serves to reveal this process. In the Enlightenment era, 'truth became anonymous', through the disappearance of the author.[21] That is, rather than a person "authoring" an analysis and conclusion situated in context and open to dispute, "knowledge" became presented as fact and the author of analysis and conclusions disappears from view. We are left not with contingent knowledges, but with truth. In this sense, Foucault's archaeology 'radicalizes our sense of the contingency of our deepest biases and most accepted necessities, thereby opening up a space for change'.[22]

His genealogy sought to explain these discursive formations, something his archaeology methodology did not address.[23] These discursive formations can be explained, in part, by the moments of rupture that interrupt otherwise cohesive historical accounts. They are explained, not by the inevitable and natural unfolding of events, but by contingent turns of history.[24] Thus, genealogy involves an explicit focus on relations of power that both shape and are shaped by discursive practices, which produce knowledge as truth. This focus upon power in Foucault's work has been subject to widespread criticism. This has included criticism from feminist standpoints.[25] In adopting Foucault's critical methodologies, it is important to keep these criticisms in mind because the concept of power operates in quite specific ways that are different for children's relationships than those for adults in relation to one another. However, by highlighting the practices of knowledge that make discourse possible, Foucault reveals how social and moral norms become politicized by relating truth claims to functions of power. Foucauldian discourse analysis, in this sense, offers a useful methodology for reconsidering the children's rights discourse anew.

Finally, his method of problematization is where this project takes its strongest cue: problematization is, for Foucault, 'the development of a domain of acts, practices and thoughts that seem to pose problems for politics'.[26] In this way, Foucault argues that he 'never tried to analyze anything whatsoever from the point of view of politics, but [instead] always [tried] to ask politics what it had to say about the problems with which it was confronted'.[27] As a methodological approach, we are asked to try 'to see how the different solutions to a problem have been constructed; but also how these different solutions result from a different form of problematization'.[28] This presents the methodology for analysing the problem with children's rights problems. It is in this sense that Foucault offers a methodology for researching the problem of problems. He writes:

> It is true that my attitude isn't a result of the form of critique that claims to be a methodical examination in order to reject all possible solutions except for the valid one. It is more on the order of 'problematization' – which is to say, the development of a domain of acts, practices and thoughts that seem to me to pose problems for politics.[29]

In revealing discursive formations and practices, his prolific works offer examples of, and direction on, how discourses operate and to what effect upon the world: political, social, moral and ethical.[30] Foucault's methodologies are not abstracted, philosophical purities of logic. Rather, they serve explicitly functional and empirical purposes, which attend to his particular interests in politics and power.[31] This, I believe, provides leave to employ Foucault's methodologies with a similar sentiment, by asking: what are the discursive limits of the children's rights discourse? And how does this inform, shape and limit how we think and talk about children, their lives and their rights?

This book is not a comprehensive discourse analysis. I do not wish to present my conclusions of this analysis as speaking to some fact or truth about children's rights. Rather, it is intended as a device that allows me to reveal the ways in which those who engage in debates about children's rights find themselves limited, and the political environment to which this speaks. To do so, it selects a range of specific controversies from across the Western world to provide examples of debates about children's criminality, sexuality and political agency. By choosing debates that pivot on whether children are risky, innocent or agentic, examples across these debates provide a broad perspective on the issues and ideas that together constitute contemporary ideas of childhood. By problematizing the discourse of children's rights, this book reveals contests over claims about who children are and what childhood should be. The purpose of doing so is to create a space in which new kinds of questions and problems about childhood, children and their rights might be raised. However, creating space presents an obligation to not then close it off with empirical or normative claims of my own. This is a methodology that is pursued for the explicit function of revealing what is political about children's rights debates. By doing so, it is possible for new kinds of questions and interrogations to be made into childhood and children's rights. My task is to open up space that makes this possible.

To explain Foucault's method of problematization, it is worth quoting at length his own understanding of this approach:

> For a long time I have been trying to see if it would be possible to describe the history of thought as distinct … from the history of ideas…. Thought is not what inhabits a certain conduct and gives it its meaning; rather, it is what allows one to step back from this way of acting or reacting, to present

it to oneself as an object of thought and question it as to its meaning, its conditions and its goals

...

This development of a given into a question, this transformation of a group of obstacles and difficulties into problems to which the diverse solutions will attempt to produce a response, this is what constitutes the point of problematization and the specific work of thought ... it is a question of a movement of critical analysis in which one tries to see how the different solutions to a problem have been constructed; but also how these different solutions result from a specific form of problematization.[32]

Foucault is seeking to look below the surface, beyond the problems that are debated, and the solutions that are claimed, to question the very problem itself. He is interested in how all the discursive practices and *prima facie* assumptions that his archaeologies and genealogies reveal determine the manner in which we construct problems and solve them. He is interested in how those practices and assumptions determine the parameters for discourse and knowledge, not only for how this sets the limits for what and how we can say that we know certain things to be true, but also for how they created the possibility of what we sought to know in the first place.

In this project, I identify reason, maturity and autonomy as continuities that exist across liberal political philosophy, liberal rights and children's rights. These concepts operate discursively to inform, shape and limit how we are able to think and talk about children, their lives and their rights. To support this claim, I analyse three broad areas of children's rights debates: citizenship, criminality and sexuality. These three debates relate to three spheres of life in liberal political communities: the political sphere, the public sphere and the private sphere. I will argue that the tensions produced by these discursive terms are evident in the rupturing of debates. In debates about children's citizenship, reason, maturity and autonomy delimit the possibility of extending to children full citizenship rights. In order to advocate for children's citizenship rights, our conceptions of childhood must be altered to account for their rational, mature and autonomous character. The attempt to do so, I argue, presents a rupture: a discontinuity in our conception of childhood as innocent. In criminality, the controversy of the murder of two-year-old James Bulger, and subsequent trial of two young boys, presents a rupture by sustaining a conception of childhood innocence on the one hand, but also identifying the "evil" (not mere naughtiness) of childhood on the other. Further, I argue that this sort of evil is only possible because it is embodied in a child, not an adult. Finally, in debates about sexuality, I offer numerous examples of how representations of children and child behaviour rupture our conceptions of childhood. All these ruptures serve to reveal discourse and discursive formations around the child subject in ways that are problematic for how we are able to define and resolve children's rights problems.

Foucault offers an historical perspective on how discourses and their foundational rationalities develop, but one that differs from history as a narrative of continuity. Instead, through his archaeologies, Foucault identifies the moments and ruptures that cause discourses to change. His genealogies, in turn, map together these moments in ways that allow us to view discourse and the manner in which we know in new ways. Foucauldian critique attempts to reveal and disrupt the very parameters of what comes to be knowledge. It challenges the idea of truth itself.

This book displaces the child as the central object of knowledge and subject for study in children's rights debates. De-centring the child subject allows my analysis to focus instead upon the knowledges and discursive formations around conceptions of childhood and knowledge of the child. This allows for problematization: raising questions about the problems of children's rights problems.

Governmentality

A common understanding of government is focused upon the state and its various institutions as the embodiment and locus of power and authority. However, Michel Foucault gives government a much broader meaning, which is not necessarily connected to the territorial boundaries of a state or restricted to the conduct of a state over its citizens. Instead, a Foucauldian notion of government describes 'a sort of complex composed of men and things', where those things might be 'wealth, resources … customs, habits, ways of acting and thinking, … [and] other things that might be accidents or misfortunes'.[33] In this sense, government refers to relations of power that exist between men and "things", rather than a relationship in which the all-powerful state *governs* passive citizens. These "men" and things are always in relation to one another. Men are not the only subjects of the state, they are also the subjects of other things, and they are also able to make other men and things subject to their own power. Further, the men Foucault refers to, are not necessarily only citizens; they may be any individual or collective that finds themselves subject to power. For this reason, it is possible for Foucault to refer to the 'government of children, of souls, of communities, of families, of the sick'.[34] It is possible to govern these children as groups, as well as the non-citizen, even though these subjects fall beyond the traditional parameters of state government. Indeed, with government understood as a complex of power that is conducted between different kinds of subjects, the state becomes only one discreet aspect of government. Rather than the state holding a monopoly of power, it becomes just one aspect of power and government. For Foucault, 'The exercise of power is a "conduct of conducts" and a management of possibilities.'[35] Individuals exist not as mere subjects of state power, but in relations of power that 'structure the possible field of actions of others'.[36] Men exist in relations of power that govern. Government refers to those relations of power, not to the state alone.

Governmentality – understood as complexes of power that set the terms of debates, draw boundaries between the political and personal, establish knowledge and truth, while also dismissing other rationalities and perspectives – can also be thought of through Jacques Rancière's concept of political dissensus. For Jacques Rancière:

> political dissensus is not simply a conflict of interests, opinions, or values. It is a conflict over the common itself. It is not a quarrel over which solutions to apply to a situation but a dispute over the situation itself.[37]

He also claims that: '[t]he essential work of politics is the configuration of its own space. It is to make the world of its subjects and its operations seen'.[38] He distinguishes between speech and "noise" in discourses of knowledge, and goes on to question:

> how can you be sure that the human animal mouthing a noise in front of you is actually articulating a discourse, rather than merely expressing a state of being? If there is someone you do not wish to recognize as a political being, you begin by not seeing him as the bearer of signs of politicity, by not understanding what he says, by not hearing what issues from his mouth as discourse.[39]

Those with the power to be heard as political beings establish legitimate discourses of knowledge.[40] For those without this power, their speech may be dismissed as nonsense or not heard at all. In this way, Rancière is able to distinguish between a private realm of noise and a public realm of speech and discourse.[41] In more grounded terms, Rancière explains that:

> Traditionally, it had been enough not to hear what came of the mouths of the majority of human beings – slaves, women, workers, colonised peoples, etc. – as language and instead to hear only cries of hunger, rage, or hysteria, in order to deny them the quality of being political animals.[42]

The ability to be heard reflects a mechanism of power: a power that can be used to participate in, and shape, knowledge and discourse. This knowledge plays a central role in his broader conception of government. Knowledge governs, by asserting an authoritative voice that influences and shapes how others conduct themselves. However, for those who are governed, the ability to assert speech also allows the possibility to govern in turn. Power in this sense is not a unilateral act of coercion of the all-powerful over the completely powerless, but a relation of power that holds human beings and other things in a constant tension with one another.

Following on from rationality and knowledge is a third condition: a moral element that attaches itself to rationality. This moral element is especially important when it concerns the care of the self. For an individual to be able to question their 'own conduct (or *problematise* it) so that he or she may better be able to govern it', that individual has already internalized the social morality attached to that area of their private conduct.[43] Foucault's understanding of government highlights obvious tension between the liberty of individuals, so highly prized by liberal political communities, and the more authoritarian aspect of the regulation of conduct. Barry Hindess discusses this at length in respect to the tension between a modern welfare state and a more liberal (perhaps libertarian) ethos of welfare.[44] The self-regulation of individuals is a way of balancing the liberty of individuals with the need for order, stability and security. In order to establish a discourse of knowledge, which an individual accepts and then employs to regulate their own conduct, moral attachments to that knowledge need to be internalized. Without a moral claim, which an individual can accept as taking priority over their own individual wants and desires, the possibility for self-government is lessened. Without a moral imperative, there is little need for an individual, in a liberal political community, to willingly regulate their own freedom. This final element of liberty, freedom or autonomy, is one of the most important conditions of government. It is also a somewhat paradoxical condition.

Government, understood as a relation of power, necessarily has freedom as one of its conditions. In order to exercise power over an individual's conduct, it is assumed that that individual has more than one choice about how to conduct themselves at their disposal. In liberal societies, individuals are presumably free to choose this conduct. Government, then, does not merely govern individuals, but freedom itself. For Foucault, it is important to see that 'power is exercised only over free subjects, and only insofar as they are "free".'[45] In this sense, slavery is not a power relationship because it is largely determined by a physical relationship of constraint.[46] You cannot have power over those who are not free to choose differently. Power is, necessarily, circular, referential and related. Thus, for Foucault, 'freedom may well appear as the condition for the exercise of power'.[47] Thus, on the one hand, liberalism operates as a political philosophy that emphasizes the freedom of individuals, including the freedom of those individuals to consent to the power exercised over them by a liberal state.[48] This aspect of consent is predicated upon a community of free individuals, and allows the liberal state to lay claim to legitimate political authority. On the other hand, free individuals in this sense, may be a great source of risk to liberal society. They are free *not* to consent to the authority of the liberal state; and, they are free to break its rules.

Foucault argues that this does not necessarily indicate an inherent contradiction within liberalism. Instead, it is an essential agonism of 'a relationship that is at the same time mutual incitement and struggle; less of a face-to-face confrontation that paralyses both sides than a permanent provocation'.[49] In respect to power, there is both freedom and constraint; in Hindess' terms, both freedom and *unfreedom*. This is not a tension that unsettles our understanding of power and of government, but rather better explains its complexity. In liberalism, this tension reveals itself between liberty and freedom, the ideal of a free-thinking, free-acting, autonomous individual and government, as the regulation of that otherwise autonomous individual's conduct. It is not a fatal tension of liberalism, but a defining one.

In these ways, then, governmentality refers to 'how we think about governing' and the rationality and reason employed to do so.[50] It is not only the rationality and morality that we come to practice upon ourselves and with others that facilitates self-regulation and social regulation, but the very production of knowledge and truth claims that allow individuals to both govern and be governed. Dean argues that 'we thus govern others and ourselves according to various truths about our existence and nature as human beings. On the other hand, the ways in which we govern and conduct ourselves give rise to different ways of producing truth'.[51] The next part of this book considers the implications of this for our understanding of reason, maturity and autonomy as key concepts that bind our social understandings of children to political understandings of subjectivity in debates about criminality, sexuality and citizenship. I then return to an analysis of governmentality that allows us to think more critically about children's rights debates and the concept of the political itself.

Notes

1　Oswell (2013: 258).
2　Eric Paras explores how and why Foucault goes 'from being a philosopher of the disappearance of the subject to one wholly preoccupied with the subject'. See Paras (2006: 3).
3　Ibid., 21. This is also discussed by Mark Bevir (1999).
4　I refer to justice in different ways in this book: here, I am using it to capture the concerns of scholars who choose not to articulate their concerns for children in terms of "rights" (such as Guggenheim (2005)); in Chapter 1, I refer to a Kantian notion of justice to explain the paternalistic paradigm; in Chapter 2, I use the language of justice where it reflects the language of the philosopher; in Chapter 4, I refer to justice in the context of the criminal justice system.
5　Foucault (2002b: xv).
6　Foucault (2002a).
7　Foucault (2002b).
8　Foucault (1994a).
9　Foucault (2006).
10　Foucault (2002a).
11　Foucault (1991).
12　Foucault (1978, 1985, 1986).
13　His genealogy followed in the tradition of philosopher, Friedrich Nietzsche: See, 'Nietzsche, Genealogy, History', in Foucault Rabinow (1984).
14　Paul Rabinow (ed.) (1984: 381–90).
15　Recently, Foucault's methodological work has been revisited in two significant ways. First, by American Erica Paras who offers an extensive historical account and context for Foucault's work, and ultimately an argument that the breadth of his work should be read in the light of intellectual shifts Foucault made late in his life. Specifically, Paras is interested in Foucault's move from a rejection of the subject as a site for critical analysis, to a preoccupation with it. This is also the interest of Bevir (1999). Bevir identifies Foucault's structuralist account of the subject in Foucault's essay 'What is an Author?' (1999) and contrasts it the post-structuralist account of the subject in *Discipline and Punish* (1991). This preoccupation with the subject in Foucault's work has also been a source of criticism: see Little (2012). Ben Golder (2009) has also sought to reconsider Foucault's work in respect to human rights and legal theory.

Again, Golder relies on Foucault's later work to suggest that he was not necessarily without normative goals (particularly in the field of human rights) or wholly dismissive of law's power.

16 Bevir (1999); Paras (2006); Golder and Fitzpatrick (2009).

17 Foucault refused to cast himself in terms of structuralist/post-structuralist and modern/postmodern, describing the choice as 'intellectual blackmail of "being for or against the Enlightenment" ', Foucault (2007: 112).

18 Foucault (2002a).

19 Flynn (2003: 30).

20 Ibid., 31.

21 Ibid; Foucault, 'What is an Author?, in Rabinow (1984).

22 Ibid., 101–20.

23 Flynn (2003: 33).

24 Foucault (2002a).

25 Nancy Fraser makes Foucault the focus of criticism in the first part of her book, *Unruly Practices*. While she acknowledges the contribution of his empirical account of power and the usefulness of a positive conception of power grounded in the 'politics of everyday life', she ultimately concludes that is 'normatively confused': see Fraser (1989: 29–31). Also see: Benhabib (1992); Hartsock (1990). For analysis of feminist uses of Foucault, both supportive and critical, see Sawicki (1994); Hekman (1996).

26 Flynn (2003).

27 Rabinow (1984: 384).

28 Ibid., 385.

29 Ibid., 389.

30 Discursive formations are the regularities and consistencies in statements and claims that together are constitute discourse. Discursive practices are a way of describing that individuals with the capacity for agency and autonomy make statements and claims in specific and particular contexts. This is a way of emphasizing grounded individuals as having the capacity to negotiate and shape discourse, within the limits operating upon them.

31 This book addresses power in two key ways. Foucault offers a complex understanding of power, which he regards as a relational concept rather than an independent one: see especially Foucault, 'The Subject and Power', in Faubion (1994). For this reason, I refer to power relations when employing a Foucauldian understanding of power. Foucault also explores power as part of the power/knowledge concept, see Gordon (1980). In parts of this book, particularly in the discussion of children's rights debates about criminality and sexuality, I use "power" in a more normative sense to capture the way that power is understood and explained in children's rights discourse.

32 Foucault and Rabinow (1984: 384).

33 Foucault (1994b: 208–9).

34 Foucault (1994c: 341).

35 Ibid.

36 Ibid.

37 Rancière (2010: 6).

38 Ibid., 37.

39 Ibid., 38.

40 This is also reflected in Foucault's power/knowledge concept: see Foucault (1980).

41 Ibid., 139.

42 Ibid., 5.

43 Dean (2010: 19).

44 Hindess (2001).

45 Foucault (1994c: 342).

46 Hartman uses power not only to explain the physical subjugation of African slaves in the United States of America, but broader relations of power that the discourse of

slavery facilitated: see Hartman (1996). While I agree with Foucault's definition of power, and accept the distinction he draws between relations of power versus physical constraint (not power), Hartman's text is an articulate reminder that physical constraint makes a whole set of power relations possible and impossible.

47 Foucault, (1994c: 342).
48 Hindess (2001)
49 Foucault (1994c: 342).
50 Dean (2010: 24).
51 Ibid., 17.

4   Criminality

Introduction

In 1993, James Bulger was abducted and beaten to death by two ten-year-old boys.[1] The murder drew enormous media attention, sparking outrage across the United Kingdom.[2] The case presents a conflict between a right to justice for James Bulger and his family and the right of two young boys, Jon Venables and Robert Thompson, to a fair trial and the possibility of reform.[3] In the United Kingdom, the United States of America and Australia, there is a shared principle that children ought to be treated differently from adults in the criminal justice system. What constitutes a fair trial for a child is substantively different from what constitutes a fair trial for an adult. Across these three jurisdictions, the principle of *doli incapax* enshrines this difference, and informs the setting of statutory ages of criminality.[4]

Exploring children's criminality illuminates how claims to children's reason, maturity and autonomy inform, shape and limit how we are able to think and talk about their rights in the criminal justice system. Differing conceptions of childhood further shape this process. Understood as sinners, children's wrongs are deeply disturbing and require a strong disciplinary response. Understood as innocents, children are incapable of criminal wrongs and should not be held to the same standards as adults. Understood as blank-slates, children's criminal behaviour gives rise to deep concern about whether they will develop into good adult citizens, prompting interventions based upon reform and rehabilitation, rather than discipline and punishment. The principle of *doli incapax* maintains that children should not be held to the same standards as adults in criminal law. Yet, as we will see with the murder of James Bulger, in the instances where children do commit grave moral wrongs, the moral panic that ensues undermines this principle. Arguments that children ought to receive the same sentencing for crimes as adults implies that children are no different from adults in terms of the rational capacities required to establish criminal culpability. However, since 2005, the United States Supreme Court has issued three decisions that continue to draw a sharp distinction between the criminal culpability of children and adults.

After a brief consideration of the *doli incapax* principle and the juvenile justice system, I turn to an analysis of debates about children's criminal culpability. I begin with a discussion of the James Bulger murder, and then three United States Supreme Court cases which, in turn, abolished the death penalty[5] for juvenile offenders, abolished life without parole sentences for juveniles who committed non-homicide offences, and established age as a relevant factor in determining when and how to inform a juvenile accused of their legal rights. Across these examples, I argue that claims to reason, maturity and autonomy are made to support children's rights claims. I argue that at the core of these debates is a concern for the future-adult subject: whether that subject is a potentially evil character who ought to have no place in society, or a subject who has the potential for complete reform, a reform that would be undermined by social exclusion. Relevant across this analysis is Michel Foucault's work on disciplinary power and, more specifically, on criminal punishment.[6] From this perspective, I argue that the juvenile justice system is oriented toward a future-adult subject, rather than a present child.

Juvenile justice

Were there no conceptual distinction between childhood and adulthood, there would be no need for a juvenile justice system. Juvenile courts in the West rely upon a modern conception of childhood that makes this distinction clear and unmistakable. The distinction has largely been drawn on the grounds that children do not possess the requisite understanding to be responsible for criminal conduct. English legal scholar William Blackstone wrote in his *Commentaries on the Laws of England* in 1765 that for a crime to be committed, both the act and the will to do the act must coincide.[7] Further, with 'infants' derived from the latin *infans*, meaning without reason, so it is that they are assumed to possess a 'defect of understanding' such that there can be 'no act of the will'.[8] Thus, 'Infants, under the age of discretion, ought not to be punished by any criminal prosecution whatsoever.'[9] In the criminal law of Australia, the United Kingdom and the United States, these principles of criminal law and of the lesser culpability of children remain in place but have been challenged by numerous examples of children who have killed. Today, the two elements that must be proved beyond a reasonable doubt to be found guilty of a criminal act include the act, known by its Latin term *actus reus*, and the intention to conduct that act, the *mens rea*. The juvenile justice system is rationalized on the basis that persons below a certain age lack the necessary *mens rea* for a criminal act, and this is captured by the principle of *doli incapax*: literally meaning incapable of deceit. In this way, criminality is tied to rationality, maturity and age.

Today, the juvenile justice system operates to provide a criminal jurisdiction that properly accounts for the unique status of children. In Australia, legislative changes across the states and territories have seen the common law principle of *doli incapax* enshrined in statutory law.[10] This principle holds that a person aged under ten years old is incapable of a criminal act and provides a rebuttable presumption that persons aged between 10 and 14 are also incapable of a criminal act.

In 1993, at the time of James Bulger's murder, the age of criminal responsibility in the United Kingdom was also ten years. The presumption was that Jon Venables and Robert Thompson were incapable of a criminal act when they murdered James Bulger, but, being over the age of ten, this was a rebuttable presumption. The presumption was successfully rebutted in court and Jon Venables and Robert Thompson were tried as adults for murder. In 1998, five years after their trial, the principle of *doli incapax* was repealed by statute: 'its removal was based on the assumption that children of ten and above can differentiate between serious wrong and simple naughtiness'.[11] The argument that children can indeed distinguish between criminal and non-criminal acts has challenged the foundation of the juvenile justice system.

Following the different conceptions of childhood outlined in Chapter 2, children may be regarded as innocents, but also as sinners. The discussion below will draw out how these two images of childhood are in constant tension with one another, in turn informing the terms of public debate about children's criminality. The principle of *doli incapax* reflects the Romantic conception of children as innocent, in the tradition of Jean-Jacques Rousseau's Émile. It reinforces that children, or at least children aged under ten, are incapable of criminal conduct. However, it remains that the juvenile justice system exists to prosecute young people for otherwise criminal acts. The child as sinner is embodied in the juvenile offender. Yet, their distinction as a juvenile delinquent as opposed to ordinary criminal also embodies the assumption that children are innocent: they commit criminal wrongs, but these wrongs are viewed differently from the criminal wrongs of adults. The conception of a child as a sinner and that of an innocent co-constitute each other: one relies upon the other to form a whole picture of the child. So it is that the juvenile justice system is designed to ensure that children who cannot be held to account *as adults*, are nonetheless disciplined and punished to minimize the risk they may pose to society in adulthood.

The first juvenile court was established in the South Australian colony in the 1880s.[12] This was shortly followed by Cook County in Chicago, with the mandate to 'regulate the treatment and control of dependent, neglected and delinquent children'.[13] The United Kingdom followed in 1908, with the passage of the Children's Act.[14] Across these jurisdictions, the juvenile court followed different standards of legal process. This historical moment coincided with the establishment of other institutions uniquely designed for children. Historian Bruce Hawes observes that in the United States, the late nineteenth century saw the emergence of Kindergartens, schools and orphanages alongside juvenile courts.[15] The rejection of child labour during the late nineteenth century reiterated the importance of education and freedom from exploitation during a young person's life, and the emergent need to keep now idle children off the streets. It was recognized that children had been exploited and abused throughout the Industrial Revolution due to a lack of concern for their young, developing selves. Thus, Kindergartens targeted children of the poor as a mechanism into the early intervention into the risks of the working-class child (feared to be a future delinquent).[16]

For all this to be possible, it was necessary to be able to know children. The rise of the juvenile courts and other institutions coincided with the rise of the social sciences.[17] In the preface to his book, *Governing the Soul*, Nikolas Rose explains his focus on the psy-knowledges by arguing that this form of expertise reshapes subjectivity by constructing images of 'what we could become'.[18] Rather than merely being cured of illness, as is the case with medicine, psy-knowledges urge us to 'help fulfil the dream of realigning what we are with what we want to be'.[19] This is true not just of our individual selves, but also of our society. It was during this time that 'Children came to the attention of social authorities as delinquents threatening property, and security',[20] and 'Childhood began to be seen as a distinct period during which bad habits could be laid down that would have a lifelong influence.'[21] In order to solve this problem, it is necessary to be able to identify and recognize risk, so that

> feeble-minded children could be ascertained in a rigorous and consistent manner such that they could be separated out from the rest of the school population and segregated in specialized institutions that would seek to awaken their moral sensibilities and increase their resistance to vice and crime.[22]

The criminal child then either alludes to the failure of our social institutions to achieve its task, or supports the sinful conception that children (or at least some children) are innately wicked. Janet L. Dolgin observes that the twentieth century saw two competing "truths" of childhood emerge. In the first half of the century, childhood is 'understood as innocent, fragile and precious'.[23] By contrast, more recent decades have viewed children as risky, bearing some reflection of original sin and non-innocence. Indeed, it was the tension between these two competing positions that characterized public debate following the murder of James Bulger.

The James Bulger murder

The trial judge described the murder of James Bulger by Jon Venables and Robert Thompson as 'an act of unparalleled evil and barbarity', sentencing the two boys to detention at Her Majesty's pleasure.[24] This is a uniquely British tariff for punishment and is a substitute for the life sentence that those aged over 21 can face. Both the trial judge and the Lord Chief Justice submitted to the Home Secretary recommendations about the appropriate period of imprisonment. The trial judge recommended eight years, the Lord Chief Justice ten, with review after five and seven years respectively. The trial judge asserted that eight years was 'very, very many years for a ten or eleven year old' and he thought appropriately accounted for their age and backgrounds.[25] The Home Secretary suggested 15 years. The Home Secretary emphasized that he had taken into account 'public concern', as well as their ages. The public concern to which the Home Secretary referred was immense. As Deena Haydon and Phil Scraton note, a petition with 278,300 signatures called for a life sentence. A further 21,281 coupons cut from the *Sun* newspaper called for a life sentence and were sent directly to the Home Office.[26] However, according to the Home Secretary, if an adult was to be subject to a minimum 25-year sentence (contrary to the trial judge's conclusion) then 15 seemed proportionate.[27]

Had Venables and Thompson been several months younger, they would not have been tried as adults as a matter of course. However, as they were over the age of ten, the principle of *doli incapax* was open to argument. The prosecution's argument to try the boys as adults was successful. Lisa Bradley has argued that the presumption is often successfully rebutted through defendant-specific psychological testimony that attests to whether or not the defendant knew the kind of act they were accused of was wrong.[28] However, she also argues that greater weight is given to the gravity of the alleged offence than to the age of the child. These are quite different concerns from whether or not the child has the capacity to participate in the process of an adult criminal court. Indeed, when the Venables and Thompson judgment was taken to the European Court of Human Rights (ECHR), it was held that the United Kingdom had breached Article 6 of the European Convention on Human Rights.[29] This Article demands the accused be able to meaningfully participate in their trial, while Article 40 further demands that court procedures should be specifically applicable to children.[30] The ECHR decision found that the United Kingdom failed to meet its Convention obligations.[31] Venables and Thompson were released as adults in 2001, with new identities, having served much less than the 15 years recommended by the Home Secretary. The case remains highly controversial, particularly following criminal behaviour that saw Jon Venables return to prison on violation of his release conditions in 2010.[32] The subject of analysis here is focused upon how this event unsettled and ruptured conceptions of childhood.

The controversy surrounding the murder of James Bulger and subsequent trial of his murderers, especially illuminates how conceptions of childhood shape understandings of children and their rights. On the one hand, the murder of a two-year-old boy strikes at the heart of a conception of childhood as innocent. Arguably, there is a greater moral wrong in taking the life of a young child, who is unable to protect himself physically against any threat to his life. For this reason, child murder is an especially grave moral and criminal wrong. On the other hand, when a child murders, the conception of childhood as innocent is ruptured. As will be argued below, a child who murders reflects the conception of the child as a sinner and employs a rhetoric of evil as the only way to explain why and how a child, otherwise innocent, could possibly take another's life. The murder of James Bulger by Jon Venables and Robert Thompson draws these two competing conceptions of childhood together into a single event. On the one hand, a commitment to children as innocents is reinforced by the outrage expressed in response to the murder of James Bulger. On the other hand, the public outrage directed toward Jon Venables and Robert Thompson, the decision to try them as adults, including calls for the death penalty to be reintroduced, point to children being conceptualized as sinners.

Allison James and Chris Jenks undertake a review of the reaction of the media to the murder of James Bulger.[33] They argue that this event radically disrupted an image of 'childhood innocence in British culture'.[34] They also suggest that the (re)emergence of the child as a sinner and a risk to society was, in part, a reaction to the more prevalent image of innocence that existed, at least in British culture, at the time. This was a system that, for several decades, had largely been treating children as not responsible for their actions let alone their own crimes. However, this is not particularly convincing. Throughout history, generations have tended to look down upon the younger criminal with condescension and even condemnation. Philippe Ariès quoted proverbs provided by French scholar Antoine Furertière's *Dictionnaire universel* in his entry on children: 'He is a spoilt child, who has been allowed to misbehave without being punished. The fact is, there are no longer any children, for people are beginning to have reason and cunning at an early age.'[35] Janet Dolgin quotes an American newspaper editorial that similarly describes children as 'the vanguard of a new, decultured generation, isolated from family and neighbourhood, shrugged at by parents, dominated by peers'.[36] It is arguable whether or not the earlier half of the twentieth century was an age of innocence for children. It seems much clearer, however, that in the modern age childhood emerges as one of the most heavily governed periods in life. In this context, the rise of juvenile justice was not an isolated event, occurring in conjunction with the rise of social sciences and a more heavily governed society. Children proved crucial to this broader project.

The public controversy that followed the Bulger murder was claimed to demonstrate that 'the innocence of childhood has finally come of age'.[37] The Romantic conception of childhood articulated so strongly by Rousseau had disappeared. The immaturity of children was no longer a condition of innocence, but rather a condition of irrational and unthinkable violence. James and Jenks describe the Bulger murder as unthinkable 'because it occurred within the conceptual space of childhood, which, prior to this breach, was conceived of – for the most part and for most children – as innocence enshrined'.[38] They argue that the moral panic that followed the Bulger murder resulted from a shift it precipitated in the understandings of childhood.

Following the trial of Venables and Thompson, Haydon and Scraton observe the following headlines in British newspapers: 'Freaks of Nature' and 'How Do You Feel Now, You Little Bastards?'[39] A similar headline followed the school shooting at Columbine in the United States: 'The Misfits Who Killed for Kicks.'[40] In these headlines, the young age of the murderers are a further indictment of their guilt. The first headline excises the two young boys from the class of childhood, even from the class of humanity: instead, they are freaks of nature. They must be understood as anomalies, as outliers and as evil. The conduct of Thompson and Venables ruptures a Romantic conception of childhood that suggests that children, while capable of naughtiness, have no capacity for moral and criminal wrongdoing. The second headline, however, does maintain a characterization of Thompson and Venables as children. As two "Little Bastards", Thompson and Venables remain children, but the term does not serve to describe merely naughty or subversive behaviour, as its colloquial use tends to. Instead, it speaks to their childishness and the evil that this childishness makes possible. As *The Times* reported, the Bulger murder was 'simply the worst possible example of *amoral childish viciousness*; horrible precisely to the degree that it was *childlike* – random, aimless, and without conscience.'[41] By casting their crime in the light of irrationality and immaturity, as a crime both outside of our imagining of childhood and only possible because of their childishness, their culpability is deepened rather than lessened. The image of the innocent child, characterized by weakness and lack of reason, is inverted and transformed. What emerges is a sinful child, whose weakness and lack of reason present as the very conditions that make such violence possible. The crime is no longer exceptional because children committed it; rather, it is possible only because children committed it.

James and Jenks described the rise of this sinner from the James Bulger murder in the following way:

> that children can and do commit acts of violence voiced the possibility that, after all, the Puritans were correct; that children are born sinful and have a natural propensity for evil unless properly and rigorously restrained. This doctrine of Adamic 'original sin' is a model of childhood ... as an image of the wilful and unconstrained potential, which has always provided the dark side or inarticulate backdrop of our contemporary and dominant images of the child.[42]

The murder of James Bulger by Jon Venables and Robert Thompson was not the first incident of child-by-child murder. Both James and Jenks, and Haydon and Scraton, discuss murders committed by Mary Bell at the ages of 10 and 11, in the United Kingdom in the 1960s.[43] However, James and Jenks argue that the murder of James Bulger was different. They argue that 'the magnitude of the public reaction to the Bulger case certainly does comprise a social phenomenon' that had not previously been witnessed.[44] In part, they acknowledge that this could be attributed to media coverage, which included video footage of Venables and Thompson leading Bulger to his death. Global media networks meant that this murder, and subsequent trial, was broadcast around the world. Despite the knowledge that very few children commit criminal acts, and even fewer commit murder, the Bulger case prompted a "moral panic".[45] This moral panic had as much to do with the death of childhood itself, as it did with the death of James Bulger.

The cruel and unusual punishment of children?

Tensions between innocence and sinfulness in childhood and the moral panics produced by criminal children play out in debates far beyond the Bulger case. In a series of decisions in the United States of America, the constitutionality of sentencing juvenile offenders to the death penalty and life without parole was considered. As a result, the last American executed for a crime committed as a juvenile was in 2003[46] and since 2005, the death penalty for juvenile offenders has been unconstitutional.[47] In June 2011, the United States Supreme Court also ruled that sentencing juveniles to life without parole was unconstitutional. By exploring the rationales for doing so, I argue that claims to children's capacities reason, maturity and autonomy are crucial. Psy-knowledges play an essential role in demonstrating these claims at a level of fact. However, empirical claims that speak to the truth of childhood do not necessarily produce outcomes that fit comfortably with normative claims that children should not be held fully responsible for their crimes.

In 2005, the United States Supreme Court considered the question of whether or not juveniles could be sentenced to the death penalty.[48] Writing from Australia, where there is no death penalty, and having a moral position that the state does not have a right to decide who lives and dies, my initial response to the various decisions offered by the Justices of the United States Supreme Court is an exasperated cry: "What's age got to do with it?" However, it is necessary to leave to one side the broader moral debate about the use of the death penalty in a criminal justice system and attend to how this debate illuminates the manner in which we think and talk about children and their rights. This section explores the question of children's criminal culpability, rather than a debate about the death penalty. No doubt, arguments about children's criminal culpability are presented especially clearly in this case because the death penalty sets the stakes so high.

The decision of *Roper* v. *Simmons* related to the sentencing of a man, who at the age of 17, planned a burglary and a murder. He then committed these two crimes, breaking and entering into the victim's house, tying the victim up, wrapping her whole head in duct tape, driving her to a bridge and throwing her from it. Two others, aged 15 and 16, knew of this plan. One participated directly, the other did not but nor did he inform anyone of what was about to occur. At trial, not only was there no evidence suggesting Simmons did not understand that the crime he was planning was wrong. In fact, there was evidence that showed he informed his two friends that they could get away with the crime because they were minors.[49]

This was a premeditated, serious crime that resulted in a violent death. There was no question of trying 17-year-old Simmons for the crime, as the principle of *doli incapax* did not apply, nor was there any reasonable doubt demonstrated at trial of Simmons' guilt. The trial jury sentenced Simmons to death. What became the question of appeals, which ended in the Supreme Court of the United States, was whether this sentence – applied to a minor – was unconstitutional on the grounds of cruel and unusual punishment. The question was not whether or not the death penalty itself amounted to cruel and unusual punishment, but whether it was cruel and unusual when applied to a juvenile. In this way, it is possible to consider the Supreme Court judgment to navigate specific and clear arguments regarding a child's criminal culpability.

In the lead majority opinion of the Court, Justice Kennedy considers how the question of Simmons' age was dealt with at trial: First, by the defence counsel:

Defense counsel reminded the jurors that juveniles of Simmons' age cannot drink, serve on juries, or even see certain movies because 'the legislatures have wisely decided that individuals of a certain age aren't responsible enough.' Defense counsel argued that Simmons' age should make a 'huge difference to [the jurors] in deciding just exactly what sort of punishment to make'.[50]

Second, by the prosecutor, who Justice Kennedy quotes:

'Age', he says. 'Think about age. Seventeen years old. Isn't that scary? Doesn't that scare you? Mitigating? Quite the contrary I submit. Quite the contrary.'[51]

At trial, the age of the defendant is not presented as a mitigating factor relevant to sentencing, but an aggravating one. Within the criminal justice system lies an exclusively juvenile justice system that is premised on the proposition that age is a factor relevant to culpability for a crime. Yet here, the prosecutor implores the jury to take the opposite position: that youth, far from being a factor that lessens responsibilities, is a factor that heightens the criminality of the act. This is what we saw above, regarding the moral panic that followed the James Bulger murder. It was the childishness evident in the 'amoral viciousness' that made the crime possible. This reflects the shift that Janet Dolgin identified in conceptualizing youth as risky.[52] It also demonstrates the supposed 'madness of youth itself'[53] and the re-emergence of the innate wickedness of the young.

For Jonathon Simon, crimes committed by children come to be seen as a 'sign of a kind of mental illness rooted in both the normal and pathological features of adolescent development'; it is the 'madness that comes from youth's mistreatment at the hands of parents, schools and society itself'.[54] This is no longer a philosophical conception of childhood in operation, but childhood and youth as a subject of knowledge: of psychology, of sociology, of individual conduct. Indeed, we see this shift from an abstracted conception of childhood, to a specific and located knowledge of *what* childhood is. In the first part of this book, I raised the developmental model of understanding childhood that emerged from the discipline of psychology. It emphasizes childhood as a biological and physical stage, in which the parameters for a full life are set. Interrupt or disrupt this childhood and you risk the future-adult subject. In this context, it is not surprising that, following the prosecutor's argument quoted above, Simmons sought a new defence counsel, who called upon clinical psychologists to testify about their evaluations of the accused. Justice Kennedy reiterated their conclusions in his judgment: Simmons is 'very immature', 'very impulsive', and 'very susceptible to being manipulated or influenced'.[55] Amnesty International, in its reporting on juveniles sentenced to death around the world, observe that many present with 'lower than average intelligence, including some with organic brain damage'.[56] Information about childhood as a developmental stage, and specific information about particular juveniles, can go one of two ways. On the one hand, it points to the lack of intellectual development as a factor that lessens the culpability for criminal conduct. On the other hand, it explains the unlawful conduct as a further reason why the justice system should respond with the full weight of the law. This is how the prosecutor was able to use age as an aggravating factor in sentencing.

Arguments about capacity did little to spare Simmons the death penalty and nothing to maintain the continued division between an adult and juvenile justice system. The argument maintains the position that young people, characterized by immaturity and irrationality, are risky and is not very useful for advocates. It risks perpetuating a fear of young people and further stigmatizing a stage of life that carries great potential (if adopting a Lockean view of the child as a blank-slate). Indeed, of all the arguments that seek to lessen children's culpability for criminal action, the potential for reform is particularly compelling. This is consistent with the narrative of childhood as a blank-slate, or of a sinful child who must seek redemption. Thus it is a narrative that must be maintained to advocate the different treatment of children in the criminal justice system. It is in this way that conceptions of childhood inform, shape and limit debates about children's criminal culpability. Later in this chapter, I will explore the implications of claims around reason, maturity and autonomy for childhood criminality. For the moment, I wish to extend the above analysis by looking to the 2011 decisions of the United States Supreme Court that clarified juvenile questioning processes and abolished life without parole sentencing for juveniles.

On 16 June 2011, the United States Supreme Court held in *JDB* v. *North Carolina*[57] that age was a relevant factor in determining whether or not a person was to be considered in custody and therefore read their legal rights, known in the United States as *Miranda* warnings.[58] Since the 1966 *Miranda* judgment, police officers have been required to inform individuals in custody of their legal rights, including the right not to answer any questions that may incriminate them. This decision concerned the Fifth Amendment right against self-incrimination and the Fourteenth Amendment protections around due process. This decision departs somewhat from the considerations undertaken in *Roper*, as it does not address directly the criminal culpability of children. Nonetheless, it does remain focused upon the capacities of young people insofar as it informs their treatment in police interrogations. The young person whose capacities were being questioned in this case, was a 13-year-old boy (*JDB*) believed to have participated in a robbery and have stolen goods in his possession. Police attended the school, and he was escorted from class by the school's "school resource officer" (a uniformed police officer on detail to the school) to be questioned by a police Investigator in the school conference room. The boy was questioned in this room, with the two police officers, the assistant principal and an administrative intern present. His legal guardian was not contacted about the questioning or allegations being put to *JDB*. During the course of this questioning, the assistant principal urged the boy to do the right thing. Asking whether or not he would 'still be in trouble' if he returned the "stuff", the boy was informed that this case would go to court regardless, raising the possibility of juvenile detention. It was at this point, according to the Supreme Court, that *JDB* confessed to the robbery. Following his confession, the Investigator informed the boy that he could refuse to answer any questions and that he was free to leave.

In the United States, the right against self-incrimination is constitutionally protected by the Fifth Amendment. The question before the Supreme Court was whether or not *JDB* could be considered in custody, for the purposes of invoking the Investigator's responsibility to give him his *Miranda* warnings. More specifically, the issue was whether the age of a child subjected to police questioning is relevant to the custody analysis of *Miranda* v. *Arizona*.[59] The majority of the Court in *JDB* held that:

> It is beyond dispute that children will often feel bound to submit to police questioning when an adult in the same circumstances would feel free to leave. Seeing no reason for police officers or courts to blind themselves to that commonsense reality, we hold that a child's age properly informs the Miranda custody analysis.[60]

The case was remitted to the trial court to properly consider the boy's age in custody analysis, in order to determine whether or not his confession could be admitted into evidence.

In reaching this conclusion, the United States Supreme Court reiterated the *Roper* v. *Simmons* observation that age is 'more than a chronological fact' and stated that 'a reasonable child subjected to police questioning will sometimes feel pressured to submit when a reasonable adult would feel free to go'.[61] Drawing on *Roper* and other past decisions, the Court identified six factors in succession to support this claim:

1 'We have observed that children "generally are less mature and responsible than adults"';
2 Children '"often lack the experience, perspective, and judgment to recognise and avoid choices that could be detrimental to them"';
3 '[T]hat they "are more vulnerable or susceptible to … outside pressures" than adults';
4 that, 'events that "would leave a man cold and unimpressed can overawe and overwhelm a lad in his early teens"';
5 that, '"no matter how sophisticated", a juvenile subject of police interrogation "cannot be compared" to an adult subject';
6 and, finally, the Court stated that 'Describing no one child in particular, these observations restate what "any parent knows" – indeed, what any person knows – about children generally.'[62]

This recognition that, at least historically, children were deemed to lack mature judgment or the capacity to fully understand the world around them sits at odds with the breadth of legislation in the United States that allows persons aged under 18 to be treated as adults in the criminal justice system.[63] This raises difficulties with the decision. Indeed, it relies upon the (problematically) 'settled understanding that the differentiating characteristics of youth are universal'.[64] This point, among others, is what Justice Alito in his dissenting judgment took issue with. Alito criticizes Sotomayer's decision for its reinforcement of the lesser capacities of children as an absolute truth. While Alito does not say so, this may ultimately not serve children's interests.[65] If age is to be a personal characteristic relevant to the *Miranda* custody analysis, Alito asks, why not other characteristics? He states that 'many persons *over* the age of 18 are also more susceptible to police pressure than the hypothetical reasonable person'.[66] He asks rhetorically whether the decision now implies that education and intellectual capacity must be taken into account. Justice Alito's point is that the analysis and reasoning of the majority of Justices turns on intellectual capacity rather than age, which he does not necessarily view to be analogous with one another.

Again, what is evident in these judgments is the naturalization of the connection between age, reason and maturity. Despite age operating in almost all respects as an arbitrary division, it is tied to actual and demonstrable intellectual and emotional capacities. The American Psychological Association evidence relied upon in *Roper* v. *Simmons* regarding cognitive maturity points to science that suggests that the brain is not fully mature until the age of 25 years. Yet, nowhere in the judgment is there consideration that this suggests that the death penalty ought to be abolished for all persons aged under 25 years. The evidence is not used to rewrite criminal law across the board. Instead, the evidence is used to support a jurisprudential principle that children are less culpable than adults for their crimes.

In 2011, the United States Supreme Court ruled in *Graham* v. *Florida*[67] that life imprisonment without parole for non-homicide offences was also unconstitutional for minors. Such a sentence, the majority held, was in contravention of the Eighth Amendment protection against cruel and unusual punishment. Prior to the decision, 37 American states, the District of Columbia and the Federal government allowed juveniles to be sentenced to life imprisonment without parole. The majority judgment questioned the trial judge's conclusion that:

> you [the defendant] decided that this is how you were going to lead your life and that there is nothing that we can do for you. And as the state has pointed out, that this [an armed robbery offence] is an escalating pattern of criminal conduct on your part and that we can't help you any further. We can't do anything to deter you.[68]

The Supreme Court noted that in making his judgment, the trial judge imposed a sentence *greater* than that sought by the prosecutor: life without the possibility of parole. In ruling this sentence unconstitutional, the Court again relied upon *Roper* to attest to the lesser culpability of young people: 'No recent data provide reason to reconsider the Court's observations in *Roper* about the nature of juveniles.'[69] The Court reiterated this decision by quoting that 'from a moral standpoint it would be misguided to equate the failings of a minor with those of an adult, for greater possibility exists that a minor's character deficiencies will be reformed'.[70] In his dissent, Justice Thomas rejected the blanket characterization of persons aged under 18 as less culpable. Once again, members of the Court find themselves at odds with one another over their conceptions of childhood and understandings of the moral and intellectual capacities of children.

Drawing the connection between age, reason and maturity in crime, Kenneth S. Levy explores psy-knowledges to ask whether or not there is a mental health problem in juvenile delinquency. He suggests that young offenders are often 'developmentally retarded' for one of eight reasons: homelessness from a young age; subjection to violence while living on the street; a weak bond to a parental home; loneliness, neglect and abandonment; sexual abuse; substance abuse; physical ailments; and psychopathological disorders such as anxiety and depression.[71] Of course, it seems reasonable that these may also be prevalent factors affecting adult offenders. This is of interest to Levy because the judicial response to juvenile crime in Australia has tended to focus on deterrence, labelling and shaming: 'these theories assume some degree of normalcy in literacy, social adjustment and mental health'.[72] A relationship is built here between crime and mental health, and specifically between youth and mental health. This points to the relationship between immaturity, by the fact of one's age that may lessen culpability, and insanity that is available as a complete defence.

As discussed earlier, Jonathon Simon also considers this rise of "psy-knowledges". He does so by considering two cases – separated by 75 years – involving young people in violent crimes in the United States.[73] The first, concerned a 1924 trial, in which two young adults (both aged over 18 at the time of the offence) faced the death penalty. The defence counsel sought to emphasize their youth (together with mental illness) as a mitigating factor in determining whether they ought to be subject to the death penalty. The judge sentenced one to 99 years plus life, the other to 111 years.[74] Nathan Leopold and Richard Loeb were tried for the kidnapping, murder and mutilation of a young boy, Bobby Franks. Jonathon Simon offers extracts from the extensive trial testimony about their psychological condition:

> The physical examination of Leopold revealed that there had been a premature involution of the thymus gland and a premature calcification of the pineal gland in the skull; that the pituitary gland was smaller than normal; that the thyroid was overactive; and that the adrenal glands did not function normally ... these abnormalities produced an early sex development and had a direct relationship to Leopold's extraordinary precocity and his mental condition.[75]

In respect to Loeb:

> The opinion is inescapable that in Loeb we have an individual with a pathological mental life, who is driven in his actions by the compulsive force of his abnormally twisted life of phantasy or imagination.[76]

It was the opinion of expert testimony that the combination of these two abnormal personalities 'made a situation so unique that it probably will never repeat itself' and that, 'There is justification for stressing the uniqueness of this case if for no other reason than that it has created widespread panic among parents of young people.'[77] History has proved that the experts were wrong on the first point and that the moral panic has been sustained.

The second case concerns the prosecution of Kip Kinkel, who pleaded guilty to murdering his parents and two high school students when he was 15 years old.[78] Kinkel was diagnosed after the murders as a severe untreated schizophrenic. Rather than presenting an insanity defence, Kinkel entered the guilty plea and then presented expert testimony at the sentencing hearing before a judge, which presented his mental condition (rather than his age) as a mitigating factor relevant to determining the sentence for the crime. Kinkel was tried as an adult and received the maximum penalty available to minors in Oregon: life without parole.[79]

The use of psychological evidence by the defence counsel regarding the mental state of Kinkel sought to reduce his culpability in the same way that psychological evidence of immaturity (related to age) might. Four expert witnesses were called – including his treating psychiatrist prior to the murders, who had failed to diagnose any mental condition. The others, a psychologist, child psychiatrist and paediatric neurologist diagnosed among other things: paranoid schizophrenia, bipolar disorder, schizoaffective disorder and that Kinkel's brain 'was literally perforated with holes and that those sectors most associated with emotional control and decision making experienced reduced blood flow'.[80]

Again, it was the question of his culpability for the crime and the punishment that ought to be exacted that concerned the court. That the punishment had to be proportionate to the crime was not an issue. That the evidence of his serious mental illness presents in terms not so different from the evidence of his age as a mitigating factor, is unsurprising but also interesting. It does not suggest that mental illness and youth are the same thing, but it points to the manner in which courts attempt to know their accused in exact and formulaic terms. How people are known in the courtroom also becomes how they are known outside of the courtroom. I suggest that for young people, this is significant in how we understand their maturity and reason.

Returning to *Roper* v. *Simmons*, it is difficult to accept that the question of culpability was not the only, or even the main, reason for Justice Kennedy's decision. Justice Scalia convincingly refutes Justice Kennedy's reliance on the shift in public standards regarding the death penalty and young people. It would seem that Kennedy's decision is as much driven by a sense that the death penalty is wrong, as it is by the assertion that young people are less culpable than adults for their criminal conduct.[81] Justice Kennedy's decision was as much, if not more, focused upon the argument that the death penalty is cruel and unusual punishment, particularly where there is potential for reform. That this potential is greater for young people seems secondary to the argument that the death penalty is only *not* cruel and unusual where there is *no* potential for reform. Such an argument has nothing to do with age; age merely becomes one factor in making that assessment. Further, the majority decision referred to the weight of international standards against the death penalty applying to children. Again, this has little to do with the culpability of an accused being altered by the fact of their age. Finally, the evidence offered as to Simmons' mental state, and the broader evidence offered as to the mental state of young people, is plainly unconvincing. More problematic is that it dramatically limits what claims can be made about young people in other contexts, where arguments about their maturity and reason would otherwise be very helpful. Justice Scalia drew the Supreme Court's attention to this in his dissent:

> the American Psychological Association, which claims in this case that scientific evidence shows persons under eighteen lack the ability to take moral responsibility for their decisions, has previously taken precisely the opposite position before this very Court ... [arguing that] juveniles are mature enough to decide whether to obtain an abortion without parental involvement.[82]

The effect is such that:

> [The] very use of categories has been a strategic legal response to external knowledge concerning the probable moral, intellectual and emotional capacities of children at various stages in their development. By solidifying these stages into fixed aged categories, law is able to reconstruct such knowledge on its own terms.[83]

The topic of criminal justice develops some of the tensions and paradoxes already identified in claims regarding children's maturity and autonomy and will continue to be developed in the next chapter on consent and sexuality. Pointing to the very tension that Justice Scalia mentions above, Elizabeth Cauffman asks: 'How could adolescents be mature enough to make their own decisions about abortion, but not mature enough to face the consequences of committing armed robbery or using marijuana?'[84] In accepting the terms of children's rights debates as being centred on claims to maturity and autonomy, we enter into these difficult tensions.

We can continue to accept being bound by the terms of this debate: an argument as to the maturity of young people and the decision-making processes they enter into. For many, it is possible to distinguish very clearly between the criminal culpability for murder and abortion on moral grounds. Even the conservative judge, Justice Scalia, is prepared to accept that this distinction might be made, despite the contradictory nature of the American Psychological Association's (APA) evidence between the cases.[85] Yet, Scalia is right to suggest that the maturity required to know that killing another person is wrong, is lesser than the maturity required to weigh the full consequences of choosing whether or not to terminate a pregnancy. It does not take a sophisticated mind to know that murder is not only criminally, but also morally wrong. It is a more challenging argument to suggest that knowing what to do in the event of an unwanted pregnancy demands less of our cognitive abilities, less of our psychological maturity. Yet, the Supreme Court, in accepting the evidence of the APA in two separate cases arguing each of these points, suggests exactly this.[86]

It is within this tension that we begin to see the challenges created by relating a young person's maturity to claims of their autonomy and rights. We begin to see how it is that autonomy claims are problematic in debates about children's rights. If we engage in an argument about the right of a young person to vote, or to have an abortion, and agree to the terms of debate as relating to that person's ability to reason and make mature decisions, what consequence follows when that same young person commits a criminal offence? Do we maintain the consistent position that young people are as mature and reasonable as adults and ought to be held accountable under the full weight of the law? Or, do we begin to draw distinctions between what a child's maturity means at the GPs office, in a bedroom, during a political election and when they commit an offence? I argue that this is exactly what happens. Yet, this is even more problematic when the evidentiary bases of these arguments are not only moral or political, but also involve the factual nature of psychological assessments and scientific knowledge, bound by the foundations set by Jean Piaget and Philippe Ariés some fifty years ago.

Across these examples of child criminality, competing conceptions of childhood are at play. When the facts of a juvenile's conduct are not in dispute, the decision of Courts necessarily turns on questions of the *mens rea* of the child defendants: they are required by the criminal justice system to account for the moral and intellectual capacity of young people to conduct a criminal wrong. This is, on the one hand, an empirical question that demands reference to expert psychological evidence in drawing the conclusion that young people are less culpable than adults. However, it is also a question that pivots on what we understand children and childhood to be. The answer to such a question is bound to sociological and philosophical constructions of childhood. Resolving whether or not a child is an innocent, incapable of commiting a criminal wrong; or, whether by fact of their immaturity, a child poses a greater risk to society; or, by fact of their neutral status as blank-slates, they have greater capacity for reform is a deeply political question. The conclusion drawn about which conception of childhood to choose in navigating toward justice (for society and for the accused) has as much to do with an empirical conclusion about who children are and what childhood is, as it does with the normative claim about who we want children to be, about what we believe childhood ought to be. This, I argue, presents us with the future-adult subject in debates about childhood criminality.

Conceptions of childhood and moral panic

The cases above present a series of controversies that are characterized by competing conceptions of childhood, and the moral panic that ensues when children commit murder. The reaction to this moral panic has been to reassert adult authority as 'imposed rather than negotiated'.[87] Haydon and Scraton identify three specific forms of this authority: correction, discipline and prevention. Correction can be translated as 'punishment – a child secured, locked away',[88] and this form of authority was asserted strongly following the Venables and Thompson trial. This punitive, retributive approach to "correction" can be distinguished from a rehabilitative approach, which otherwise characterizes juvenile justice, and to a lesser extent the broader criminal justice system. Discipline is also asserted through existing institutions of childhood – in schools and the family – and continues as an effort to shape young people into good, responsible members of society. However, just as the discourse begins to shift toward a conception of sinful children, and the risk and threat they pose to society, a response of 'moral renewal' pushes back.[89] A faith that 'interprets the crimes of children as indicative of a "breakdown of morality associated with a feckless underclass, dysfunctional families and a parenting deficit"'.[90] In America, multiple shootings at Columbine High School and elsewhere have prompted debates about gun control laws, signalling a broader social ill as a condition that makes child-by-child killing possible.[91] The child, though no longer innocent, presents in this response as a blank-slate rather than a sinner. Indeed, amongst the moral panic following James Bulger's murder there were reports of the deprived lives of Jon Venables and Robert Thompson.[92] Naughty children are produced by the failures of society and family. In this way, the child as an image of potential, rather than as innately sinful or innocent, emerges.

Michael Freeman makes a similar argument, but in different terms. He contrasts the public reaction and condemnation of James Bulger's murderers with a very similar case in England in 1861. In this case, two young boys also brutally murdered a two-year-old. Peter Barratt and James Bradley (both aged eight) were convicted of the manslaughter of George Burgess, but not his murder. As with Thompson and Venables, there was no doubting the guilt of these boys. However, the sentiment of the sentencing judge was quite different:

> I am afraid you have been very wicked, naughty boys, and I have no doubt that you have caused the death of this little boy by the brutal way to which you used him. I am going to send you to a place where you will have an opportunity of becoming good boys.[93]

In *The Times* commentary on the judgment, this sentiment was supported:

> As far as it went [their conscience] was as sound and as genuine a conscience as that of a grown man: it told them what they were doing was wrong ... [But] conscience, like other natural facilities, admits of degrees: it is weak, and has not arrived at its proper growth in children, though it has a real existence and a voice within them ...[94]

These statements demonstrate an attempt to hold two competing understandings of childhood alongside one another. The children have, knowingly, committed serious wrongs. However, this knowledge, awareness and criminal conduct does not fully displace children's special innocence. In this earlier case, Michael Freeman demonstrates that it is still possible to choose to emphasize their presumably greater capacity for redemption prior to adulthood, despite the seriousness of the criminal act. The earlier case maintains a conception of childhood innocence alongside evidence of a serious and knowing wrong. It is possible to have rational capacities to know right from wrong, but maintain that children are different enough from adults in order not to be held fully responsible. To choose to do this demands a faith in the potential of children, despite evidence of a very risky future. For Michael Freeman, the earlier case occurred at a time when there was 'no psychology or psychiatry'.[95] By the time of the Bulger trial, psy-knowledges had taken up a role in trials to establish legal responsibility, but not, Freeman argues, to 'explain or excuse'.[96] The result, he argues, was fortunate for the United Kingdom government:

> Had the child psychiatrists' evidence failed to establish that the boys were unable to distinguish naughtiness from serious wrong, or found that they lacked the mental capacity to stand trial, where would they [the government] have been? With no trial, with identities and biographies suppressed, the killing of James Bulger could not have been used as an object lesson for pontificating about evil.[97]

The murder of James Bulger was far more than the murder of a young boy. It was also, in these ways, the death of childhood innocence. Whether one agrees with the justice served by the court that tried Jon Venables and Robert Thompson, it remains true that their trial was also a trial of childhood; a trial of good versus evil, of innocence versus sin. No longer could childhood be allowed to encompass these competing, contradictory terms and instead it had to be reduced to one or the other.

The James Bulger murder and subsequent controversy demonstrates competing moral conceptions of childhood. For James and Jenks, one image was that of an innately sinful child, the other was a composite creature, an "adult-child".[98] Either of these images of childhood, they argued, allowed the public to reject the inclusion of Venables and Thompson into the category of child, in turn 'reaffirming to itself the essence of what children are'.[99] A sinful child, or adult-like child is not a child at all. Children can be innocent, which may also create the conditions for serious violence to be possible. Or, they might be sinful, with the capacity of redemption or not, but always providing society with an opportunity for moral renewal. On either of these accounts, despite ruptures in specific moments by specific acts, the discourse of childhood is able to remain intact.

Moral panic also serves as a useful concept to consider the future-adult as the political subject of children's rights. Stanley Cohen, in his seminal text *Folk Devils and Moral Panics: the creation of the Mods and Rockers*, explored the phenomena of moral panics, particularly those associated with youth.[100] His 1972 analysis of British youth subcultures and public responses to these subcultures introduced the concept of moral panic into sociological literature, which revealed the complicit and complex roles of the media, the public, political leaders and interest groups, in identifying 'a condition, episode, person or groups of persons ... as a threat to social values and interests'.[101] In 2002, in a third edition of this text, Cohen explicitly considers the James Bulger murder as an example of how an 'utterly unique' crime 'triggered off an immediate and ferocious moral panic'.[102] The murder became 'a potent example of everything that had gone wrong in Britain'.[103]

Informed by Cohen's analysis, Erich Goode and Nachman Ben-Yehuda argued in the early 1990s, that:

> During the moral panic, the behavior of some of the members of a society is thought to be so problematic to others, the evil they do, or are thought to do, is felt to be so wounding to the substance and fabric of the body social, that serious steps must be taken to control the behaviour, punish the perpetrators, and repair the damage. The threat this evil presumably poses is felt to represent a crisis for that society: something must be done about it, and that something must be done now; if steps are not taken immediately, or soon, we will suffer even graver consequences.[104]

The graver consequences to which Goode and Ben-Yehuda refer apply not only to the individual victims of evil but, more importantly, to society at large. In respect to children, this risk is two-fold. First, children might be the subject of moral panic; for example of sex panics regarding sexual abuse and paedophiles living in a community;[105] these concerns place childhood itself at risk. Second, the moral panic might refer to a panic about the decay of society such that 'the young and the morally weak, wavering, and questionable are dabbling (or might dabble) in evil, harmful deeds'.[106] That is, children might be the subject of evil or the potential doers of evil. Even as the subjects, or victims, of evil acts such as paedophilia, there is a risk that persists beyond the immediate physical harm. Similarly, Foucault's history of sexualities also points to the fear that premature sexual exposure will somehow compromise the welfare of that person in later life.[107]

Goode and Ben-Yehuda point to five elements that indicate a moral panic: concern, hostility, consensus, disproportionality and volatility.[108] Concern is distinguished from fear, and is evidenced by quantitative indicators of public opinion; hostility is then directed toward those who are understood to give rise to this concern; consensus is established that this concern is a real and serious matter, which is caused by the group of people toward which hostility is shown;[109] the panic is disproportionate to the established risk; and, these panics are volatile by nature, arising suddenly, perhaps even unexpectedly, and likely to be short-lived. The discussion of James Bulger's murder above, and of the decision by the United States Supreme Court decision to rule the execution of juveniles unconstitutional, are broadly indicative of debates concerning young people's violence not just their criminality. John Springhall offers a survey over school shootings in North America in his discussion of moral panic.[110] Though

Springhall does not undertake this analysis himself, school shootings can be further understood through assessing the incidents in terms of Goode and Ben-Yehuda's criteria for moral panic. Enormous concern was demonstrated in North America following, for example, the Columbine school shootings. Hostility was shown against teenagers who were viewed as sharing the characteristics of the shooters (the Trench Coat Mafia, Goth apparel, loners).[111] Further, Springhall's discussion reveals that a consensus was established following the shootings that youth violence was on the rise, prompting calls for legislative change and public policy changes. In turn, this resulted in a panic that was disproportionate to the established risk, which did not indicate a rise in violence across the youth population generally. Finally, it represents an extremely volatile public debate; one that arises with grave seriousness at the time of shootings, but does not persist strongly between shootings. The impact of a moral panic about youth violence, Springhall argues, distracts from the seriousness of the actual events.

The moral panic that followed the Columbine shootings prompted a search for explanations which was necessarily informed by the indicators of panic: hostility and disproportionality especially. Springhall argues that the search for explanations in this context led to four key areas of analysis: access to guns, violent youth cultures, the social world of the American High School and, finally, personal and psychological factors.[112] Springhall argues that policies concerning gun control, security, night curfews, movie rating systems and media self-censorship all emerged in response to Columbine. Laws were tightened to ensure that persons aged under 18 could not easily access weapons, despite the fact that one of the weapons used by the Columbine shooters was already outlawed.[113] Night curfews were also introduced, despite little evidence of increasing levels of youth violence.[114] Stronger media regulation through classification and self-censorship followed in the aftermath of the shootings, even though media exposure was never established as a causal factor.[115] Importantly, these responses were explicitly age-focused, as adult criminal acts do not tend to illicit curfew and stricter media regulation. In this way, the age of the criminals, rather than the crime itself, informed public policy responses.

The child as a violent offender ruptures more prominent views of childhood as an innocent or blank-slate. However, the violence of adults does not call into question our understandings of adulthood in a similar way. Where adult violence might be regarded as an aberration of adulthood, the violence of children is positioned as embodying a greater moral concern. There is a fear that "misfits", who are otherwise regarded as troublesome but innocuous, if gone unchecked will kill.[116] Moreover, as Springhall stresses, in North America, two-thirds of murdered American children are killed, not by other young people, but by adults.[117] Thus, it is not the murder of children that necessarily elicits a moral panic, but murder by children. The aberration is not children as the victims of violence or violent adults, but violent children.

The violent child is the child as sinner, one that must be disciplined and reformed before earning one's place in adult society. The violent child, however, is also the risk of failing to realize an ideal liberal adulthood. The moral panic surrounding school shootings elicits concerns about the demise of society. This reinforces claims that the next generation are de-cultured vanguard: that the next generation presents the end of a liberal society, and not its replication or progression.[118] Debates about children's criminality, then, are also debates about maintaining and reproducing this political community, which is about realizing adults who will meet the standards of a rational, autonomous and liberal adult citizenship. As Jonathon Simon has argued, being young in discourses of crime is regarded similarly to being mentally ill: he argues that crimes committed by children come to be seen as a 'sign of a kind of mental illness rooted in both the normal and pathological features of adolescent development'.[119] For Michel Foucault, 'madness was childhood'.[120] The irrationality of criminal actions in this way is to be considered childlike. Therefore, it is against this irrationality, embedded in the adolescent mind, that the child must be disciplined and educated. It is the awakening or indulgence of this irrationality by young people in engaging in violent acts that presents the great risk to society that prompts moral panic. It is this innate irrationality that is read as an innate criminality, an innate sinfulness. The danger of these qualities in children is not only tied to the kinds of children they might be, including those children who might murder, but also to the kinds of adults they might one day become. These children are the future-adult citizens that will constitute our future liberal political communities. When young people demonstrate these qualities, concern arises that the next generation of adults will not satisfy the conditions of their political subjectivity as good, liberal citizens. It is this future-adult subject that emerges as a primary concern of the juvenile justice system.

The future-adult subject

In *Discipline and Punish*, Foucault famously observed that, 'One must calculate a penalty in terms not of the crime, but of its possible repetition. One must take into account not the past offence, but the future disorder.'[121] Criminal behaviour is evidence of the failure to become a good, liberal, adult: where adulthood is understood as the realization of reason, maturity and autonomy. However, as discussed, the rise of juvenile justice coincided with other social institutions and the development of disciplines that sought to know children. This shift began to change the way society viewed children by pointing to the fact of their immaturity, mapping the linearity of their psychological and physical development, marking out phases of growth that families and societies must support in order to realise a full-fledged, mature and responsible, autonomous adult.[122] In 1951, Jean Piaget published *Psychology of Intelligence* and a decade later, Phillipe Ariès followed with *Centuries of Childhood*.[123] The rise of developmental psychology further sought to quantifiably measure and account for the condition of childhood. The relationship between human evolution and individual development has been established.[124] Variation in evolutionary development occurs in adulthood, with the modern adult's physiological development meeting the exacting standards of an Enlightened individual in Kantian terms, including the figure of

Kant's Enlightened individual as a man. This modern adulthood differs, then, from our ancient ancestors' adulthood, which in modern society is reflected in the "higher" animals, "savages" and women, as well as in childhood's immaturity.[125] John Morss quotes Alexander Chamberlain, who considers the comparison thus: 'the child and the savage meet on this ground, some young boys and girls being as firmly impressed with the reality of their dreams as are the Brazilian Indians'.[126] This conflation of immaturity, with prehistory and with savagery, informs the sense of childhood as untamed and risky.

Establishing a science for knowing children and mapping their growth into adulthood in developmental terms has seen the terms of maturity, reason and cognitive capacity become central in debates about children's rights. For those who seek to demonstrate the greater autonomy of children, it becomes necessary to demonstrate in these known terms, the greater cognitive capacities of young people. Priscilla Alderson has attempted to do this in the area of medical treatment.[127] While David Archard attempts to grapple with emerging maturity, it nonetheless remains very difficult to escape the dichotomies of child/adult, irrational/rational, immature/mature, citizen-in-waiting/citizen, becoming/being. Elizabeth Cohen, in attempting to reject a choice between protection and autonomy rights, sought to theorize "semi-citizenship" for children. She did so, not by rejecting claims about innocence, vulnerability or reason and maturity, but by attempting to account for all those competing claims.[128] This is problematic because it obscures the complex spaces and environments that children live in: where they are more than a measure of (im)maturity and their world is one of more than innocence and risk.

By the 1970s this thinking was informing a well-established juvenile justice system in Western countries. As shown in previous chapters, the issue of how children ought to be treated within the criminal law turns on matters of maturity, reason and autonomy. With these concepts once again at the heart of debate, we find ourselves arguing about issues that have much less to do with children as they do with what adulthood ought to be. By seeking to fix an empirical basis for normative claims about what childhood is and what adulthood ought to be, we configure the debate of children's criminal culpability around truth claims that bind us all.

As discussed, the juvenile justice system is premised upon the different treatment of children on account of their lesser culpability for criminal acts. This position is attached to claims about reason, maturity and autonomy and to a Romantic conception of children as innocents. However, this lesser culpability is not a fixed idea. It emerges from a particular historical moment and has, ever since, been in a state of constant negotiation. As shown above, this negotiation is evident in criminal trials and public debates. This is consistent with Michel Foucault's rejection of the criminal justice system as a neutral site of liberal instrumentalist reason. On the contrary, in *Discipline and Punish*, Foucault conducts an archaeology of crime that reveals crime and justice (along with other institutions, most notably schools) as a highly politicized domain of disciplinary power.[129] Disciplinary power operates in this way for children as well as adults.

Foucault identifies the emergence of the modern criminal justice system at a juncture in which the state's 'right to punish ... shifted from the vengeance of the sovereign to the defense of society.'[130] The defence of society presents as a more considered object of criminal law, and allows punishment as a goal in and of itself to be superseded by more modern goals of deterrence and rehabilitation. Foucault demonstrates this historically by pointing to the move away from public spectacles and torture, toward the privatization of punishment – in enclosed and secure jails that separate the criminal from the rest of society. The defence of society, however, is a very broad and necessarily political goal. In this way, I argue that the defence of society no longer concerns conduct that is offensive to the state, but rather conduct that undermines individual liberty and freedom in a liberal state. That children may lack the necessary *mens rea* on the one hand, does not discount the enormous risk that disobedient and criminal children present to society as a whole. When Foucault writes that 'A stupid despot may constrain his slaves with iron chains; but a true politician bind them even more strongly by the chain of their own ideas',[131] he highlights the importance of childhood. In order to constrain a person by their own ideas, those ideas must be shaped, informed and internalized from the earliest of days. Children who present with behaviour that is contrary to the goals of liberal society are an enormous risk and require intervention to ensure the preservation of the liberal state. I have argued this in the earlier chapter on liberal rationality.

Foucault describes the citizen as one who:

> is presumed to have accepted once and for all, with the laws of society, the very law by which he may be punished. Thus, the criminal appears as a juridically paradoxical being. He has broken the pact, he is therefore the enemy of society as a whole, but he participates in the punishment that is practiced upon him. The least crime attacks the whole of society; and the whole of society – including the criminal – is present in the least punishment.[132]

This juridically paradoxical being is all the more paradoxical if one imagines the child as the criminal. Children, after all, are not citizens in the fullest sense. Thus, they are not yet members of the "pact" that Foucault identifies as having been broken. Nonetheless, by demonstrating behaviour that is contrary to the interests of society, children who conduct criminal acts also demonstrate their incapacity to be members of society. Criminal punishment then demands the necessary reform to ensure that they are placed back on the path toward good, liberal, adult citizenship. This is emphasized in the cases discussed above of the greater potential of child offenders for reform.

However, by rupturing the conception of children as innocents, the criminal child invokes a particular kind of fear – or, a moral panic – that calls for far greater serious intervention. The inability to reconcile criminal behaviour with a conception of children as innocents is what prompts the claims that offenders such as Venables and Thompson are evil, that the Columbine shooters were "monsters". Such characterizations sidestep the need to reconcile our conceptions of children as innocents with children as sinners. Instead, they are not only no longer children, but they are also no longer human. Maintaining their humanity, and child status, and emphasizing reform over punishment compels us to accept that children can commit grave moral and criminal wrongs. In turn, this prompts serious consideration that children should not be subject to differential treatment in the criminal justice system. Whether to do so or not, I argue, does not turn on an empirical truth of who children are. Instead, it is a political choice that has as much to do with our understandings of what childhood and children ought to be and their idealized role in the maintaining of a liberal state.

As Nikolas Rose observes, in the nineteenth century: 'childhood began to be seen as a distinct period during which bad habits could be laid down that would have a lifelong influence',[133] compelling the need for the sinful child, in need of reform and attention, to be appropriately disciplined and governed before reaching adulthood so that he or she would become a good and productive citizen. Nikolas Rose discusses the implications of this at length, identifying the processes of "normalization" that provide a quantifiable benchmark against which all children can be measured. He expresses concern that the 'soul of the young citizen has become the object of government through expertise', specifically the expertise of scientific truth.[134] Rose argues that 'a powerful "counter-discourse" has taken shape, which has sought to limit incursions into the freedom of the family in the name of the protection of children'.[135] Meanwhile, the normalization of individual development has informed how we conceptualize and know young people. Politically, this serves a very specific purpose: not to realize an autonomous Kantian individual, but to form a self-regulating member of liberal society; to form, in Rose's terms, a governed soul.

Conclusion

In this chapter, I have argued that the juvenile justice system is premised upon the different treatment of children from adults, on account of their lesser culpability for crime. This lesser culpability is not fixed. Instead, it emerges from a particular historical moment in which children began to be seen as fundamentally different from adults. This modern-day concept of the child coincided with three alternative conceptions of childhood. Debates about criminality, especially, highlight the competing conceptions of childhood as a time of innocence and as a time for naughtiness or outright wickedness. So it is that debates about criminality are fraught with tensions about holding children properly accountable for what are, sometimes, very distressing and violent crimes while, at the same time, giving weight to children's greater capacity for redemption and society's own interests in perpetuating childhood as a time of innocence. These debates are attached to claims about reason, maturity and autonomy. These claims are made not just anecdotally or through attention-grabbing news headlines, but in science, medicine and psychology. These "knowledges" of childhood, I argue, are made possible by existing social conceptions of childhood, but then also serve to make these conceptions concrete in law. The James Bulger murder, in particular, disrupts these conceptions of childhood. On the one hand, it was the murder of a toddler who was physically unable to defend himself against two older boys. It was an innocent life taken. On the other hand, the two murderers were also children but portrayed as the very opposite of innocent. Robert Thompson and Jon Venables, despite their own neglect, were deemed to be knowing and deliberate in their crime. They represent the child sinners: an unintelligible evil, but also an evil only possible because of their childishness. That children are naughty is not at all controversial. However, when mere naughtiness is also a criminal wrong it trespasses into a public domain that children do not belong to. They do not belong to this public domain, because they do not yet possess the adequate reason, maturity and autonomy. The criminal child is a serious threat, not only because of how it ruptures discourses of childhood but also because it undermines the very purpose of childhood: to become a good, adult, liberal citizen.

Notes

1 James Bulger was two years old when he was abducted and murdered on 12 February 1993. The Coroner's post-mortem findings were reported in depth, including that that he died as a result of approximately 30 blows to his body, after which his body was left on train tracks and his body severed: Jonathon Foster, 'James Bulger suffered multiple fractures', *Independent*, Wednesday 10 November 1993.
2 The media attention is discussed at length by Haydon Scraton (2000).
3 In this chapter, "justice" relates specifically to the criminal justice system and the principle of remedying a criminal wrong. For a general discussion of theories of punishment in Australia's criminal justice system. See Edney and Bagaric (2007).
4 *Doli incapax* is a Latin term meaning incapable of deceit. As a principle, it presumes that children aged under ten are incapable of a criminal wrong. In Western legal traditions this principle is rebuttable between the ages of ten and 14. It will be discussed in greater depth in the next section of this chapter. The common law principle has been superseded in England and Wales by the *Crime and Disorder Act 1998*, and there is no longer a presumption that children cannot be criminalized under the age of fourteen. See Muncie (2009: 275–6).
5 Robyn Linde has analysed the abolition of the death penalty from states around the world, to argue how normative claims about children's rights are able to usurp state interests. See Linde (2014).
6 Here, disciplinary power refers to mechanisms that regulate the activity and behaviour of individuals and, together, society. It refers to a range of different apparatuses, including schools, prisons and hospitals. See Foucault (2006, 1991).
7 Blackstone (2001).
8 Ibid.
9 Ibid.
10 For a summary of the Commonwealth, state and territories legislation, which establishes that children aged under ten cannot be held criminally responsible and that the principle of *doli incapax* operates from ages ten to 14 see Australian Institute of Criminology (2005).
11 Haydon and Scraton (2000: 420).
12 Graham Parker (1976: 171). Other colonies were settled as convict populations, which included children that had been tried for criminal acts and sent to Australia (it

is estimated that 25,000 people aged under 18 arrived in Australia as convicts), Kociumbas (1997).
13 Victoria (2000: 29).
14 Hirschel and Wakefield (1995: 325).
15 Hawes (1991: 2).
16 Ibid., 36.
17 For an analysis of how sciences of knowing entered into criminal law, see Michel Foucault (1975).
18 Nikolas Rose (1999).
19 Ibid., xiii
20 Ibid., 123.
21 Ibid., 152.
22 Ibid., 137.
23 Dolgin (1999: 421).
24 Haydon and Scraton (2000: 431).
25 Ibid., 432.
26 Ibid.
27 Ibid., 433.
28 Bradley (2003).
29 *T.* v. *The United Kingdom; V.* v. *The United Kingdom*, joint decision of the European Court of Human Rights (1999).
30 *The Convention for the Protection of Human Rights and Fundamental Freedoms.*
31 Haydon and Scraton (2000: 436–47).
32 Venables and Thompson were released on certain conditions, Venables did not face further criminal charges but having been found in possession of child pornography, was immediately returned to prison.
33 James and Jenks (1996: 318).
34 Ibid., 316.
35 Ariès (1962: 28).
36 Dolgin (1999: 421); Hymowitz (1998).
37 James and Jenks (1996: 315).
38 Ibid.
39 Haydon and Scraton (2000: 423).
40 John Springhall (2008: 50).
41 Haydon and Scraton (2000: 424).
42 James and Jenks (1996: 321).
43 In 1968, Mary Bell, aged ten, was sentenced for the murder two boys aged three and four. See Sereny (1995). The case is also discussed by Haydon and Scraton (2000).
44 Ibid.
45 Stanley Cohen (1972).
46 In 2003, Scott Allen Hain, aged 32 was executed in Oklahoma for a crime he committed as a 17-year-old boy. For a current list of child executions since 1990, see website: Amnesty International (1990).
47 *Roper* v. *Simmons*, 543 United States Reports 551 (2005).
48 Ibid.
49 Justice Kennedy's summary of facts, ibid.
50 Justice Kennedy, ibid.
51 Justice Kennedy, ibid.
52 Dolgin (1999). Also see, Brownlie (2001: 519–37).
53 Jonathon Simon (2004: 80).
54 Ibid.
55 *Roper* v. *Simmons.*
56 Amnesty International (1990)
57 *JDB* v. *North Carolina*, 564 United States Reports unbound (2011).

58 *Miranda* v. *Arizona*, 384 United States Reports 436 (1966).
59 Ibid.
60 Justice Sotomayer, *JDB* v. *North Carolina*, 1.
61 Justice Sotomayer, ibid., 8–9.
62 Justice Sotomayer outlines these at ibid., 9.
63 Sixteen- and 17-year-old children are tried as adults in the states of Connecticut, New York and North Carolina. Seventeen-year-olds are tried automatically as adults in ten other American states.
64 Justice Sotomayer, *JDB* v. *North Carolina*, 10.
65 Reinforcing the lesser capacities of children makes arguments about their rights in other domains more difficult.
66 Justice Alito, dissenting, *JDB* v. *North Carolina*.
67 *Graham* v. *Florida*, 560 United States Reports unbound (2010).
68 Justice Kennedy, ibid., 5.
69 Justice Kennedy, ibid., 17.
70 Ibid.
71 K. S. Levy (1998: 521).
72 Ibid., 523.
73 Simon (2004).
74 Ibid., 82.
75 Ibid., 86.
76 Ibid., 89.
77 Ibid.
78 Ibid., 91–111.
79 Ibid., 80.
80 Ibid., 93.
81 Two other issues, the relevance of international standards, including the United Nations Convention on the Rights of the Child and the theory of punishment as a deterrent toward young people, were relevant to the decision but are not of interest here.
82 Justice Scalia, *Roper* v. *Simmons*.
83 King and Piper (1995: 107), quoted in Haydon and Scraton (2000: 420).
84 Cauffman (1999: 408).
85 Justice Scalia, dissenting, *Roper* v. *Simmons*.
86 Of course, there is not always a moral or criminal distinction made between murder and abortion. At time that Justice Scalia writes, there is a criminal distinction between those two acts in American law.
87 Haydon and Scraton (2000: 423).
88 Ibid., 447.
89 Ibid., 431.
90 Ibid.
91 Springhall (2008: 51–3).
92 Bedell (1993). Also discussed in Freeman (1997b).
93 Ibid., 129–30.
94 Quoted in ibid., 131.
95 Ibid.
96 Ibid.
97 Ibid., 131.
98 James and Jenks (1996: 323).
99 Ibid; Also see Jenks (2005: 129).
100 Morss (1995: 24). Also see Cohen (2002).
101 Stuart Hall (1978). Hall extended Cohen's analysis of moral panics as a sociological phenomenon into more political terrain whereby moral panics are employed to legitimize greater state control over social life.

102 Cohen (2002: 9).
103 Ibid., ix.
104 Goode and Ben-Yehuda (1994: 31).
105 Such as those discussed in Krinsky (2008).
106 Goode and Ben-Yehuda (1994: 31–2).
107 See especially, Foucault (1978). This is referred to in more detail in Chapter 6.
108 Goode and Ben-Yehuda (1994: 33–4).
109 Consensus here is not necessarily a majority of the population, but is substantial or widespread, or perhaps just influential enough to shape public debate and even public policy.
110 Springhall (2008).
111 Springhall describes the 'Trench Coat Mafia' as a 'jock term of contempt for a group of pariah students at Columbine High School who jointly fascinated the media', despite the Trench Coat Mafia playing no role in the Columbine shootings as the shooters were not a member of this social group. The clothing the shooters wore resembled that of the Trench Coat Mafia and was likened to that of the American Goth rock, musician Marilyn Manson: ibid., 56–8, 59.
112 Ibid., 51–63.
113 Ibid., 53. Springhall reports that two shotguns and a rifle used in the Columbine shootings were purchased legally by a third party, who then gave the weapons to Eric Harris and Dylan Klebold and in doing so committed no crime. A fourth illegal weapon was sold to Harris and Klebold, and this was the subject of a criminal prosecution.
114 Ibid., 64.
115 Ibid. Springhall also argues that school bullying and harassment was a more likely causal factor than media or ineffective gun control: ibid., 60–1.
116 Ibid., 50.
117 Ibid., 64.
118 Hymowitz (1998).
119 Simon (2004: 80).
120 Foucault (2006: 489).
121 Foucault (1991: 93).
122 Morss (1995).
123 Ariès (1962).
124 Ibid., 16.
125 Ibid., 22–4.
126 Ibid., 24.
127 Alderson (2007); Alderson *et al.* (2006).
128 Cohen (2009).
129 Foucault (1991).
130 Ibid., 90.
131 Ibid., 103.
132 Ibid., 89–90.
133 Rose (1999: 55).
134 Ibid., 131.
135 Ibid., 203.

5 Sexuality

Introduction

In the previous chapter, ideas of reason, maturity and autonomy operate to determine the criminal culpability of children. In debates about sexuality, these three ideas operate to determine whether or not a child is able to consent to certain sexual activities. This chapter begins with a consideration of how consent comes to operate as the key device that distinguishes illegal from legal sexual conduct. With respect to debates about children's sexuality, I look at three broad areas: medical treatment relating to contraception and gender reassignment, sexual relationships and representations of children's sexuality. In these debates, I argue that conceptions of children as innocents, sinners and blank-slates are evident. The positions these conceptions inform, I argue, are all oriented toward a concern for the future-adult subject.

The transformative effect of consent

David Archard observes that in the game of sex, the only rule is consent.[1] This is due to the morally transformative effect of consent. It regulates relationships between parties where there is a power differential[2] enabling one party to determine whether or not another has authority over them. This transformative effect is also evident in the social contract of the liberal state. In the absence of the consent of the governed to be governed, an authoritarian regime dictates. Through a hypothetical social contract, a citizen trades their absolute and complete freedom for some restrictions that otherwise protect the greater public good. In liberal societies, just as consent transforms illegitimate political authority into legitimate political authority, consent transforms an illegal act, into a legal one. For example, when reduced to an act of physical penetration, rape and sex speak to identical conduct.[3] What distinguishes rape from sex is the absence of consent. What is otherwise morally unacceptable and criminal in a liberal state becomes both acceptable and legal. It is for this reason that consent is so important. As philosophers Neil Manson and Onora O'Neill explain, informed consent is the:

> assurance and evidence that a proposed action will not involve or be based on force, fraud, deceit, duress, constraint or coercion, and the like, and so

will neither force the body nor overwhelm or undermine the will. Consent matters because it can be used to protect ... against grave wrongs.[4]

By mitigating against force and coercion, the requirement for consent, whether in political communities, medical treatment or sexual relationships, operates to justify and legitimize certain acts. However, there are certain acts that cannot be consented to: in Australia you cannot consent to your own death, as evidenced by the absence of a euthanasia regime; nor can you consent to your own enslavement;[5] or, to your own harm.[6] Further, for Manson and O'Neill, 'informed consent is needed in order to secure respect for autonomy, which is presumed to be fundamental to ethics.'[7] Consent relates to autonomy insofar as it requires the decision of an individual to determine conduct that affects his or her own physicality independent of others' desires.

It is in this sense that consent speaks to an act of rational, autonomous choice. This arguably requires the exercise of reason, a degree of maturity and the autonomy of an individual. These three ideas are what children are defined against. As a result, children below a certain age (an age that is presumed to coincide with the lack of these qualities) have generally been presumed to be unable to give consent. Before considering explicitly the role of consent in debates about children's sexuality, I spend some time unpacking consent as a transformative device and the concomitant reason, maturity and autonomy it relies upon.

Neil Manson and Onora O'Neill explore what is required for an individual to demonstrate consent. In doing so, they distinguish between "rational" and "mere choice".[8] Understood in a minimal sense, they argue that mere choice refers to an understanding of individual autonomy which requires that all choices must be protected, irrespective of their basis. Rational choice, by contrast, only recognizes individual autonomy as demonstrated through reason and reflection; it is a demonstrable rationality that establishes autonomy. Manson and O'Neill describe it in the following terms:

> If we think of autonomy as a matter of mere choice, arguments will be needed to show why all choices (however irrational, however poorly informed) should be protected. If, on the other hand, we think of autonomy as a matter of reasoned or reflective choice, further arguments will be needed to show why only these choices should be protected, and it will be hard to show why only these choices should be protected, and it will be hard to show that actual consent (so often less than rational, so often unreflective) operationalizes autonomy. If individual autonomy is seen as fundamental to ethics, but merely as a matter of choice, then the only permissible restrictions on choice will be those required to protect others' individual autonomy.... Nothing will be prohibited as unacceptable between consenting adults.[9]

For Manson and O'Neill, 'autonomy-based justifications of consent requirements are problematic'[10] and raise the following questions: which conception of autonomy do we adhere to? And why should respect for individual autonomy trump other ethical considerations, such as care and public health? How must consent requirements be structured to ensure individual autonomy, if that is what we maintain is a priority? Indeed, why must all choices be protected, and how does a particular conception of autonomy mandate this? What about the choices that are good or bad, prudent or risky, informed or ignorant? In response to these questions favour tends to lie with a rational choice, rather than a mere choice approach. However, this raises an ethical conundrum:

> Appeals to conceptions of rational autonomy may justify too much where individuals choose dire alternatives in the appropriate way: would consensual cannibalism, consensual torture or consensual killing be acceptable, provided victims choose them in the appropriate way?[11]

In these ways, consent may actually operate to obscure the harm or violence of an act. Hence, there are some acts, such as murder and slavery, that liberal political communities have decided cannot be consented to. With respect to children, expressions of consent premised upon reasoning suggest that choice is impossible for children. Defined by their immaturity, their lack of capacity to reason, and their dependence on others, children are deemed unable to make a decision in their own best interests: and, therefore, unable to consent.

In exploring the relationship between autonomy and consent, Manson and O'Neill rely upon a Kantian conception of principled autonomy, which says that: 'Autonomy of the will is the sole principle of all moral laws and of duties in keeping with them.'[12] For Kant, consent is important in certain contexts, such as his idea of the social contract. It reflects respect for an autonomy that is the property of individuals and theirs alone to exercise in their own independent interests. Informed consent protects individual choice and independence; it protects as well as expresses individual autonomy.

For Manson and O'Neill, the interaction between consent and autonomy is particularly important in the field of bioethics, which is largely concerned with public health and public goods. This sits in tension with the focus of autonomy upon individual choice. Indeed, as the discussion that follows shows this same tension arises in debates about sexuality: on the one hand, it is a deeply private and individual domain; on the other, it has public health implications that affect society broadly.

The Gillick competency test: assessing children's capacities

The 1986 House of Lords decision *Gillick* v. *West Norfolk and Wisbech Area Health Authority*[13] provided a legal test to determine children's ability to consent to medical care and treatment. The High Court of Australia has since approved it, introducing the principle into Australian common law.[14] This decision held that a 'parental right yields to the child's right to make his own decisions when he reaches a sufficient understanding and intelligence to be capable of making up his own mind on the matter requiring decision'.[15] And the decision led John Eekelaar to claim that as a result, 'children will now have, in wider measure than ever before, that most dangerous but most precious of rights: the right to make their own mistakes'.[16] The case concerned children accessing contraceptive treatment and advice from medical professionals without the involvement and agreement of their parents. Specifically, the government of the United Kingdom issued memoranda to public health clinics to support the provision of this advice. The judges' decision sought to emphasize the period of adolescence as one in which parents 'relax their control gradually', so as to allow children to develop and become increasingly independent.[17] This supports the notion that in extending to individuals degrees of autonomy they further develop the skills required to be fully autonomous members of social and political communities.

Victoria Gillick took action against the Department of Health and Social Security for its issue of the memoranda to health authorities condoning the provision of contraceptive advice to children below the age of sexual consent.[18] She argued that any staff at her local health authority that gave advice about, or treatment for, contraception to her children without her consent would be unlawful.[19] The House of Lords split, with three in favour of the UK government and two in favour of Gillick. All five Law Lords agreed that the three key parties to the decision about contraception were the parents, the child and the doctor. That is, they all agreed that the parents were a relevant party in a matter concerning a child's medical treatment. In his dissenting judgment, Lord Brandon determined that the statutory duty to provide contraceptive treatment to "persons", where no age requirement was mandated, nonetheless did not include girls under the age of 16. If it did, it would serve to encourage or facilitate sexual intercourse among those of an age for whom such activity would be deemed criminal. This logic, he argued, would hold irrespective of the rights of parents.

Lord Templeman, also in dissent, gave much greater weight to the capacity of children to make a decision. Like Lord Brandon, other statutory provisions (in criminal law) indicated that girls under the age of 16 were not 'sufficiently mature' to consent to sexual intercourse. Thus, he decided 'such a girl cannot therefore be regarded as sufficiently mature to be allowed to decide for herself that she will practise contraception for the purpose of frequent or regular or casual sexual intercourse'.[20] For Lord Brandon, the age of sexual consent cannot be separated from the age for seeking independent medical advice about sexual health.

The Lords who disagreed with Gillick held that parental rights exist for the benefit of the child, not the parent. They also emphasized that it is an ordinary part of parenting to gradually relax control over children, allowing them to take on increasing responsibilities in line with their developing capacities. Finally, they held that consent can be valid if the child has 'sufficient understanding' of what is proposed and is capable of expressing his or her own wishes.[21] Lords Fraser and Scarman placed less emphasis on criminal law provisions and the age of sexual consent, and more emphasis on entitlement to medical treatment. Lord Scarman concluded that:

as a matter of law the parental right to determine whether or not their minor child below the age of 16 will have medical treatment terminates if and when the child achieves a sufficient understanding and intelligence to enable him to understand fully what is proposed.[22]

The contrast between those recognizing children's consent and those that do not turns on whether or not children can be regarded as persons in law, and the acceptance by all that a "sufficient maturity" is required for this to be possible. Whereas those Lords in dissent accept an arbitrary line that separates person from non-person according to ages of sexual consent as stated in criminal statutes, the Lords of the majority accept that each individual person develops maturity differently. Further, it is the responsibility of parents, the court and the state to recognize this process and encourage the gradual autonomy of the child rather than inhibit it. As Lord Scarman went on to describe:

> The law relating to parent and child is concerned with the problems of growth and maturity of the human personality. If the law should impose on the process of 'growing up' fixed limits where nature knows only a continuous process, the price would be artificiality and a lack of realism in an area where the law must be sensitive to human development and social change.[23]

However, in practice, the Gillick competent child has created uncertainty and difficulty for legal and medical practitioners alike. Indeed, the measure of competency as described by Lord Scarman is not designed to create uniform practices. Yet, professionals working for and with children have to be consistent.

The decision has led to greater uncertainty about when young people can and cannot make decisions regarding their medical care and treatment. It has also brought into view very serious questions that need to be asked about how we assess maturity and the capacity for decision-making. In addition, it creates a context for debating why reason, maturity and autonomy to give consent are so central to determining the rights of children.

It is worth noting that the focus of this decision is necessarily on girls rather than boys. Indeed, we live in a world where boys do not require medical advice or treatment to practice safe sex. Boys, at any age, are able to go to a store to buy condoms. Vasectomy aside, boys and men have no need to seek medical advice for contraceptive purposes. The most obvious reason for this is that the contraceptive pill is a hormone and a drug that, arguably, needs to be administered by a professional. Contrary to the concerns of the dissenting judges, I would argue that to view girls' seeking responsible contraceptive methods of which they can be in control of, rather than at the whim of their sexual partners, is far from immature. However, in a decision that comes to focus so heavily on the relative capacities of young people, arguments that are grounded in the context of young people's everyday lives fall to the periphery and become less relevant.

In Australia, the Gillick competency test was introduced into common law by the High Court in *Secretary, Department of Health and Community Services* v. *JWB and SMB*, known as '*Marion's Case*'.[24] In *Marion's Case*, the young person was severely deaf, epileptic and suffered from mental retardation. Thus, this young person was not deemed to be Gillick competent. It would seem unlikely that even as an adult, this person would necessarily be deemed competent enough to make independent choices of their own. It is interesting, that this decision has become the Australian authority for the fact that children failing to demonstrate Gillick competency cannot have the capacity to give consent. That is, the Australian authority for denying children competency rests with an example of an acutely disabled person who would not have that competency even as an adult.[25]

Controversially, the Gillick competency test in Australia has gained most prominence in cases of adolescents seeking sexual reassignment surgeries.[26] In *Re A*, the person in question had been born intersex and underwent genital reconstruction to be given the characteristics of a female. *A*, a transsexual, identifying with the male gender, sought sexual reassignment at the age of 14. In *Re Alex*, the child was a 13-year-old person with unambiguously female chromosomes and sexual characteristics. Alex was a transsexual with diagnosed gender identity disaphoria/disorder (GID) seeking sexual reassignment surgery. In Australia, neither young person was deemed to be Gillick competent. In *Re A*, the deciding judge stated:

> In the present case I am satisfied on the evidence that A understands the problem and, in general terms, the way in which it is proposed that such problems be resolved and further, that the child has expressed a desire that such resolution take place. However, I am not satisfied that A has sufficient capacity and maturity to fully appreciate all aspects of the matter and to be able to assess objectively the various options available to him.[27]

In *Re Alex*, the judge stated:

> It is one thing for a child or young person to have a general understanding of what is proposed and its effect but it is quite another to conclude that he/she has sufficient maturity to fully understand the grave nature and effects of the proposed treatment.[28]

The law in these cases becomes quite complicated. These cases move from questions of when a parent or guardian can give consent, to questions of when the Family Court is able to give consent. The focus here is simply on how the children were assessed in terms of their competency. What was also relevant to these decisions was the nature of the medical treatment being sought. The distinction between therapeutic and non-therapeutic treatment, between ordinary medical treatment and special medical treatment are not insignificant. Indeed, in Judge Nicholson's decision in *Re Alex*, it would appear that Gillick competent or not, no child could be regarded as having the sufficient maturity to consent to special medical treatment, whether it is therapeutic or not:

> There is considerable difference between a child or young person deciding to use contraceptives as in Gillick and a child or young person determining upon a course that will 'change' his/her sex. It is highly questionable whether a 13 year old could ever be regarded as having the capacity for the latter, and this situation may well continue until the young person reaches maturity.[29]

Moral and political objections about gender reassignment aside, the treatment required for sex reassignment, including hormone therapy, is much more effective and easier to manage prior to or during adolescence rather than in adulthood. It is a difficult point of tension that the most effective and least intrusive medical treatment for achieving sex reassignment relies on a person's biological immaturity while the capacity to decide the treatment you seek is premised on the demonstration of your maturity. For this reason, I argue that the relevancy of consent and the interest in adhering to children's consent over their own medical treatment has far less to do with their maturity, than it does with the relative moral controversies their treatment elicits. Just as the moral panic surrounding child crime in the previous chapter revealed the complexity of competing conceptualizations of childhood, here the moral controversy surrounding child sexuality allows a simplification of the child as an asexual innocent, shedding little light on the complexity that the question of children's consent raises in liberal society.[30]

In a different context, Priscilla Alderson has sought to demonstrate the capacities of young people subject to health treatment.[31] In particular, she considers the management of young people with diabetes. Her purpose is to consider children's status in decision-making beyond an age of consent. She observes that the statutory age of consent to medical treatment varies around the world between 12 and 19 years.[32] Alderson points to numerous documents and authorities to suggest that moving beyond a fixed age of consent is justified. The Gillick competency test, explained below, comes from the authority of the House of Lords in the United Kingdom and has been endorsed by Australia's High Court. The test acknowledges that it is not reasonable for a fixed, arbitrary age to be the determining factor of competency to consent. Instead, it recognizes that a child can demonstrate their competency in a number of ways. The United Nations Convention on the Rights of the Child also demands that there should be respect for 'informed, free, express and specific consent' (Article 12).[33] On these grounds, the question is transformed from a normative choice about whether or not children ought be able to consent to medical treatment, to a quantifiable, empirically-based assessment that determines competency on a case-by-case basis.

Alderson observes that there is a presumption that adult research subjects are competent unless obvious incompetence is demonstrably evident. This presumption is reversed in the case of children. That children are taken to be *prima facie* incompetent does not necessarily mean, however, that they are 'intellectually and morally incompetent, despite enduring beliefs about their limited reasoning and morality'.[34] Further, Alderson observes that 'efforts to protect children from having to decide about healthcare research and treatment may protect adult power as much as children's interests'.[35] In assessing competence, Alderson points to numerous standards. Four main standards of mental competence common in assessments include: understanding of the relevant information; retention of the relevant information; weighing information in order to make a reasoned choice; and making voluntary and autonomous decisions. Two further standards are: the ability to communicate the decision and the ability to believe the information. However, she argues that rather than being empirical and strictly objectively determined criteria, these standards and the assessment of children according to these standards are informed by understandings of how 'childhood incompetencies are socially constructed'.[36] Alderson maintains that children's competencies are not necessarily tied to age and physical growth, but to experience. Furthermore, many young people, particularly those undergoing medical treatment, have a wealth of experience that can result in them being highly informed and confident.[37] She observes that children with long-term illnesses know a great deal about their illness and condition. Children as young as two are able to identify and describe the purpose of each of their cancer drugs; children as young as three and four are able to manage illnesses like Type 1 diabetes and cystic fibrosis for themselves.[38] In identifying and acknowledging that children often do demonstrate competency to manage their own illness, an argument is made that children ought also to be able to make decisions regarding their treatment. For Alderson, the empirical observation that children are able to manage their illness informs the normative claim that children ought, therefore, to make decisions for themselves in their medical treatment. However, for Alderson, this is not strictly a matter of determining an age of consent but rather of assisting in shaping health care professionals' ability to assess and appropriately engage with young people seeking treatment.

Children's sexual conduct

Sexual consent raises issues of sexual morality and sexual permissibility. As in other contexts, consent has a morally transformative effect.[39] Through consent, what would otherwise be immoral and impermissible (even criminal) becomes acceptable. As a criminal offence, rape is an act of sexual penetration without consent.[40] Consent, as discussed above, requires an individual to have the capacity to rationally weigh options and risks for the purposes of making and communicating a decision. Children do not have the capacity to give consent. Thus, children are not able to consent to sexual activities. In law, the crime of statutory rape recognizes children's inability to give consent to sexual acts, thus protecting them from exploitation by setting a social and moral norm. In addition, where this law is not enough to protect children against the risk of sexual exploitation, it creates an avenue for redress and justice. In contrast to crimes against adults, the absence of a capacity to give consent removes the possibility of the accused arguing that their actions were morally permissible and legal because a young person communicated in more or less terms, "yes".

In these terms, little is controversial. Children are particularly vulnerable. The risk of their exploitation, sexual or otherwise, extends from their dependency on adults around them. Like adults, children depend on others to afford them care and dignity. For children, when adults fail to provide this or when the risk for this becomes apparent, they are less powerful to act against it. Often, they lack the physicality (to fight back), the economic independence (to leave a risky home, for example) and the influence necessary to be taken seriously.

In the absence of controversy, it is important to explain what is at stake in the debate regarding the age of sexual consent. There are two issues that must be considered more carefully to ensure that an age of sexual consent serves the best interests of children.[41] First, an age of sexual consent does not merely assist in the prosecution of statutory rape charges, nor does it merely create a social and legal norm that exists in isolation from other children's issues. As discussed by Lord Brandon above, if a child is unable to give consent to sex until they reach the age of 16, then on what grounds do policy and lawmakers evaluate whether a 14-year-old child can seek medical advice for contraception? On what grounds do we evaluate whether a 14-year-old person can fill a prescription for the contraceptive pill, without their parents knowledge? Further, how might we ensure that 14-year-old children can fund contraception, without the ability to work? How do we ask even more difficult questions about a child's ability to seek advice and to make a decision regarding a pregnancy, to choose parenthood or termination? When we seek to protect children from the risks of being sexually exploited, what other risks do we fail to address? The policy issues go further than this to more fundamental expectations about sexual education, not merely about whether or not children ought to have sexual education available to them in schools, but also what that sexual education includes. In these ways, the private domain of sexual conduct begins to take on broader public concerns. The answers to these questions inform how we view the sexual behaviour of children. However, the asking of these questions in the first place also says something about how we already view the sexuality of children. I will not argue here that children have the capacity to consent to sex, or that there should be no age of sexual consent. These are not my positions. However, by interrogating how consent operates in respect to children it is possible to reveal a little more about how claims to reason, maturity and autonomy inform, shape and limit debates about children's rights, including debates about children's sexuality. Claims about children's best interests inform a variety of issues that extend beyond the issues of a specific case. Justice Brennan in *Marion's Case* stated that the best interests approach 'depends upon the value system of the decision-maker' and that 'absent any rule or guideline that approach simply creates an un-examinable discretion in the repository of the [judicial] power'.[42] It is in this sense that the best interests of the child can be revealed as more than an objective legal principle. Instead, the principle of best interests operates as an extension of existing conceptions of childhood and understandings of who children are. As demonstrated in Chapter 2, even within a Western liberal tradition these conceptions and understandings are grounded in different philosophies and produce different normative meanings, informing different claims about children's rights and interests.

Debates about children's sexuality thus far have been premised upon the need to maintain a moral and legal norm that sex with children is impermissible. By using consent as the key device that distinguishes legitimate from illegitimate, and legal from illegal behaviour, the debate necessarily comes to focus upon children's lack of capacity. What I wish to problematize here is whether or not consent really has to matter when we're talking about the harm and exploitation undertaken by adults.

For Archard, the "Principle of Consensuality" remains central because of its role in distinguishing the moral from the immoral.[43] It states that 'a practice, P, is morally permissible if all those who are parties to P are competent to consent, and the interests of no other parties are significantly harmed'.[44] The Principle of Non-Consensuality, by contrast, states that

> a practice, P, is morally impermissible if at least one of those who are parties to P, and who are competent to consent, does not give their valid consent, even if the interests of no other parties are significantly harmed.[45]

The relevance of morality to consent, and the political and policy debates it underpins, becomes central. The moral ambiguity of certain practices is resolved, or at least made clearer through consent. It appears that consent actually becomes increasingly relevant where the moral status of a practice is more ambiguous and controversial. I would argue that it is the morality of these issues, in a political debate, which creates the condition that makes consideration of consent relevant. It is moral claims about sexual conduct that places the issue of consent at the heart of these debates. That is, in debates about children's sexuality it is an already existing morality surrounding children's sexual conduct that centralizes the importance of consent; not children's capacities for reason, maturity and autonomy. Whether an act is right or wrong is less important than recognizing that morality and its relationship to politics is crucial here. This relationship has a significant impact on determining the parameters for debate. With consent central to these debates, issues around consent and competency to consent become the key sites for contest. Informed consent raises issues of coercion and other relations of power that may impact upon whether a competent adult gives consent or not. However, in respect to children it is the very competency to consent that is called into question (if not disregarded entirely).

Archard later offers guidance on how we might better assess an appropriate age of sexual consent.[46] However, my purpose is different. Whether the age of consent is higher or lower is of little interest to me. Instead, it is crucial that we understand why we have a sexual age to consent, separate from other legal ages of majority: to vote, to work, to be held criminally culpable, to marry, etc. It is equally important to understand how that age then shapes broader debates. In exploring sexual consent, we have an opportunity to understand with greater clarity why consent is the only question in the game of sex. We can question and disrupt with more focused purpose the competency that consent requires. By doing so, it is also possible to question how this competency coincides with understandings of autonomy and maturity that operate against paternalistic practices in other contexts. This both informs and limits debates about children's sexuality. David Archard argues that four factors are relevant to determining an age of sexual consent: different ages, for different sex; sexual maturity; intergenerational sex and the sexual abuse of authority.[47] In considering these four factors, I suggest that Archard's approach has less to do with consent than it does with the risk of exploitation. Indeed, by the end of his argument, what remains is not a thesis of 'sexual consent' as much as a thesis on the regulation of exploitative sexual relationships. Once again, this has much less to do with children and their reason, maturity and autonomy than it does with the moral terrain of sexuality and power.

Briefly, Archard dismisses the idea that different ages might be set for different kinds of sex: whether it is "levels" of sexual interaction, or homosexual versus heterosexual practices. Indeed, in some jurisdictions there are different ages for homosexual and heterosexual ages of consent.[48] Of course, there are many jurisdictions that criminalize homosexual activity outright. The justification for higher ages of consent to homosexual activity, as Archard writes, is untenable.[49] It relies upon misinformation and prejudices that have nothing whatsoever to do with maturity and decision-making capacity. Those prejudices will not be entertained here.

By contrast, Archard's second factor – sexual maturity – is very much related to the question of a young person's capacity to consent to sexual relationships. Sexual maturity, for Archard, includes physical and intellectual maturity.[50] It seems uncontroversial that emotional maturity might also be relevant. Physical maturity, marked by the onset of puberty, distinguishes the child from the adolescent. The physical changes, including physiological changes and hormonal influences, foster experiences of lust and, of course, love. However, while young girls may be able to sustain and nurture a pregnancy from the onset of puberty which may be at eight, ten or 13, there are few arguments that girls this young should be sexually active, or that they should be able to marry. By focusing explicitly on physical maturity, debates about sexual maturity and the sexual age of consent might exist without the moral overtures. However, David Archard's point is that physical maturity alone cannot determine an age of sexual consent and also an intellectual understanding of its consequences. Further, our social and moral norms, as well as historical conceptions of childhood, have shifted very little since the Enlightenment, with conceptions of innocence, sinfulness and blank-slates continuing to play out in debates. The consequence is that we are not particularly inclined, as social and political communities, to engage seriously with the sexual curiosities and activities of young people irrespective of their physical maturity. I explore "sexual maturity" as a factor relevant to determining an age of consent in much more depth below.

Gary Melton writes that competence to consent has obvious psychological dimensions.[51] Although, this is not a piece of psychological research or analysis, some engagement with the discipline is necessary to show how consent – a concept fundamental to the political life of liberal democracy – operates as more than a political tool, but as the subject of science. Psychological interest in consent centres on seeking evidence of how individual people demonstrate an autonomous decision. In respect to children, a primary concern, writes Melton, is that if they have a recognized capacity for consent they 'will be harmed by the consequences of making bad decisions'.[52] Further, the self-determination of a child can safely be denied because the state has a duty as *parens patriae* to protect dependent persons from harm,[53] presumably and particularly from the potential harm of their parents[54] who generally act as their de facto decision-makers until adulthood. However, in suggesting that competence goes hand in hand with harm, that incompetence is a necessary condition for that harm arising seems untenable: harm results from the exploitation of a power differential exercised by one over another and not only solely from the absence of consent. Consent has become a legal and philosophical concept that may vindicate individuals from responsibility for otherwise harmful acts.[55] In respect to sex acts, the question comes to centre on the action or inaction of the individual who claims they have been harmed. Harm is not the result of incompetence of the victim; harm is the result of action by the perpetrator, or the inaction of a person in a position to help. Consent may serve to limit the possibility for redress. Melton argues that consent is designed to enhance children's welfare or minimize harm,[56] but it seems unclear how it does this beyond transforming the moral landscape so that what might be viewed as harmful becomes ethically sound and by providing a framework through which legal redress is possible.

Jane Fortin observes that in the UK context, which holds true for Australia and the United States, the 'law withholds the right to adult autonomy from all adolescents until they attain the age of eighteen'.[57] In exploring the question of whether or not adolescents (she does not discuss younger children) have the development capacity to shed their status as a minor before the age of 18, she contrasts the arguments of child liberationists and other children's rights advocates. Advocates of children's autonomy rights particularly seek greater civil and political rights to be extended to children. They refute the assumptions made by Jean Piaget and other psychologists, who sought to establish the rational limitations of children. Instead, they draw on evidence of children who demonstrate autonomy in a range of different ways – including in the work of Priscilla Alderson and her colleagues.[58] However, like Melton, Fortin points out that to do so carries the risk that the decisions children make may result in 'considerable psychological cost'.[59] Yet, it may be as much the experience of pain or hardship that may result in this considerable psychological cost as the experience of making a decision about how to best manage or remedy that experience.

Children, Fortin points out, have a right to protection that is just as – if not more – valid than the right to choice or decision-making. Further, she suggests that the moral right a child may have to make a choice if it exists at all is to be contrasted with the moral right of that child not to have to make such a choice in the first place.[60] This analysis goes some way towards attempting to recognize the autonomy a child may or may not possess, and accounting for this in the decisions that adults may make on their behalf. In the USA, the decision of *In re Gault* indicated for the first time that children were persons within the meaning of the Fourteenth Amendment, making the Bill of Rights applicable to the states.[61] This decision undermined the concept of *parens patriae* for the first time, suggesting that parents and the state do not necessarily have unreserved control over minors. Yet, this decision, significant in the field of children's rights, did not have to grapple in any detail with the question of children's consent: minors were per se, incompetent. Rather, this was a case regarding criminal process and the equal application of rules of law to young people as well as adult citizens.

Writing generally about the crime of rape, Victor Tadros argues for a 'differentiated offence of rape': an offence 'which can be completed in a number of different ways that cannot be captured in a simple definition'.[62] In particular, he considers the role of consent in shaping and limiting our understanding of sexual violence. In defining rape around consent, he argues that: 'Violence, it appears, is merely evidence of something else ... a lack of consent.'[63] As Tadros explains it tends to 'put the victim on trial'.[64] Doing so places the focus of evidential inquiry and questioning on the alleged victim, including on their sexual history and behaviour, rather than on the actions of the alleged perpetrator. It is an unusual shifting of the burden of proof that does not tend to occur in other areas of law.

Tadros, while writing about rape in an adult context, argues that the concept of consent ought to be used as little as possible[65] because 'definitions of rape which revolve around consent do not properly capture the wrong perpetrated by the defendant in any particular rape case'.[66] His analysis is primarily of UK statutes, and, in particular, of the rape provisions rather than provisions regarding crimes against children. His analysis, even in this context, is strained at times by drawing analogies between the crime of rape and property offences that he at least acknowledges.[67] In doing so, he seeks to provide examples of how property law has accounted for varying types of harms more effectively than criminal law. It is in response to these limitations of criminal law that Nicola Lacey calls for the 'violation of trust, infliction of shame and humiliation, objectification and exploitation' to be better accounted for in rape law.[68] Where consent is the key focus of rape trials, little focus is given to these experiences in establishing the criminal act. They are relevant to sentencing guidelines, but in themselves they constitute no part of the wrong. By contrast, were consent to be the only focus of property offences, there would be outrage. How could consent, as a single concept and device, be adequate in fully accounting for the various factors that give shape to property offences: fraud, deception, blackmail, force and coercion, as well as consent and capacity.[69] To be specific, it is not that a person violates trust, exploits their power over another either physically or emotionally (by lying, for example), inflicts shame, humiliation and pain and objectifies another person that constitutes the crime of rape. It is that the subject of the crime did not consent. The harm and exploitation stands apart from consent. It is not the harm and exploitation that establishes the offence, but the lack of consent.

There is an obvious reason for this, and it brings us back to broader moral concerns. Sado-masochistic sexual practices might be viewed as morally abhorrent or deviant. However, arguably, if the parties involved consent to such practices it ought not to be impermissible. Anastasia Powell offers an analysis of sexual consent as an embodied gendered practice.[70] She writes in a strictly heterosexual context of young people aged between 14 and 24. Her particular interest in gender roles and embodied gendered practices is not central to the analysis she presents, but her observations regarding how these roles and practices inform young people's negotiation of sexual consent is insightful. Further, her interest in creating a reflexive space for young people to consider these roles and practices informs the possibility of alternative approaches and focal points for policies around sexual education and the prevention of sexual violence.[71]

For Powell, gender roles in which women are expected to be passive and accommodating, and men are presumed to be assertive and pursuant, result in a 'theoretical understanding of pressure and consent that [means it is] ... women who are responsible for communicating their refusals clearly'.[72] In this way, it is not consent itself that is problematic but rather its gendered construction and the implications that has for women. Building on the work of Moira Carmody's Foucauldian notion of reflexivity, and using Pierre Bourdieu's work on 'gendered habitus', Powell seeks to develop a reflexive space that has room for alternative negotiations of consent. That is, consent beyond the mere articulation of yes and no, where consent becomes 'bodily communication and practice at the intersections of structure and agency' that accounts for gendered practices and social contexts.[73] She argues that it is the recognition of a gendered habitus, that is 'the taking on of gendered norms in bodily practice ... in the very ways we think, feel and respond to others', that creates room to identify how young people negotiate consent, as well as room for society to recognize sexual consent as a complex social interaction, rather than mere communication.[74] The failure to do so, while maintaining a focus on explicit verbal communications, 'significantly contributes to existing "miscommunication" analyses of the "grey area" of sexual violence'.[75] It is indeed a significant problem of consent. Powell's purpose is not legal reform or even the rejection of consent, but rather to promote and encourage 'young women and young men to pay attention to a partner's body language, and to the ways in which people may communicate their consent or non-consent to sex less explicitly'.[76] To do so, she argues, creates greater potential for sexual violence prevention strategies to actually prevent sexual violence.

Powell observed elsewhere that the focus of sexuality education in Australian schools tends to focus on the policing of young women's sexual practices.[77] Articulated in terms of risk, about how to say no and the dangers of sex (pregnancy, as well as sexually transmitted infections), arguably this approach limits the potential for young women to 'actively negotiate and make choices'.[78] It pre-sumes that all sexual advances are necessarily unwanted and does not emphasize practices for negotiating consent to sex; practices for saying yes. It also reflects the notion that we are more likely to be at risk of a mugging than the sexual assault of a friend or family member. Sexual education in these limited terms is about saying no and only recognizing violence as a threat, rather than more nuanced forms of pressure and coercion such as those highlighted above by Powell.

The argument follows that if a person is deemed to have the intellectual matu-rity required to weigh options, account for risk and communicate a decision to others, it is as relevant to one's ability to vote, as it is to one's ability to choose a sexual partner. It may be that the risks involved are dramatically different, but if the focus is on intellectual maturity, surely the ability to weigh those risks is not altered by the context. This isn't a strong position: intellectual maturity is often undermined by more physical or emotional desires. However, these mitigating factors are relevant to grown adults, as well as young adults. The depth of experience a grown adult has to regulate these factors comes from having been a young adult who had to do the same. It follows that if we recognize intellectual maturity as a relevant factor in determining a sexual age of consent and we value the development of this maturity in young people, then education and access to information must be the ways in which we develop this maturity,[79] not merely in terms of risk as discussed in the context of Powell's analysis above, but in positive and meaningful terms. Indeed, by valuing this intellectual maturity, we might find the space necessary in sexuality education and health policies for an understanding of social reflexivity that Powell advocates so convincingly. Indeed, Foucauldian reflexivity and Pierre Bourdieu's gender habitus are rather intellectual endeavours. If young people are given the opportunity to explore these ideas, and demonstrate their potential, they may prove to have greater sexual awareness and maturity than any generation that has preceded them.

Returning to David Archard's four factors that he considers relevant to deter-mining an age of sexual consent, it is worth noting that his third and fourth factors are closely related. His third factor concerns intergenerational sex and, understood in terms of an age differential between sexual partners, may be related to his fourth, which concerns the possible sexual abuse of authority,[80] not least because an age differential likely results in other power differentials, in turn creating the risk of exploitation. However, in following Archard's argument through these two points, it is worth suggesting that it has very little to do with the capacity to consent. Thus, it is perhaps not that relevant to determining an appropriate age of sexual consent. Instead, it is about whether or not a young person *ought* to be able to consent to these kinds of relationships. Alternatively, it could be argued that it is a question of whether or not consent is possible within an exploitative relationship. Feminist analysis of prostitution has explored this question extensively.[81] The inability to consent in this sense is about the nature of the relationship (premised on particular relations of power), rather than the capacity of those who are in the relationship. The reason why the age differential in sexual relationships becomes significant is because it underpins other differentials: financial power, physical power and the ability to influence others.

Considered in these terms, it is apparent that the age differential between a 25-year-old and a 40-year-old individual is less significant than the age difference between a 12-year-old and a 25-year-old. Both the 25-year-old and 40-year-old are adults, with all the legal rights and autonomy that this implies and with degrees of power that go beyond being able to work and live independently. Physical power differentials are likely to still be relevant, not necessarily due to age, but rather to sex. For a 12-year-old, there is no financial independence, their physical power is negligible against an adult's (although female school teachers may attest to the contrary), they have limited opportunities for complaint and less influence on those around them. Most importantly, children are educated to defer to the authority of adults. The potential for exploitation between an adolescent and an adult is obvious, between a child and an adult even more so. By contrast, the age differential between a 14-year-old and a 15-year-old is much less significant in terms of various power differentials.

All relationships involve degrees of power. Power is not necessarily exploitative, though a power differential creates the potential for exploitation.[82] Jeffrey Weeks' argues that 'It is not sex that is dangerous but the social relations which shape it'.[83] The risks of a significant power differential in an intimate relationship are greater than those of a smaller power differential in the same context (i.e. two adolescents). The risks are different again regarding a power differential in a workplace context rather than an intimate one. Adults are often exploited by power differentials in different relationships. It is far more confronting, however, to see children exploited. Our sense of moral outrage – that visceral reaction that can lead to anger and tears of compassion in the same moment – is not because that an adult engaged sexually with a person *who could not give consent*. It is because to engage in sexual acts with a child or a young adolescent, is to exploit their innocence, their vulnerability, their apparent powerlessness in the world. Children are vulnerable not because of an incapacity to reason, due to their immaturity, but because of the power of adults around them. The sexual exploitation and abuse of children has nothing to do with consent.

This would be of little consequence, except that consent as a device for delineating non-criminal from criminal, moral from immoral and right from wrong hinders as much as it helps. For Archard, 'someone who does not have the right to make sexual choices is effectively considered to be a person without sexual desires, an asexual being'.[84] This idea fits neatly with modern understandings of childhood. Indeed, it probably puts many a parents' mind at ease. But it also clouds the developmental process of human biology, cognitive capacities and the changes that have occurred over the past century in terms of sexual development. It insists on defining children by their lack: their lack of maturity, their lack of power and the impossibility of their action or assertiveness. It denies children their curiosity and casts shame and judgement upon their actions where there has not necessarily been any harm. It sets the parameters of our ability to argue for different social and health policies: for access to contraception, to information and debates about sexuality and sexual practices, indeed about sex and gender as concepts which shape our social relations every day, as girls and boys and the women and men we become. Consent limits our ability to engage with these complex social relationships and the norms that underpin them. Further, the absence of a consent doctrine does not necessarily increase the risk that we will not be able to effectively and appropriately regulate and mitigate against the sexual abuse of children. After all, consent has nothing to do with the sexual abuse of children: whether they have the capacity to give consent, or not.

In thinking about consent in this way, there are legitimate questions to be raised about whether or not consent ought to be the only question in the sex game. Certainly, there are serious considerations to be made about how consent shapes, informs and limits our understandings of children's sexuality in terms of their development and autonomy, as well as their vulnerability and abuse.

The fact that consent is the only rule in the game of sex has proved problematic. A 2010 report by the Australian Law Reform Commission into family violence acknowledges that the continued focus of sexual assault trials is largely about competing evidence of consent and refusal. This focus upon consent necessarily focuses upon the actions of the alleged victim, 'inextricably linked to the focus on credibility, where women and children – particularly when they raise allegations about sexual violence – have generally been seen as less credible'.[85] Thus, while children are on the one hand excluded from the burden of having to establish a lack of consent in sexual assault trials, consent remains heavy in the construction of the crime: 'For adult complainants this is intertwined with the issue of whether the activity was consensual. For children (as well as for adults) it is about whether their evidence can be believed.'[86] So, while consent operates as the key concept distinguishing legitimate and criminal sex, in ways that ought to protect children, it does so in a limited way. Further, one must remember that this issue of consent only comes into play after the commission of an alleged sexual assault. The concept of consent is not a negotiating tool in and of itself; it is not a claim that children can hold up in front of their bodies to prevent a potential harm.

Representations of children's sexuality

Victoria Gillick's objections to her daughters receiving medical advice about contraception reflect a concern about the loss of innocence in childhood, that she believes results from purportedly premature exposure to sex.[87] Similar concerns were addressed in the 2008 'Australian Senate Inquiry into the Sexualisation of Children in Contemporary Media', which noted that 'preventing the premature sexualisation of children is a significant cultural challenge'.[88] Typical of this protectionist perspective on children's rights, one pair of parents submitted that, 'childhood is a time of joy and innocence, and *this should be an absolute right for all our children.* They become adults soon enough, and childhood is a time to be cherished'.[89] The Report noted that 'Submitters frequently equated "innocence" with a form of right allowing children to grow up free of adult concerns and to mature at their own pace: '[young people] ... have the *right of innocence*'.[90] That is, a narrative that has traditionally served to justify the denial of rights to young people, until they reach adulthood, now underpins a new sort of rights claim: to innocence itself. Nonetheless, the concern about the corruption of innocence is understood to be very real. The Report expressed some concerns that the 'premature sexualization' of children created a 'risk of psychological damage'.[91] This suggests that what is at stake in these debates about children's premature exposure to sexuality is the risk that children will be "damaged", that their development will be obstructed, and that they may not grow up to be healthy adults. Again, I argue that in these terms, the concern reflected here is tied more strongly to the future-adult subject than to the child. As Jonathon Bignell argues:

> the root of this anxiety about the child's media interaction is the assumption that the child is determinant of the adult, and this legitimates a discourse about how media may produce a socially undesirable child who in turn becomes a socially undesirable adult.[92]

In these terms, lamentations about the loss of childhood are as much to do with adult anxieties about sexuality as children's experiences of sexuality.

The private submissions to the Senate Inquiry differed in emphasis from expert submissions, which expressed greater concern for the need for broader research on how young people engage with the media and its representations of sexuality. Acknowledging that children (like adults) are not necessarily passive recipients of media images and messages, Catherine Lumby and Katherine Albury point out that 'The media do not have an autonomous ability to either sexually corrupt children or to sexually "liberate" them'.[93] In the absence of an existing body of research, the Inquiry recommended a major longitudinal study into the effects of 'premature and inappropriate sexualisation of children' and in doing so, presumed its effect from the outset as 'premature and inappropriate'.[94] They even detailed the forms of harm they wished to see further research into, including body image, self-esteem and sexual behaviour. The report maintained that the 'lack of research demonstrating the effects of premature sexualisation' was in tension with anecdotal claims that 'suggested that many people believe exposure to sexual imagery in the media is harmful to children's development'.[95] Narratives of innocence and sin in conceptions of childhood set these terms of debate. In setting the parameters for discussion around harm, body image, self-esteem and sexual behaviour, the Inquiry risks answering its question by the very formulation of it. Further, the Inquiry agreed with the submission of Professor Handsley of the Australian Council on Children and the Media, that 'any potential for harm to children justifies a prescriptive or interventionist response'.[96] That is, the narrative of innocence here is so strong, that even without an evidentiary basis of the risk of harm to that innocence, its possibility alone is the only justification necessary for recommending greater regulation of media content directed at children.

In these two examples, narratives of childhood innocence merge with concerns for a young person's development. The concern for harm encompasses both the harm to the child at the time and also the harm to that child's potential development, which risks being stunted, thus preventing them from maturing into adulthood (as an autonomous individual). Children's rights as a discourse must protect the innocence of children, not only because of the harm to children as children, but also because of the potential harm to the future-adult.

This protection of childhood innocence also reflects the alternative narrative of the child as sinner. While innocent children are at risk of being prematurely sexualized, sinful children are those that engage in sexually promiscuous and (age) inappropriate behaviour. This is the risk of giving young people greater autonomy over their sexual lives. Lacking the requisite rational capacity to make good decisions about intimate relationships, facilitating their participation in the illicit world of sex creates a great risk for those young people and liberal society more broadly. Anxieties around these risks are well documented.[97] However, as Affrica Taylor argues, it is possible that these narratives around childhood innocence and the risks of sexualization may serve to cast a 'paedophilic gaze onto children's bodies ... effectively casting children's bodies as dangerous in and of themselves, and implying, '... that they can somehow provoke sexual abuse by what they wear or what they don't wear', reflecting a concern around women's sexuality more generally.[98] As discussed in the previous chapter, the distinction between children as innocents or sinners also plays out in debates about children's criminal culpability.

The future-adult subject

I have raised a number of texts that demonstrate how claims to reason, maturity and autonomy shape how we think and talk about children and sexuality: the Gillick competency test, the *Re Alex* decision, statutory rape laws and the Australian Senate Standing Committee on the Environment, Communications and the Arts' Report on the Sexualisation of Childhood in the Contemporary Media. I am arguing that these examples demonstrate how the subject of these debates transforms from a view of the child as a child, with attendant concerns to children's present-day experiences, into a view of the child as a future-adult subject, with attendant concerns to how those experiences will impact on their adult life. I argue that this future-adult subject is the political subject of these debates, obscuring from view the ways in which children negotiate sexuality as children.

A controversy that gained minor public attention in 2010 concerned an advertising campaign that launched a children's clothing range by hitherto adult fashion retailer, Witchery. On 29 September, the director of kids free 2B kids [*sic*], Julie Gale, contacted major clothes retailer "Witchery" regarding its WitcheryKids label and associated advertising material. Kids free 2B kids describes itself as an organization 'which raises community, corporate and political awareness about the early sexualisation of children'.[99] Gale's concern with the WitcheryKids campaign was that 'children are being catapulted out of early childhood into the teen years and are increasingly portrayed as "mini-me" adults'. She goes on to link this premature exposure of children to an adult world with 'body image problems, eating disorders, anxiety and depression'.[100] There is no doubt that such issues are harms, in and of themselves, and that there is a genuine concern here that children may experience these harms as a result of exposure to an adult world. However, the organization is more broadly 'committed to children developing their full potential – without exposure to sexualised imagery before they are developmentally ready to process it'.[101] That is, the concern for children-as-children is folded into concern for children-as future-adults. Implicit in this aim is a concern that premature exposure presents a developmental harm: that a child exposed too soon to materials that they are not biologically and psychologically able to accommodate will be disrupted in their emergence into a fully functioning adulthood. This raises a number of issues that need to be unpacked: first, that this concern for the future-adult alters the political subjectivity of the child; second, that the child enters public space as a passive innocent, unable to negotiate or critically engage with the context of media advertising; and third, that as a result either the public space needs to be more heavily regulated or children's exposure to public space needs to be more heavily regulated. These will be considered in turn in the final part of this chapter.

In 2009, Julie Gale and other concerned advocates successfully campaigned against clothing retailer CottonOn to cease the production of children's clothing bearing slogans like "I'm a tits man", "I'm bringing sexy back", "They shake me", and "Milk today, beer tomorrow".[102] These statements play on the objectification of women's bodies and child abuse as a source of humour, yet the T-shirts themselves neither objectify women's bodies nor abuse children. Nonetheless, these T-shirts come to be conveyed as the harm itself. In a *Herald Sun* article detailing the complaint of Julie Gale's Kids free 2b kids lobby group against CottonOn, Gale argued that 'They [CottonOn] don't get that it's … harmful. It's all part of a continuum of sexualisation of kids. It's about the mental health of our children.'[103] Child psychologist, Stephen Biddulph was reported in support of the Kids free 2b kids lobby group:

> Children exposed to sexual messages too young get a cheapened idea of what love is about, before they are old enough to form better ideas.... The sad thing is that smarter parents protect their kids, but as the media environment and shopping malls deteriorate, the kids with not very bright parents have their mental health and sexual health degraded.[104]

In this way, concern for children is expressed not only in terms of a present harm but a future harm: a harm to normal development. However, these slogans, irrespective of any offence, are not directly harmful to women or to the children who wear them, who cannot read them and have limited context for their meaning. They may be harmful for other reasons, such as perpetuating the gendered role of women's bodies being for men and articulating child abuse ("They shake me") as a laughable rather than criminal offence. These are, however, adult concerns about adult practices of sexuality, gender and associated violence. To convey these problems as children's rights issues becomes enormously problematic.[105] As feminist scholar, Meagan Tyler argues:

> [t]he real problem then is not simply that children are exposed to sexual imagery per se but that they are exposed to a particular model of sexuality (i.e. an objectified sexuality with a notable power imbalance) which is deemed objectionable.[106]

This problem is not a children's problem, but a social problem: one that includes children and adults. To reduce it to a problem of 'child sexualization' as Tyler argues, presents pornography as a problem but only a problem for kids: 'No-one is asking why adult women should have to put up with frequent exposure to images of women being "endlessly sexually available" '.[107] For Tyler, this is a problem in the way it limits debate about pornography and pornographication; here, this is a problem in the way that it presents children as somehow separate and apart from these broader social (adult) issues. Pornography is characterized as only a problem for children because it risks sexualizing young people in ways that are undesirable. Thus, as Tyler explains, the problem of pornographication is transformed into a problem of child sexualization. Child sexualization turns on concerns for development, for the future lives of young boys and girls. The child in this debate is transformed into a future-adult subject.

While the CottonOn slogans have explicitly sexual content, the 2010 WitcheryKids campaign is not at all sexual. Where the former example demonstrates concern about the "sexualization" of childhood, the WitcheryKids campaign concerns the "adultification" of childhood. It is not only a problem that children are exposed to sexual imagery, but also that they are represented in ways that duplicate adult life. It is no longer just a problem of children growing into particular forms of sexualized adults, or of being prematurely exposed to sexualized media content. It is now a problem that, in being exposed to images of adult life – images that merge happiness with consumerism and prettiness and style with self-confidence – children might come to be plagued by adult problems: problems of body image, anxiety and depression as mentioned above. It is no longer about the sexualization of children, but about a defiant objection to children's exposure to adult life, lest children come to have problems that only adults should bear. This objection turns on a claim to innocence. Children, in the absence of being exposed to a public world would, apparently, not have problems, suggesting that it is somehow possible to either remove children entirely from public space, or necessary to transform public space for the benefit of children (not for adults) alone. The issue of innocence is problematic in ways that were unpacked in an earlier chapter. The issue of public space is an important one that Tyler draws out: constructing these issues as children's rights problems calls for the transformation of public space (by censoring, for example, pornography in public spaces) for the benefit of children are positioned as somehow different from the benefits of adults.[108] In these terms, we have a narrative of innocence and risk to that innocence constructing conflicting claims over public space.

By constructing an image or text as harmful to children but not to adults, which developmental arguments tend to do, attempts to transform public space are undermined. On the one hand, childhood is a period in which we learn to be adults: the adults we learn to be are those that are demonstrated to us during our formative years. This elicits concern that children are passive becomings that cannot engage critically in the world around them. It constructs childhood as a time in which children will uncritically mimic the roles of the powerful adults they see: girls will practice at playing "mum" to a baby doll, boys will not; girls will practice dancing like strippers, boys will watch. In a heteronormative society this "play" arguably dictates whom these boys and girls ought to grow into and the roles they must fulfil. However, to suggest that girls who play with dolls will be good mothers and girls that dance like strippers will be teenage – and hence bad – mothers, presumes that children have no analysis of the world they occupy.[109] Understanding child play as an explicitly passive experience suggests that somehow, the context of their childhood is their only possible destination. Jonathon Bignell says this:

> the root of this anxiety about the child's media interaction is the assumption that the child is determinant of the adult, and this legitimates a discourse about how media may produce a socially undesirable child who in turn becomes a socially undesirable adult.[110]

The concern that the child passively becomes an adult obscures from view the ways in which children do negotiate their place in, and experience of, the world around them.

As Anastasia Powell has demonstrated in her study of young peoples' experiences of sex, young people negotiate the terms of sex (and of consent) in all sorts of ways, even if they do not demonstrate the particular form of rationality that Foucault illuminates in his histories of sex and madness.[111] The limitations of young people's capacity to negotiate are not exclusively related to age, maturity and experience. She observes that young middle-class girls from a private school demonstrated a more active form of negotiation.[112] However, the terms of negotiation these young people employ reflect a gendered and heteronormative society more generally. That is, the scope of their verbal negotiations is tied to the language of sexual consent that must articulate either yes or no. The actual negotiations of sexual conduct that these young people describe, Powell argues, is embodied.[113] These young people negotiate the grey areas of sexual conduct that the law has struggled to articulate by reading and deploying acts of "consent" that may still result in "unwanted" sex. For children negotiating sex, the lack of emotional, physical and intellectual maturity operates to preclude consent from consideration: children are not able to provide consent due to a lack of these forms of maturity. These are maturities that are required not only for verbal consent, but also for Powell's more embodied concept of consent.

Joanne Faulkner reflected on similar tensions in her analysis of the Bill Henson affair. Anxiety about children's sexuality emphasizes a vulnerability that means 'their innocence is always at risk – children become society's greatest liability as well as its most precious asset'.[114] This was especially so in Bill Henson's exhibition that depicted not children, but adolescents, with their sexuality in a state of emergence rather than being. In his images, we are confronted not with an image of obvious innocence, nor of obvious sexuality. We are confronted instead with a cleavage in time, where it is no longer certain that children are innocent and asexual but nor have we yet come to terms with risk that their sexual development presents. The "children" in Henson's exhibition are confronting because they are neither children nor adults. Joanne Faulkner refers to the argument of David Marr, who wrote of one particular image that:

> Without breasts or with full breasts this image would ... have caused less fuss. ... But these were budding breasts, rarely seen and almost never celebrated. In our culture budding breasts are extraordinarily private.[115]

It is, however, not just that this moment in an individual's life is private, it is that this moment of emerging sexuality is, in itself, unintelligible. To make its public display intelligible requires a retreat to a conception of childhood as innocence and, therefore, of this disclosure as exploitative, or, to defend it not as a literal and embodied disclosure of a person's sexuality but, instead, as art. In Joanne Faulkner's words:

> She is in the ambiguous zone of no-longer-not-yet that is hidden from view in our culture because ... we're not quite sure how we should categorise it. ... The budding breast refers obliquely to a budding sexuality and the stirrings of a desire we cannot control.[116]

Anxiety about an emerging sexuality highlights, once again, the risk attached to the promise and vulnerability of the next generation of adults. It is not just the risk of an individual, but also the risk of society that emerges in these debates that we otherwise name "children's rights".

This concern for the future-adult, premised as it is upon a passive and apolitical child, extends from particular understandings of sex and sexuality. The innocence of the child presents risks to that innocence as inherently problematic. Foucault's histories of sexuality provide some direction in how to understand its risks in childhood and beyond. In the discussion of medical advice and treatment above, giving children greater autonomy over their sexual lives coincides with an increase in risk. Foucault observes the place of children in discourses of sex as changeable. He argues there was an earlier age, in which 'direct gestures, shameless discourse, and open transgressions, when anatomies were shown and intermingled at will, and knowing children hung about amid the laughter of adults' were permissible and normal. This period, he argues, gave way to a later age when:

> Everyone knew, for example, that children had no sex, which is why they were forbidden to talk about it, why one closed one's eyes and stopped

one's ears whenever they came to show evidence to the contrary and why a general and studied silence was imposed.[117]

However, this shift was not a sudden and absolute change. Instead, he demonstrates that concerns for the risks of sex are evident in texts from Ancient Greece. In these texts, sex presents as needing regulating in both private and public life. Indeed, for Foucault, the history of sexuality is also a history of self-regulation and care so central to modern liberal society.

Foucault observes that sex has been regarded as 'dangerous, difficult to master, and costly; [and] a precise calculation of its acceptable practice and its inclusion in a careful regimen had been required for quite some time'.[118] The 'art of self', Foucault argues, comes to 'give increasing emphasis to the frailty of the individual faced with the manifold ills that sexual activity can give rise to'.[119] It also, he says 'underscores the need to subject that activity to a universal form by which one is bound, a form grounded in both nature and reason, and valid for all human beings'.[120] Sexual practices came to be the subject of medicine and of hygiene, which asks questions of 'their nature and their mechanism, that of their positive and negative value for the organism, that of the regimen to which they ought to be subjected'.[121] Accounting for sex, knowing sex, in medical and biological terms, gives rise to its risk. Increasing inquiry into sexual activity and its effect upon the self, in a quantifiable and scientific way, results in increased anxiety and vigilance about sex. Sex, if practiced the wrong way, might become a disease; or, if practiced the right way, might be therapeutic. For Foucault, the following statement by Stoic philosopher Musonius Rufus sums it up:

> Those who indulge in sexual relations and especially those who indulge without much caution need to take care of themselves in a much more rigorous fashion than others, so that, by putting their body in the best possible condition, they might experience less harmful effect of these relations.[122]

This knowledge, anxiety and vigilance demands regimes around sex that make one prepared and ready for it. This allows one to extract from it its greatest benefits, while minimizing its greatest risks. This knowledge, however, also produces a particular rationality. It requires a level of rational capacity to be able to make such calculations and judgements in order to care for the self appropriately. Most importantly, it demands the suppression of sexual life driven by impulse and desire, instead of by reason. Children, defined against reason and maturity, find themselves unable to engage in this rationality.

Conclusion

In this chapter, I have sought to demonstrate how conceptions of childhood in the private realm of sexuality nonetheless become serious public controversies. Again, I have argued that this is due to a preoccupation with the future-adult subject, as much as any genuine concern for the child, as a child. Reason, maturity and autonomy remain present as key limiting terms of debates about children's sexuality, determining the limits of what a child can and cannot do. These debates highlight the physicality of autonomy claims that literally give rise to a consideration of whether or not children have the right to determine matters affecting their own body. Yet, debates about medical treatment are distinguished from debates about sexual activity despite being premised on a shared concern about a child's rational and mature capacities to give consent. I have argued that this is political. It arises out of a concern about what kind of adult that child will grow into. It arises out of a concern that a child's life is cared for, and regulated, in ways that provide them with opportunities as adults. It arises out of a concern that children should not make choices when they are young that they will have to live with as adults; or that they should not be exposed to ideas, images and experiences that will disrupt their normal development into healthy, (hetero)sexual, adults. By no means do I criticize efforts to protect children from sexual and other forms of physical exploitation (including unnecessary medical procedures). My point is that the narrative of children's rights debates around these issues are premised upon broader claims than the integrity of children and their bodies: they are premised upon a political claim about what childhood should be, and who children should be free to become.

In these discussions of criminality and sexuality I have stressed how the focus of debates shifts from children as present beings to children-as-future-adults. The child is the precursor to the good, liberal citizen and so debates about children's citizenship are oriented toward this future. In accounts of criminality, conceptions of childhood as inherently innocent, or at least neutral, result in child criminals presenting a deeply confronting reality: they are not mere aberrations from the norm, as adult criminals might be, but evil personified. Children's sexual encounters have the capacity to inhibit their ability to be a good adult, with a healthy and rational sexuality. As much as any concern for sexual harm that children may experience as children, it is the risks that threaten a healthy adult life that are at the heart of the debates discussed above. At the discursive level childhood is, paradoxically, both an age of perfection and imperfection: as an age of perfect innocence, any risk to this – or evidence that this conception of childhood is misplaced – disrupts dominant discourses of how we think and talk about childhood, children and their rights. As an age of imperfection, the discourse of children's rights must be oriented toward ensuring that children's lives present every opportunity to ensure that they develop into good, liberal, adult citizens.

Notes

1 Archard (1998a: 2). Archard notes that he is sympathetic to this view, but does not always defend it.
2 Even by understanding power as a relational concept in Foucauldian terms, encompassing both the possibility for powerful conduct and resistance to that conduct, it does not mean that power exists as an equal relationship.

3 As an example, see the definition of the crime of rape at s. 38 of the *Crimes Act 1958*, (Victoria, Australia).

4 Manson O'Neill (2007: 17).

5 Locke (1993: 125–7).

6 *R* v. *Brown*, 1 AC 212 (1994). This case convicted five adult men consenting to sadomasochistic acts, who made no complaint about the harms done to them. It can be contrasted to the decision of *R* v. *Wilson* (1996) 2 Cr App Rep 241 in which the English Court of Appeal held that a woman could consent to being branded by her husband with a hot knife.

7 Manson and O'Neill (2007: 17).

8 Ibid.

9 Ibid., 20.

10 Ibid., 70.

11 Ibid., 70–1.

12 Ibid., 18.

13 *Gillick* v. *West Norfolk and Wisbech Area Health Authority*, 3 All ER 402 (1985).

14 *Secretary, Department of Health and Community Services* v. *JWB and SMB* (*'Marion's Case'*), 175 Commonwealth Law Reports 218 (1992). *Marion's Case* made the Gillick competency test a part of Australian law, which has since been developed through subsequent case law. For discussion of the development of the Gillick test as applied in Australian law see NSW Law Reform Commission (2008: 83–7).

15 As summarized by Fortin (1998: 72).

16 John Eekelaar (1986: 182). Also quoted by Fortin (1998: 63).

17 *Gillick* v. *West Norfolk and Wisbech Area Health Authority*.

18 Ibid.

19 For extensive discussion of this case see Pilcher and Wagg (1996).

20 *Gillick* v. *West Norfolk and Wisbech Area Health Authority*, 431.

21 As discussed in Pilcher and Wagg (1996: 85), with reference to the original decision.

22 *Gillick* v. *West Norfolk and Wisbech Area Health Authority*, 423; Also quoted in Pilcher and Wagg (1996: 86).

23 *Gillick* v. *West Norfolk and Wisbech Area Health Authority*, 421; Pilcher and Wagg (1996: 87).

24 *Secretary, Department of Health and Community Services* v. *JWB and SMB*.

25 Disability presents a separate, but related, area of discussion that also turns on questions of reason, maturity and autonomy. Martha Nussbaum uses disability to develop her capabilities approach. See Nussbaum (2007).

26 Parlett and Weston-Scheuber (2004); Jeffreys (2006).

27 Judge Mushin, *In Re A*, 16 Family Law Report 715 at 719 (1996).

28 Judge Nicholson, *Re Alex*, 180 Federal Law Review 89 at 118 (2004).

29 Ibid., 120.

30 Just as an analysis of moral panic was undertaken in respect to childhood criminality, it would also be possible to undertake an analysis of moral panic in respect to children's sexuality. However, the focus of this chapter seeks to remain on consent and claims to reason and maturity that are made in relation to this.

31 Alderson (2007); Alderson *et al.* (2006).

32 Alderson (2007: 2273).

33 'Convention on the Rights of the Child', (United Nations General Assembly 1989).

34 Alderson (2007: 2276).

35 Ibid., 2277.

36 Ibid., 2278.

37 Ibid., 2281; Alderson *et al.* (2006).

38 Alderson (2007: 2276–77).

39   Archard (1998a: 3).
40   See, for example, the *Crimes Act 1958*, (Victoria, Australia) s. 38.
41   Here the term "best interests" refers to the concept in family law (rather than the United Nations Convention on the Rights of the Child).
42   Justice Brennan, dissenting, *Secretary, Department of Health and Community Services* v. *JWB and SMB ('Marion's Case')*, 271.
43   Archard (1998a: 2), discussed in length at: 148–51.
44   Ibid.
45   Ibid.
46   Archard (2004: 105–11).
47   Archard (1998a: 120–9).
48   Ibid., 121–23.
49   Ibid; Archard (2004: 109).
50   Archard (1998a: 124).
51   Melton (1983: 21).
52   Ibid.
53   Ibid., 22.
54   Alderson (2007: 2276).
55   This is discussed broadly by Pamela Haag (1999).
56   Melton (1983).
57   Fortin (1998: 63). Shulamith Firestone also called for a much more expansive conception for rights for children. See Firestone (1970). Also see Farson (1974); Howard Cohen (1980).
58   Alderson *et al.* (2006).
59   Fortin (1998: 65).
60   Ibid.
61   *In re Gault*, 387 United States Reports 1 (1967). This decision established the principle that the United States Constitution applies to children as well as adults. Specifically, it held that Fourteenth Amendment rights to equal protection and due process in law applied to children and that each of the states was required to uphold these rights within their own juvenile justice jurisdictions.
62   Tadros (2006: 515).
63   Ibid., 517.
64   Ibid.
65   Ibid., 518.
66   Ibid., 519.
67   Ibid., 536–8.
68   Lacey (1998: 106).
69   Unconscionable dealings in contract law do introduce the concept of consent into property dealings, but it remains the case that consent is not the sole concept of property offences in the way that it is for sexual offences.
70   Powell (2008).
71   Ibid., 179.
72   Ibid., 170.
73   Ibid., 173.
74   Ibid., 172.
75   Ibid., 181.
76   Ibid.
77   Powell (2007).
78   Ibid., 23.
79   Ibid.
80   Archard (1998a: 126–8).
81   Jeffreys (1997, 2000.
82   As already mentioned, for Foucault power operates as a relationship rather than an

independent function. Wherever there is a power relationship, there is also the potential for resistance and acquiescence.

83 Quoted in Archard (1998a: 128).
84 Ibid., 120.
85 Australian Law Reform Commission (2010), section 24.71.
86 Ibid., section 24.72.
87 Concerns that children are growing up too fast, that their innocence is being lost, or that childhood itself is being destroyed are addressed in David Buckingham and Sara Bragg's analysis of sex, media and young people. See Buckingham and Bragg (2004). Joanne Faulkner at the University of New South Wales has been researching innocence and characterizes innocence (not specifically in relation to children) in two alternative ways: as either victims or becomings. See Faulkner (2011) Also see Faulkner 2008) here, she argues, among other things, that innocence might come to characterize agency, not just victimhood. There is also literature that addresses child behaviour and attitudes directly, in a range of contexts including sexual activity and criminality. For example, Louisa Allen's study of New Zealand schoolchildren's attitudes to sex, sexuality in the context of sex education both at school ("official") and beyond ("erotic"); see Allen (2005). This literature is useful in providing a child-centred basis for engaging in an analysis of what rights children should or should not have. However, once again, this is not the task of the research at hand. In the main, children do not represent or speak for themselves in scholarly literature. So, the site of analysis in this research is to consider *how* children are represented and spoken for in this literature, and how this shapes debates about children's rights. It is not the task of a research paper to attempt to know *who* children are, in order to better represent or speak for them.
88 Communications and the Arts ('SCECA') The Senate Standing Committee on Environment, 'Australian Senate Inquiry into the Sexualisation of Childhood in the media', (Canberra2008), Recommendation 1, v.
89 Ibid., 21.
90 Ibid.
91 Ibid., 22.
92 Bignell (2002: 139).
93 The Senate Standing Committee on Environment, 'Australian Senate Inquiry into the Sexualisation of Childhood in the media', 22. For a critical discussion of children and the media, see M. Gigi Durham's exploration of the sexualization of children in the media in the United States, accounting for risk whilst also trying to reveal possibilities for resistence by parents and children: Durham (2009). Jonathon Bignell approaches the interaction between children and the media in a two-fold manner: first, that 'Children's interaction with media is on one hand a question of discourse' and second, that 'the relations between children and media are a matter of action, including the procedures for parents' control and prohibition of media use, legal regulation and censorship, and policy debate'. See Bignell (2002: 127). As a discourse, David Buckingham and Sara Bragg also argue that the media is an interactive space that children do not necessarily process passively, but actively. They interviewed 120 young people (British children aged nine to 17) in 100 interviews, surveyed 800 young people, and interviewed around 70 parents. They concluded from this research that the children they encountered were '"literate", and often highly critical, consumers' of sexual content in the media, see Buckingham and Bragg (2004: 238). John Tobin also writes about the media and children, though in a much more optimistic and positive frame, arguing that the media can play a positive and pro-active role in supporting the United Nations Convention on the Rights of the Child. He explicitly acknowledges that in a consumer-driven world the consequences for children (he specifically refers to prostitution and child labour) can be devastating. He also agrees that:

... the media in all its forms have the capacity to be harmful and even exploit and violate the rights of children. Just witness the proliferation of child pornography, the relative invisibility of racial groups and cultural differences, gender stereotyping and the levels of violence to which children are exposed in the media.

(Tobin 2004: 141)

94 The Senate Standing Committee on Environment, 'Australian Senate Inquiry into the Sexualisation of Childhood in the Media', 26.
95 Ibid., 30.
96 Ibid., 38.
97 Buckingham and Bragg (2004).
98 Affrica Taylor (2010: 51).
99 Gale (n.d.).
100 Ibid.
101 Ibid.
102 Doherty (2010).
103 Gale (n.d.).
104 Critchley (2009).
105 Tyler (2010).
106 Ibid.
107 Ibid.
108 Ibid.
109 Rush and LaNauze (2006).
110 Bignell (2002).
111 Foucault (2006, 1978, 1985, 1986).
112 Powell (2010: 97–103).
113 Ibid.
114 Faulkner (2011: 122).
115 Ibid., 124.
116 Ibid., 124–5.
117 Foucault (1978): 3 and 4 respectively.
118 Foucault (1986): 237.
119 Ibid., 238.
120 Ibid.
121 Ibid., 104.
122 Ibid., 123.

6 Citizenship

Introduction

The previous chapters have demonstrated how children come to be positioned as future-adult subjects, with empirical claims about children's (lack of) reason, maturity and autonomy coinciding with normative claims about what childhood ought to be. Scholarship at the intersection of citizenship studies and childhood studies is rapidly expanding and has been the focus of much attention and debate.[1] The breadth of scholarship in this area is deserving of, and has already been the subject of, whole books. The analysis undertaken in this chapter is necessarily more limited in scope, and looks to a specific debate in the scholarship that exemplifies the shift toward "rethinking" citizenship for children. This chapter considers a narrow selection of arguments that have sought to re-theorize citizenship in ways that are more inclusive of children by challenging our understandings of citizenship rather than our understandings of childhood. The purpose of doing so is not to synthesize or resolve the enduring questions of children's citizenship status: whether children are, could be, or ever have been citizens.[2] Rather the purpose is to relate the conceptions of childhood in political philosophy and policy debates about crime and sexuality, to an explicitly political context. To do this, the chapter looks at debates regarding voting ages in Australia as a grounded example that scholarly debates about citizenship reflect and inform. The theme of citizenship captures understandings of the concept of the political at the broadest level and the status of individuals who are included in it and excluded from it. The work of Elizabeth Cohen, Andrew Rehfeld and Ruth Lister, in particular, grapples with the limits of liberal accounts of citizenship for children. Their attempts to re-theorize citizenship for children are pushed further in this chapter by drawing upon the work of radical democratic theorist Chantal Mouffe and the philosopher Hannah Arendt. I argue that debates about children's citizenship remain tied to the concepts of reason, maturity and autonomy. I do so to understand the seemingly irresolvable tensions in debates about whether or not children do, or should, have status as citizens and belong properly to the political realm. What is revealed is that children do not just challenge understandings of citizenship, but our understandings of the concept of the political too.

The paternalistic paradigm evident in Chapter 1 emphasizes autonomy as an antidote to political exclusion. This individual autonomy underpins a claim to citizenship in liberal democratic societies. Thus, the women's rights movement of the nineteenth century, asserting rational capacity and political autonomy, successfully advocated for voting rights. Similarly, Aboriginal and Torres Strait Islanders rejected claims about their intellectual inferiority in order to seek inclusion in the national census and therefore recognition as citizens of the Commonwealth of Australia, culminating in the successful 1967 referendum.[3] These are two examples in which the principle of individual autonomy was employed to lay claim to citizenship rights as a way of redressing paternalistic practices. In respect to children, who are excluded from public and political life, it can be argued that paternalistic practices can only be redressed if children are heard and accounted for within a liberal democratic society on their own terms. As this chapter will further explore, even though many do not advocate the full range of citizenship rights for children, some continue to argue that a greater recognition of children's citizenship rights are necessary.

Empirical and normative divides in theorizing children's citizenship

It is this tradition that Jeremy Roche points to when he suggests that 'the "story" of citizenship over the past 150 years has been one of struggles for inclusion'.[4] In this vein, Iris Marion Young has observed that:

> Liberalism has traditionally asserted the right of all rational autonomous agents to equal citizenship. Early bourgeois liberalism explicitly excluded from citizenship all those whose reason was questionable or not fully developed ... poor people, women, the mad and the feebleminded, and children were explicitly excluded from citizenship, and many of these were housed in institutions modelled on the modern prison: poorhouses, insane asylums, schools.[5]

By contrast, Tom Cockburn has demonstrated that citizenship is a category that is actually defined by practices of exclusion rather than inclusion.[6] He argues that while scholarship traditionally focuses upon geographical boundaries at the site of "Othering", in fact children demonstrate that citizenship also "Others" those within such boundaries.[7] David Archard describes a citizen as 'someone who participates in the government of their society and, where that government is democratic, does so by casting votes in elections'.[8] While recognizing that a right to vote may have 'little instrumental value', he argues that the vote remains 'central to citizenship'.[9] For Archard, citizenship is largely and symbolically tied to voting and other rights. He claims that 'it is arguable that citizenship is constituted by a cluster of rights and duties that can be acquired progressively rather than all at once', suggesting that citizenship rights may be understood as developmental and incremental.[10]

Despite recognizing citizenship as a set of practices broader than the right to vote alone, Archard views citizenship explicitly in terms of rights, consistent with a liberal understanding of citizenship. This liberal tradition is evident in the work of T. H. Marshall, whose three aspects of citizenship – civil, political and social – each invoke a different set of rights.[11] In contrast to this perspective is a republican tradition of citizenship that Hannah Arendt and, more recently, Chantal Mouffe have favoured. This work will be explored in the final section of this chapter.

As mentioned in the Introduction, thinking about children presents scope to rethink political questions more broadly.[12] Jeremy Roche also acknowledges this when he argues that in thinking about children's citizenship, we are required to think beyond the state–individual or state–civil society relationship that citizenship debates tend to emphasize. Instead, a focus upon children demands consideration of horizontal dimensions of citizenship that 'looks at relations within civil society and how children are positioned' in order to reveal 'new questions of power, requiring justification'.[13] In doing so, Roche accepts that children are 'social agents' undertaking responsibility in a range of contexts and also accepts the normative claim that the absence of a child-friendly citizenship is to the 'detriment of all'.[14] This follows in the tradition of citizenship claims made by women and marginalized racial groups. Roche discloses this connection directly, pointing to the wealth of feminist literature that has helped to unmask 'the standard citizen as male, white and provider'.[15] It is the role that feminist thinking has played in transforming understandings of citizenship and the political that compels Roche toward a theory of citizenship attendant to children. He argues that, 'just as women have altered understandings of citizenship and belonging, a politics inclusive of children will produce a further shift in understanding'.[16]

This is something that both Elizabeth Cohen and Ruth Lister take up when considering the dual status that children hold within the nation-state.[17] On the one hand, they are citizens insofar as they hold nationality and passports. It is in this sense that children are generally recognized as citizens: they belong to a nation-state.[18] However, on the other hand, children hold no civil and political rights that ordinarily coincide with citizenship of a nation-state. They are, at once, both citizens and non-citizens. By revealing this tension, Cohen and Lister both seek to offer altered understandings of citizenship that children as a class embody in liberal democracies.

When Ruth Lister identifies two ways of thinking about citizenship – as legal status and as a socio-political practice[19] – she is pointing to the liberal and republican traditions. In a liberal tradition, Lister explains that citizenship, as a legal status, views citizenship as a bundle of rights that enable 'people to act as agents'.[20] On the other hand, in a republican tradition, citizenship as a socio-political practice 'represents an expression of human agency'.[21] Individual autonomy makes agency possible. This agency is reflected in a lived citizenship, a set of practices that occur in day-to-day life, irrespective of whether or not formal citizenship rights exist. However, in the absence of formal citizenship rights, these practices may go unrecognized, or actually be undermined by insisting on the exclusion of some groups from public and political life. So, while citizenship can be practiced without citizenship rights, those practices will be enhanced by rights protection. Further, citizenship practices support claims for citizenship rights. If a citizen has the capacity to act politically, as an autonomous individual, and engages in citizenship practices in the course their day-to-day life, then that citizen should be recognized and protected by law. If a citizen is not protected, and instead he or she is excluded from public and political life, then a key principle of Kantian liberalism has failed: the autonomy of an individual, necessary for the legitimacy of the liberal state, has been denied. Within a liberal social contract theory, this both undermines the legitimacy of the liberal state and presents an injustice by denying an autonomous individual their autonomy. In this way, these two ways of thinking about citizenship are not paradoxical, but mutually supportive.

However, for Jessica Kulynych, the rights-based approach to children's citizenship is problematic. It has, she argues, 'actually disabled serious discussion of children as political actors'.[22] For Kulynych, the liberal emphasis on citizenship as rights comes at the expense of recognizing children's lived citizenship practices. Instead, she argues that it is necessary to leave the rights approach to the side and instead 'focus on citizenship as a form of political identity'.[23] In order to develop this political identity, Kulynych must deconstruct social constructions of childhood. In its place, one could offer an empirical claim about childhood that identifies and emphasizes actual citizenship practices that children engage in. This speaks more closely to a republican ideal of citizenship, rather than a reconsideration of citizenship itself. Kulynych's consideration of children's citizenship as a form of political identity is not a call to reconsider understandings of *children* but understandings of *citizenship*.[24] Further, Kulynych finds herself employing descriptions of children rather than redescriptions of citizenship to make her argument.[25] This is important, because if the emphasis remains on a reconsideration of children, as it does for Roche and Lister, then analysis is always compelled toward an empirical account of childhood and children's political practices. Where this occurs, any theoretical work that has opened up space for reconsiderations of children's citizenship is closed off again by truth claims about who children are, what childhood is and how children conduct themselves politically.

Interestingly, while Kulynych – compelled toward this empiricism – does offer a few statements from young people as evidence of certain forms of children's citizenship practices,[26] she is not actually providing an empirical account. Her argument remains a theoretical one. In the context of liberal and republican notions of citizenship, her anxiety about leaving open an empty theoretical space around children's citizenship void of any empirical claims for childhood is understandable. However, this anxiety is the valuable result of cleaving open space that is necessary for the transformation of our understandings of citizenship and the political. Once these understandings have been challenged and considered anew, it may be possible to seriously rethink children's political identity, which she takes as her central task. Further, deconstructing social meanings of childhood in this process (that is, by rejecting the desire to redeploy empirical claims about children) creates a void in what we know children to be. The desire to fill this void with an empirical or normative claim about what children are or should be looms large. However, to replace a social construction of childhood with an empirical or normative account only reproduces truth claims about what children are. I argue that any such claim is problematic.

Andrew Rehfeld touches on one aspect of why this is problematic. He argues that the benefits of citizenship are discontinuous: one either has the right to vote, or does not.[27] On the other hand, if there can be said to be a generally accepted "truth" of childhood, it is that childhood is a developmental, continuous, process. Children are educated, socialized and disciplined over many years to practice citizenship. Children are understood as having emerging capacities for civil and political life. Attempts to offer definitive accounts of what children are, at any given point in time, can only serve to fully exclude or fully include children in civil and political society. Such an approach disallows more critical analysis of how ideas of children and ideas of citizenship come to be understood in fixed and reflexive terms. A more rigorous analysis of this will be undertaken in this chapter, and utilizes a governmentality analysis to do so.

Children's citizenship: debating capacity and autonomy

As I have previously claimed, there are two broad approaches to children's rights: a protectionist mode and an autonomy mode. A protectionist mode appeals to an innocent conception of childhood, but, as I will show below, can also be supported by sinner or blank-slate conceptions in respect to citizenship rights debates. A protectionist mode emphasizes welfare and protection rights that are designed to protect children until they are fully rational and mature. An autonomy mode does not directly refer to child liberationists claims – that children should have the full gamut of adult rights – but to the arguments that have been drawn from this more radical movement. This less radical approach is an autonomy mode insofar as it emphasizes children's autonomy, while recognizing that this is likely to be an emerging autonomy and therefore stops short of claiming equal rights. These two competing approaches to children's rights are evident in debates about citizenship.

Andrew Rehfeld identifies an emphasis in the CRC upon children's welfare and protection, at the expense of participation rights. Contrary to Elizabeth Cohen,[28] he considers this appropriate. He states that 'Children are, by nature, an at-risk population, and their inclusion, as political citizens, must rank behind their basic security.'[29] Here, the protectionist approach to children's rights extends from a claim that children are, as a matter of fact, without reason, and risky, weak and vulnerable as a result. Unquestioned, this natural claim would suggest that it is both necessary and appropriate that children's rights be focused upon the development of children into adults. Consistent with a stage theory understanding of development, Rehfeld identifies the inadequacy of children's citizenship in the following way: '[children] are a population that is incrementally developing among institutions that are usually all-inclusive or all-exclusive'.[30] This creates an impetus to develop a conception of children's citizenship that allows for children's emerging cognitive, emotional, physical and communicative capabilities.[31] To highlight the importance of these capabilities for rights-holders, Rehfeld relies upon Robert Goodin and Diane Gibson's arguments regarding both choice (will) and interest theories of rights and the manner in which children fail to meet the standards of both.[32]

Rehfeld goes on to argue that while setting an age that one acquires citizenship is arbitrary, it is not the case that age distinctions are *necessarily* arbitrary. He argues that, while the difference between a 17- and 18-year-old might be difficult to determine, it is possible to highlight the differences between a four-year-old and 17-year-old.[33] This is easily accepted: four-year-olds and teenagers present as physically different, and there is a clearer distinction in cognitive skills and life experiences in a way that cannot be said for the difference between a 17- and 18-year-old. However, it is problematic to rely, as this argument does, upon fixed and definitive claims of characteristics that are tied to and determined by age. Indeed, this collapses the concept of childhood into a conception of childhood, albeit one based upon scientific claims rather than social meaning.

Rehfeld goes on to suggest that it is similarly obvious that '25-year-olds have greater political maturity than their younger cohorts'.[34] This is a more difficult proposition. The selection of the age of 25 is not random; Rehfeld earlier defers to the domain of cognitive psychology that is currently settled on the conclusion that the human brain is not fully developed until the age of 25.[35] In this way, Rehfeld is suggesting that it is possible to draw a sharp distinction between ages in a non-arbitrary manner. A 25-year-old brain is physically different from a 24-year-old brain. However, Rehfeld is not arguing for the delay of citizenship rights until full political maturity is reached but, on the contrary, argues for the extension of some forms of citizenship practices (if not rights) to younger persons to facilitate the development of cognitive capacities that are required at maturity. Rehfeld relies on Harry Brighouse's argument that 'Children cannot come to be competent agents without some experience of agency. They must have the experience of choice before it makes sense for them to be seen as having the right to choice.'[36] For Brighouse, this leads to the conclusion that 'the child can be said to have a right to an upbringing that prepares her for competent agency (which will include many opportunities for agency) but not to have agency rights'.[37]

For Rehfeld, the importance of reflecting children's development capabilities in political institutions serves a dual role: 'the promotion of children's capacity as politically mature citizens and the mitigation of harms that their political immaturity would cause them and the polity'.[38] He further identifies four practices that serve this dual role: according fractional votes to children; having national constituencies based on age, rather than only geographic regions; political spending accounts to fund political campaigns and interest groups devoted to particular age groups; and, finally, using federalism to allow young people to first participate in local politics, then state, then federal.[39] Together, what these approaches emphasize is children's lesser, not just different, political capabilities. These approaches do recognize that children have different political interests than those of adults. However, they do not emphasize children's participation in order to represent their choices as a collective body, or their collective interests. Instead, the value of these designs is oriented toward realising the future-adult subject, a blank-slate; and mitigating the risks of a potentially bad citizen, a sinner. So while Rehfeld does, valuably, think more creatively about the ways in which we thought-lessly exclude children from political citizenship, and seeks to create more mean-ingful ways for children to gain greater experiences of political citizenship, this is not done with a view to transforming the political status of children. Rather, it remains tied to the future-adult subject and the good of the liberal democratic polity to which they belong.

Like Rehfeld, Jeremy Roche is concerned about failing to account for the incremental attainment of citizenship. He seeks to avoid a "zero-sum" or all-or-nothing approach to children's citizenship, and instead proposes "partial citizen-ship".[40] For Roche, citizenship is both about 'governing and being governed'.[41] Roche does not offer examples of political participation for children that might realize this partial citizenship. Instead, he points approvingly to the attempts by other scholars to think about how to achieve increasing degrees of participation for children. David Archard, for example, focuses specifically on the question of the right to vote rather than citizenship more broadly.[42] However, his thinking around the right to vote could equally sustain an argument about broader citizen-ship rights.

Ruth Lister emphasizes the social practices of children's citizenship over cit-izenship as a set of formal legal rights. Drawing on feminist thinking, she also emphasizes relations within and across political communities, rather than the relations of a citizen to the state.[43] Together, Lister describes this socio-political understanding of citizenship as a "lived citizenship". This emphasis on the socio-political is distinct from Rehfeld's more legal approach. In this way, Lister and Roche arguably share in a republican conception of citizenship, rather than a liberal conception. This will be discussed at length below. For now, I wish to consider further how these broader conceptions of citizenship are claimed for children by considering Ruth Lister's argument and its implications for how we think about equality in liberal citizenship. I will also consider Elizabeth Cohen's theory of semi-citizenship,[44] and its implications for how we think about capa-city in the republican theory of citizenship.

Lister identifies the ways in which children are portrayed as becomings, rather than beings in theories of citizenship. She observes that citizenship literature has implicitly equated 'citizenship with adulthood, or has portrayed children as citizens of the future: variously described critically as "citizens-in-waiting," "learner citizens," or "apprentice citizens" ',[45] or T. H. Marshall's "citizens in the making".[46] Lister is sceptical of this future-oriented perspective and expresses her concern about how this perspective translates into an economic view that children represent "citizen-workers of the future".[47] In an age of neoliberal political economy, children are not just future-citizens, as discussed here, but also future-workers and future-consumers. Lister argues that thanks to sociological deconstructions of childhood, it has become possible to think more critically about this "becoming" view of childhood. She argues that:

> The contemporary sociology of childhood's construction of children as social actors with agency and varying degrees of competence opens up possibilities for the recognition of children as active citizens in a way that a construction of them as passive objects of adult policies and practices did not.[48]

Further, our understandings of children are problematically simple. Lister employs the research of Alexandra Dobrowolsky to further the argument:

> [b]ecause the figure of the child is unified, homogeneous, undifferentiated, there is little talk about race, ethnicity, gender, class and disability. Children become a single, essentialized category.[49]

For this reason, I would argue that empirical debates about whom and what children are can be seen as unhelpful for realizng a theory of citizenship for children. Both Ruth Lister and Jeremy Roche, whom Lister relies upon, find themselves forced to counter the claim that children lack the capacity for citizenship. When Roche argues that '[t]he arguments for the increased participation of children in decision-making affecting their lives are both practically and theoretically more compelling the older the child is',[50] he is reinforcing reason and maturity as the foundation for individual autonomy, and therefore liberal citizenship. When Lister cites his argument, she does so to point to research that emphasizes younger children's capacities for participation.[51] Neither find themselves able to overcome reason, maturity and autonomy as the foundations of a person's citizenship status and associated rights.

Employing a feminist analysis, Lister goes on to unpack the problematic concepts of capacity, independence, the public/private divide and equality in citizenship claims. However, on the one hand Lister acknowledges the question of rational capacity as a foundation for citizenship while, on the other, she continues to offer empirical evidence of children's sufficient rational capacities for citizenship.[52] Lister more successfully utilizes feminist analysis to disrupt the connection between dependency and protection, at the expense of participation rights.[53] Similarly, in respect to the public/private divide, she rejects claims that while the majority of children's experiences may exist within the private realm of family life, this does not disclose the latter from the political realm.[54] Finally, Lister raises the important difficulty within citizenship debates about whether or not citizenship should be rationalized on the sameness of children to adults, or their differences.[55] Assertions regarding the rational capacities of children, of their degrees of independence and responsibility within the family home, tend to emphasize their sameness. However, Lister argues that the question: 'does children's citizenship then tend to devalue the right of children to remain children with all its implications – such as playfulness, lightness, and "childishness"?' – posed by Daiva Stasiulis[56] – problematizes this approach.[57] Indeed, this is often the question that debates about children's rights come to centre on. Does extending children adult rights on the basis of their adult-like (or emerging adult) capacities, undermine the qualities that make them a child? This is an important question: if extending children's citizenship is pursued to further expand our concept of the political, as Jeremy Roche argues it should be,[58] then including children on the grounds of their sameness to adults is highly problematic.

I now unpack some of the broader political implications we might take from these debates about children's citizenship. I agree with Jeremy Roche that, 'In our arguments about childhood, children's rights and citizenship we are arguing about ourselves and our place in the world: it is an argument about politics and how we want to be and live our lives.'[59] As argued in the previous chapter, the future-adult subject comes to figure heavily in debates about children's rights. Further, this future-adult subject does not emerge accidentally, but is a necessary element of political philosophy. A future-adult subject is central to how we are able to imagine and theorize an ideal political community. Roche's statement allows us to recognize that we cannot extricate ourselves or our concept of the political from how we think and talk about children and their rights. Having unpacked some of the key difficulties of theorizing children's citizenship above, I turn to an example of this debate in the context of the voting age, before moving on to the broader implications for our understandings of the concept of the political.

The citizenship right to vote in Australia

This analysis is largely conceptual, and later I theorize further how these questions of children's citizenship delimit our understandings of the concept of the political. However, we can still look to voting as a specific site of debate about children's citizenship. Below, I offer a snapshot of Australian debates about the voting age. The first relates to the successful campaign to lower the voting age from 21 to 18 in the 1970s, the second relates to a more recent campaign to lower the voting age from 18 to 16. This discussion demonstrates the discursive concepts of reason, maturity and autonomy in debates about children and their rights. It will also demonstrate that the voting age is largely arbitrary in nature. Notwithstanding the emphasis upon young people's reason, maturity and autonomy, the decision of the Australian Parliament about the appropriate voting age remains an arbitrary political choice.

In Australia, the right to vote itself is a contentious matter of jurisprudence, with the High Court of Australia reluctant to recognize an express constitutional right to vote.[60] The absence of an express constitutional protection makes it particularly difficult for disenfranchised groups (prisoners and children being two current groups) to claim the right.[61] The issue of age has only been considered once. In *King* v. *Jones*, the High Court interpreted "adult" as a key limiting term in section 41 of the Australian Constitution. The term "adult", the Court held, was to be read literally and fixed at the age of 21 until the Commonwealth legislated differently. The Commonwealth did so the following year, in an amendment to the *Commonwealth Electoral Act 1918*. This reflects the difficulty of lowering the voting age: within the legal framework, a child in order to claim a right to vote, would have to define themselves as adult rather than being able to take issue with the fact of adulthood as a non-negotiable basis of autonomy and citizenship rights. This is very different from claiming a child's right to vote, and arguing that children, as children, have citizenship rights. Consequently, the legal framework makes it necessary to emphasize children's *adult* qualities in order to claim voting rights. This is a paradoxical proposition and does nothing to develop a theory of children's citizenship. Indeed, this is the approach that many seeking to extend the right to vote to those aged under 18 rely upon: an emphasis upon 16-year-old's adult-like qualities (they work, pay taxes, drive cars, can leave school, etc.) and their emerging rationalities.[62] Regardless of these legal limitations, the extension of the right to vote has been driven by political, social and cultural shifts in the way the empowered voting majority has viewed the rights of the politically marginalized. Thus, it is appropriate to situate children's rights claims within political frameworks as well as legal frameworks.

In *King* v. *Jones*, two central arguments were put to the High Court of Australia. One, that South Australian legislation, which lowered its voting age from 21 to 18, therefore also extended to those persons the right to vote in Commonwealth elections by virtue of section 41 of the Constitution. Second, that section 41 itself, ought to be read as including persons aged 18 and above, effectively extending to all Australian persons of that age the right to vote, irrespective of the South Australian legislation. This interpretation of section 41 could be possible, by reading 'no "adult" persons' to mean 'no "mature" persons', and therefore not referring to a specific age. Justice Menzies claimed that this argument was made on two alternative propositions: first, that mature persons reflected an age that, in fact, demonstrated maturity; second, that mature persons refers to an age at which persons *ought* to be recognized as mature. The first, of course, makes an empirical claim about the maturity of 18 years, while the second makes a normative one. The Court was unanimous in rejecting both arguments and any proposition that section 41 could include persons aged under 21 years of age. Chief Justice Barwick reasoned that

> the word mature may possibly be used to express a person's suitability to exercise a capacity in relation to some subject matter or in relation to some specified purpose or activity ... [but] it does not follow that a person expressed to be mature in relation to some stated activity or in relation to some attitude or behaviour is mature in relation to all matters or activities or in relation to all purposes. A capacity to engage in contracts, to make a will, to borrow money or to drive a motor vehicle is quite disparate from a capacity to exercise a franchise. To decide to accord the one is not to compel, or perhaps even persuade, a decision to accord the other.[63]

On this basis, Chief Justice Barwick argues against the interpretation of section 41 of the Constitution to be read as allowing all mature persons, rather than adult persons to vote. He goes on to defend the arbitrary divisions of age, arguing that 'It has always been necessary for the law to select age for the purpose of determining the capacity of a person to do various things.'[64] The Constitution, written in 1900, Barwick concludes, used the term adult to refer to persons of or above the age of 21. In the absence of express legislation to the contrary, the Court has no basis for lowering (or raising) the voting age. However, Justice Menzies explicitly makes clear that the Commonwealth (not the states) have the power to amend section 39 of the *Commonwealth Electoral Act 1901* to lower the voting age at their will. The Commonwealth of Australia did just this the following year. Since 1976, the voting age in Australia has been 18 years. Arguments to lower the voting age to 16 in more recent times have, therefore, focused upon political lobbying for legislative change, rather than the court system.

In 2004, the Victorian Electoral Commission released a discussion paper on lowering the voting age. It sought to establish a framework on the question of voting age in order to be 'logical and consistent in terms of whom we allow to vote'.[65] The two main framing questions for the Commission were: 'on what criteria do we decide whether or not to allow people to vote in Victorian elections?' and, 'on what criteria do we decide to exclude people who meet the criteria in answer to [the previous] question?'[66] The Commission identified that a primary criteria for why a Victorian has a right to vote in state elections is because that Victorian has a substantial stake in the state's governance. It also identified that 16- and 17-year-olds were persons who had such a stake. However, on the second question, it was reasoned that Victoria restricts the vote to those who are 'incapable of understanding the nature and significance of enrolment and voting'.[67] The discussion paper further identified four main ways in which it is often argued that young people are incapable of this: lack of maturity; not enough life experience on which to base decisions; lack of interest; and ignorance.[68] The Commission did not find these arguments compelling enough to justify the exclusion of 16- and 17-year-olds from the right to vote. However, the voting age in Australia, at the Federal and state level, has not been lowered.

The election of the Australian Labor Party in 2007 saw a renewed interest in lowering the voting age to 16. In the following year, then Prime Minister, Kevin Rudd, held two national summits: the Australia 2020 Summit, and the Australia 2020 Youth Summit. This Youth Summit included in its discussions and final paper the recommendation that the voting age be lowered to 16. The paper argued that this was necessary for a more participatory political system.[69] This is quite distinct from an argument (that was also made, but with less emphasis) that 16- and 17-year-olds possess a requisite level of reason, maturity and autonomy. Instead, it emphasizes the plurality of the political realm. This recommendation was then considered in the 2009 Green Paper on Electoral Reform, which identified three possible proposals for doing so: the extension of a compulsory vote to 16-/17-year-olds; the extension of voluntary voting to 16-/17-year-olds; and, voluntary enrolment for 16-/17-year-olds, with voting to be compulsory for those who opted to enrol.[70] No conclusions were drawn by the report as to the best approach. Since the Green Paper, the issue has once again slipped to the margins of Australian policy debates.

These debates demonstrate, once again, how claims of reason, maturity and autonomy operate to inform, shape and limit how we are able to think about children and claims to a right to vote. However, Chief Justice Barwick's acknowledgement of the arbitrariness of age thresholds as a social, legal and political function is one that has been lost in more recent debates. It is no longer acceptable to defend arbitrary age limits for voting and broader citizenship rights, and yet Chief Justice Barwick's claim resonates strongly. Also, the 2020 Youth Summit emphasis on political plurality as being for the good of politics (not just good for young people) is an argument that remains underdeveloped in the literature. It is worthy of more serious consideration. In the next section, I develop my own analysis of children's citizenship through an explicit consideration of the concept of the political. Specifically, I consider Elizabeth F. Cohen's theory of semi-citizenship for children in more depth. I also raise the implication for understanding children's political natality through the work of Hannah Arendt. My main focus, however, is on Chantal Mouffe's more radical conception of democracy. Through this terrain of political theory, I argue that the exclusion of children from the political realm is constitutive of it. Therefore, any efforts to theorize children's citizenship must attend to the tension of inclusion/exclusion at the threshold of the political realm. This analysis is not concerned with our understandings of childhood, but instead turns to our understandings of the concept of the political itself.

Elizabeth Cohen's theory of semi-citizenship

So far, I have outlined the terms by which children's right to vote is debated, turning on claims to reason, maturity and autonomy. The Australia 2020 Youth Summit, in publishing its recommendation to lower the voting age to 16, emphasized the importance of expanding the franchise for the good of the political process itself.[71] In the interests of politics, Elizabeth Cohen theorizes semi-citizenship for children as a response to the 'conceptual and practical need for a category between citizen and non-citizen'.[72] Children are citizens because of their nationality, but they are also 'judged to be incapable of citizenship in that they cannot make the rational and informed decisions that characterize self-governance'.[73] However, as I will argue, Cohen's theory is constrained by a number of ideas that delimit possibilities for children's citizenship. These constraints do not arise from deficiencies in Cohen's own analysis or reasoning. Instead, as will be shown in subsequent chapters, they are constraints that can be read across the children's rights discourse more broadly. To explore this, I offer a critique of a liberal rights approach to children's citizenship through the critical perspective of Chantal Mouffe. Employing Mouffe's radical theory of democracy,[74] I will argue that children can be understood as a constitutive Other, defining the limits of the political realm. This can be argued in both a liberal conception of the political, as well as in Mouffe's radically democratic conception of the political. In this radically democratic conception, Mouffe relies on a republican notion of citizenship and it is to this that I attend. While the discussion that follows will explore the place of children in relation to the political at a broader level, it does so through a continued consideration of citizenship debates. Cohen's theory of semi-citizenship is an attempt not just to think about children differently by deconstructing conceptions of childhood that have seen in previous attempts, but an attempt to rethink citizenship itself.

As discussed, the turn toward citizenship as a means of accounting for children's lives politically follows in the path of other liberal rights movements. By emphasizing the individual and moral autonomy of women and Indigenous peoples, it was no longer possible to rationalize their exclusion from civil and political life on the grounds that they were childlike. However, as argued in Chapter 1, children cannot be metaphors for themselves, so understanding claims to children's citizenship in terms analogous to other groups is problematic. Second, Cohen cannot escape a subject of liberal political philosophy who remains an ideal liberal citizen. A citizen who is necessarily adult. Third, Cohen's analysis remains tied to a dichotomous relationship between protectionist and autonomy perspectives that inform debates across children's rights discourse. This relationship emerges from a continued and unquestioned commitment to reason, maturity and autonomy, as key limiting terms for how we think about adult citizens and child potential citizens in liberal political philosophy.

Cohen's theory of semi-citizenship is an explicit attempt to address a conceptual gap between citizen and non-citizen. While I draw on her discussion around childhood, for Cohen it does extend to other groups.[75] Children's exclusion from full citizenship reflects the notion of citizenship as a form of self-governance, in a Kantian tradition of autonomy. It also reiterates rationality and informed decision-making as key characteristics of citizens. As will be discussed later, these foundations of citizenship make thinking about children's citizenship particularly difficult.

In developing her theory of semi-citizenship, which she argues captures actual forms of citizenship, Cohen grapples with two perspectives of childhood that serve their exclusion.[76] The first is a paternalism view, which 'allows adult ownership of children's higher level interests ... confining them to the private realm of the family and excluding them from public affairs.'[77] This view reflects the paternalistic paradigm I have discussed in the histories of women and Indigenous peoples. The lack of rational capacity operates in this way to exclude certain persons for membership in the political community, in their own best interests. This is supported by what Cohen describes as the 'coverture analogy', which regards children as the beneficiaries of their parents' fiduciary interests: that is, that parents serve children's best interests and thus children require no citizenship rights of their own. The second perspective is the "minor" view, which 'treats children as a means to achieve adult ends'.[78] This view is preoccupied with children's status as future-adults.[79] It rationalizes the exclusion of children from citizenship on the grounds that their exclusion is temporary. Its effect, according to Cohen, is that it allows policies to overlook the 'political interests of the perpetually present class of minors' in democracies.[80] This view is concerned not only with ensuring that society does not become burdened by neglected children, but that childhood is maintained as a crucial time in life to ensure that children are educated to become future citizens.

However, having eloquently expressed what is at stake (not only for children but for democratic politics) in debates about children's citizenship, Cohen's final conclusion can only point to an expanded role for various Ombudsmen as a means for children to be considered semi-citizens, while acknowledging that 'they can't really enforce civil rights'.[81] Her cursory view of voting rights considers lowering of the voting age to 14 or 15 to be appropriate, even if those votes only count for a quarter of an adult's vote.[82] In short, Cohen's attempt to theorize citizenship for children results in a compromised and diluted form of adult citizenship, rather than a coherent rethinking of citizenship that might provide an account of children as having a political status of their own. As stated earlier, this does not emerge from any weakness in Cohen's analysis. Rather, it is a product of a liberal rights discourse that sets the limits for how we can think about children's rights. Cohen's work here is an overdue and welcome enterprise. However, given the lack of work and thinking around this area, Cohen's theory of semi-citizenship falls short of transforming the political status of the child.

First, the paternalism view that Cohen uses is, indeed, reflective of a paternalistic paradigm evident in other political movements. However, as discussed, it is not directly analogous to questions of children's rights and political status. In the first chapter, I offered two examples from Australia of how assertions of equality were tied not just to one's moral status and humanity, but also to the exercise of reason. Both women and Indigenous people around the world had to displace misunderstandings that they were less rational than European men, unable to represent their own interests on their own terms. Both groups found themselves having to demonstrate their equal *rational capacities* as a means for establishing their equal moral worth. By drawing an analogy between other political movements and children's rights, Cohen's theory of semi-citizenship presents conceptual difficulties.

To treat an adult like a child implies an inherent injustice because adults are assumed to be autonomous individuals and free from the dictates of another. It disrespects individual autonomy, the moral worth of another person, and belies any possible political status of that individual as an equal member of society. To treat an adult like a child is to exclude them from an adult, public and political world. By contrast, the power relationship between children and adults is necessarily skewed. Rejecting a paternalistic paradigm risks rejecting the parental relationship between children and significant adults in their lives, including parents, carers and teachers. Overcoming the paternalism view in debates about children's rights requires a reconsideration of how we understand paternalism during childhood, and a different path for countering its foundations in a lack of reason and capacity for self-governance. This is something that Cohen and others have not succeeded in doing.

The second constraint operating on Cohen's thesis goes toward the more abstract question of who the political subject of liberal political philosophy is. I argue here that the political subject is an ideal, future-citizen, who is necessarily an adult. Childhood is a very important period in the life of an individual in a liberal state. In various ways, the years before a person becomes an adult and acquires the status of *citizen* are spent protecting innocence, mitigating risk and realizing the potential of the individual. I argue that this is necessary to produce the kind of individual that liberalism identifies both as its destination and the only source of its political legitimacy; that is, the realization of a rational, autonomous adult citizen is liberalism's end: it is Enlightenment; the Age of Reason. This autonomous citizen also provides the hypothetical consent required by the social contract to be governed.

Finally, as mentioned previously, Cohen points to two alternative positions that inform debates about children's citizenship: a paternalism view and a minor view. There are, however, two other positions that inform debates about children's rights more broadly: the protectionist and autonomy modes. This is the third constraint operating upon Cohen's theory of children's citizenship. The protectionist mode, which largely captures both her paternalism and minor view, is premised upon the child's need for protection from exploitation, as well as their own immaturity. The autonomy mode regards this protectionist mode as inadequate. The counterarguments to Cohen's theory of children's citizenship draw upon this autonomy perspective. They emphasize civil and political rights as the best basis for addressing children's lives, following the need to overcome paternalistic practices evident in other social and political movements. There are those who seek to protect children on the basis of their innocence and inherent vulnerability. There are those who seek to provide greater autonomy on the basis of their demonstrated capacities for reason, in the belief that children need the freedom to protect themselves.

In order to take children's rights seriously, Michael Freeman argues that it is necessary to consider both the actual and potential autonomy of children: to 'confine paternalism ... without entirely eliminating it'.[83] In some ways, this is also what David Archard supports when he suggests that children be accorded greater autonomy in line with a principle of 'minimum rationality', that most young people (if not very young children) can be regarded as possessing.[84] The point here is that competing claims to protection and autonomy present two opposing concepts that determine the terrain of children's rights. In navigating debates about children's rights, one must operate between these two positions. It is very difficult to talk about anything in children's rights other than these competing claims, and the foundations they rest upon: the development of reason and maturity. Should children have a right to vote? To answer this question, the debate focuses on questions like: are children mature enough to identify what's in their own best interests? Do children have the rational capacity to make a meaningful choice between two alternatives? Are children significantly enough affected by policy that their parents' representation of them is inadequate? Having determined the parameters for debate, the discourse delimits possible responses to the problems facing children. In respect to citizenship, this means overcoming both a commitment to a Kantian reason and capacity for self-governance that characterizes the political subject of liberal political philosophy, and its commitment to the ideal future-citizen. These two commitments are not grounded in debates about who children are, but in how we understand the concept of the political itself.

One of the difficulties that emerge in the analysis above is the disjuncture between our understandings of children as *not* equal to their adult counterparts in terms of citizenship, which is premised in a liberal understanding upon the equality of citizens. The inequality of children is not necessarily an inequality in moral status, but turns on their lesser capacity to conduct themselves as rational and mature citizens. Part of this problem is illuminated by Iris Marion Young, who argues that:

> Modern political theory asserted the equal moral worth of all persons, and social movements of the oppressed took this seriously as implying the inclusion of all persons in full citizenship status under the equal protection of the law.[85]

In attempting to realize an inclusive model of citizenship, liberal political theory has universalized what it means to be a citizen by discounting the particularities and differences between individuals, operating against the plurality that a fuller citizenry might otherwise realize. This is Young's paradox of democracy. For children, liberal political theory asserts a form of rationality that only adults can be deemed to possess. If children can demonstrate a liberal rationality that would allow them to understand the consequence of – and to make a meaningful choice when – voting, this demonstrates their adult-like maturity. In order to make sense of the citizen child, it is necessary to emphasize their adult-like qualities over their child-like qualities. Thus, it remains that liberal political theory relies upon its citizen as a future being.

In the attempt to reconcile the position of child liberationists who advocate for children's full citizenship on the same terms as adults' citizenship and the position of more contemporary children's rights advocates that value a citizen with emerging rational and mature capacities, Elizabeth Cohen cannot help but present a compromise designed to provide some forms of democratic participation by the young, without actually bringing them into a theory or conception of politics that accounts for children on their own terms. For Young, the better means for inclusion is based upon self-organisation,[86] but this too presumes that children might be recognized by others as legitimate participants within the political sphere, and that children share in the liberal rationality demanded by democratic citizenship. It is in this way that the very terms of citizenship and democracy make conceptualizing children's citizenship so difficult.

Beginnings

For Hannah Arendt, 'the new beginning inherent in birth can make itself felt in the world only because the newcomer possesses the capacity for beginning something anew, that is, of action'.[87] Children are born with a potential that creates new possibilities for politics, and yet this status as a beginning is also one that limits the possibility for our understanding of politics in children's lives and the concept of the political itself. So long as one is *becoming* a political actor, one is not yet that political actor; so long as one is *becoming* a good citizen, one is not yet that citizen, and, indeed, is vulnerable to the possibility of becoming a bad citizen instead. The potential inherent in beginning is both vulnerability and assertiveness, both a risk and a hope. Conceptions of children as blank-slates, innocents and sinners are one way to make sense of these contradictions and tensions. These contradictions and tensions also speak to the difficulty of accounting for the complexity of children's lives that are at once vulnerable and assertive, risky and hopeful. Children's rights debates oriented around a dichotomous tension of protection versus autonomy claims embody a futile effort to reach a final conclusion as to which set of claims reflect the truth of childhood. There is no such truth. The only truth of childhood to be discovered is the truth of our own, adult, social and political ideals informed by a set of governing norms and values that we have come to embody in order to practice upon ourselves and each other. The only truth of childhood that can be discovered is one that discounts the natality that Arendt describes; one that rejects a new beginning and instead reiterates states of being that have already become:

> even the children one wishes to educate to be citizens of a utopian morrow are actually denied their own future role in the body politics, for, from the standpoint of the new ones, whatever new the adult world may propose is necessarily older than they themselves. It is in the very nature of the human condition that each new generation grows into an old world, so that to prepare a new generation for a new world can only mean that one wishes to strike from the newcomers' hands their own chance at a new.[88]

This reflects the tension between valuing children for the possibilities that they present to social and political life on the one hand, and the necessity of ensuring that children come to be educated within the already established political order. Indeed, Hannah Arendt is quite forceful about the absurdity of calling for children to be free from the authority of adults.[89] Jessica Kulynych summarizes Arendt's position as one that regards children's exposure to the public world as destroying political natality.[90] Arendt does not view children as ready for politics, and, in the case of Elizabeth Eckford referred to in the Introduction, viewed placing the child in a political debate as a mistake.[91] It was a mistake, not only by risking harm to the child, but also by posing a risk to the realm of politics:

The responsibility for the development of the child turns in a certain sense against the world: the child requires special protection and care so that nothing destructive may happen to him from the world. But the world, too, needs protection to keep it from being overrun and destroyed by the onslaught of the new that bursts upon it with each new generation.[92]

Hannah Arendt's view of childhood, and of the separation of the private and political realms, lends itself very well to a protectionist mode of children's rights. However, what it also reveals is that the importance of protecting children from public and political life is not only good for children's interests, but good for public and political life. All this serves to reiterate my argument that the discourse of children's rights cannot be considered separately from an analysis of the concept of the political. Following Arendt, we are compelled to reveal that our concern for the protection of children is also a concern for the protection of the political realm. Even in choosing to exclude children from political life lies a political motivation. By holding children outside of politics until an arbitrarily determined threshold of maturity and rationality is reached, both childhood and politics is preserved, and made possible. The exclusion of childhood from the political is also constitutive of it.

Understood in this context, debates about children's citizenship reveal a political problem with the limits of liberalism, rather than a problem with the limits of children's rights. To explore this, I consider Mouffe's ontological commitment to Carl Schmitt's friend–enemy distinction as definitive of the political.[93] I argue that while we may not easily view children as "enemies" according to this distinction, they nonetheless can occupy Mouffe's idea of a 'constitutive Other'.[94] In this way, I argue that children defined against reason, maturity and autonomy, are definitive of adult liberal citizenship. Therefore, attempts to use citizenship as a means for children's political inclusion are made at the risk of dissolving the political realm itself, collapsing it into the merely social. This suggests that it is neither desirable nor possible for children to be citizens. However, this should not necessarily compel us to view children as pre-political or apolitical beings. On the contrary, by the fact of their exclusion, children are definitive of the liberal political realm. This may not be a foundation for claiming children's citizenship rights, but it should have consequences for how we adults, who belong to this political realm, think about childhood, children, their rights and liberal political philosophy more broadly. The child as a constitutive Other may well have a claim to be included, and this is a claim that needs to be taken seriously. However, the nature of this claim is grounded in different conceptual terrain than previous citizenship debates have adhered to.

Chantal Mouffe has argued that citizenship has been reduced to a mere legal status, which determines the relationship of the individual (who belongs already) to the state, at the expense of a fuller understanding of citizenship and the political. In this way, she offers a useful point of departure from the previous literature. Citizenship rights capture Mouffe's articulation of the democratic paradox.[95] On the one hand, the concept of citizenship speaks to belonging to a political community, a *demos*: a political community that, following Schmitt, is homogenous in nature; a political community that emphasizes equality and unity. On the other hand, rights extend from a liberal tradition that emphasizes individualism and plurality. Citizenship rights, then, carry with them the possibility to transform the political status of their holder by bringing them into the political realm. Therefore, citizenship rights are characterized in such a way that potential citizens need to demonstrate their equality, as sameness, with the rest of the political community. This risks having a depoliticizing effect, undermining the plurality necessary for the political realm.

Indeed, it is by accepting citizenship as little more than legal status that Cohen looks for scope within existing policy-making practices (rather than across politics more broadly) for children to participate.[96] By doing so, she has no choice but to accept citizenship as a concept that is founded upon a certain rationality and maturity that children are defined against. This being the case, children are not easily theorized into citizenship and so must be satisfied with some lesser form of citizenship than adults. Raia Prokhovnik has characterized the work of early Enlightenment philosopher Baruch Spinoza as against this modern conception of citizenship, whereby a rational and autonomous citizen presents in the modern world as an abstract being who is thoroughly depoliticized.[97] Relatedly, Tracey B. Strong regards Schmitt's critique of liberalism as turning in part on its depoliticizing and dehumanizing affect, resulting from substituting political procedure for struggle.[98] Chantal Mouffe's characterization of this tension between liberalism and democracy as a democratic paradox highlights the emphasis of individualism and rights on the one hand, and homogeneity and equality on the other.[99] In this way, citizenship rights embody the democratic paradox: by seeking admission to a democratic political community premised upon equality on the one hand, but asserting the importance of individualism and plurality on the other.

Following Carl Schmitt, Mouffe adopts the friend–enemy distinction as the ontological foundation of her conception of the political. Where the political is premised upon an antagonistic relationship, it presents the ever-present possibility of contestations, if not outright combat. Children are not easily characterized as the enemy in this articulation of the political.[100] However, they can be understood as a constitutive Other, in that they represent the frontier of the political. For Schmitt, this foundation is reflected in the ever-present possibility of combat, which characterizes political matters.[101] "Friends", in this characterization, are reflected in a homogenous, political realm that is defined against its "enemies", which fall outside of this realm. In international politics, this is demonstrated in relations between nation-states. However, it also operates within domestic politics, such as establishing the conditions within a nation-state for civil war. In both contexts, the distinction highlights the ways in which two opposing groups share within themselves a homogeneity that is defined against a shared enemy. For Mouffe, 'Schmitt highlights the fact that democracy always entails relations of inclusion-exclusion.'[102] Therefore, Mouffe must depart from Schmitt because she remains committed to the democratic project. However, in order to strengthen democracy rather than dismiss it (as Schmitt does), without abandoning Schmitt's ontological foundations, she transforms an antagonistic and possibly violent relationship into an agonistic, relatively peaceful one. In order to understand Schmitt's friend–enemy distinction in ways useful for democratic pluralism, Mouffe turns to a broader we–they relation that holds within it the possibility for antagonism.[103] This broader relation is an extension of what Mouffe regards to be Jacques Derrida's "constitutive outside",[104] highlighting difference as a precondition for identity formation.[105] This allows Mouffe to contemplate we–they relations that are not necessarily characterised by an explicit friend–enemy distinction. Instead:

> the friend/enemy distinction can be considered as merely one of the possible forms of expression of the antagonistic dimension which is constitutive of the political. We can also, while acknowledging the ever present possibility of antagonism, imagine other political modes of construction of the we/they.[106]

To transform antagonism into agonism, Mouffe points to an adversarial model of democracy as a mechanism for doing so.[107] This process, Mouffe stresses does not eliminate antagonism altogether. On the contrary, it remains an ever-present possibility. Instead, democratic procedures condition the antagonism so that what is played out in political contests is not outright violence, but a confrontation between adversaries.[108]

What the friend–enemy distinction reveals, according to Mouffe, is the futile effort of producing a fully inclusive political community. This, she says, 'can never be achieved since, as Schmitt tells us, in order to a construct a "we" it must be distinguished from a "them", and that means establishing a frontier, defining an "enemy"'.[109] This is an enemy who has a potential claim to be included within the political that the citizens defend themselves against. Therefore, for Mouffe, there exists a permanent constitutive outside, that makes the political community possible. Mouffe, of course, rejects what the distinction means for Schmitt: the constitution of a normative and social homogeneity. Instead, she uses it to present a challenge that liberal democracy must better respond to: the plurality of social life and the ever-present possibility of conflict (if not outright war) that it produces.[110] It is only in retaining this possibility for dissent and contestation that the concept of the political exists, and it is this, Mouffe argues, which liberalism pacifies. In order to retain the political, without producing war, Mouffe seeks to "tame" the violence at the heart of Schmitt's rejection of liberal democracy. However, the ever-present challenge at the threshold of the political also suggests a more dynamic paradox than Mouffe allows for. At the threshold of the political, the bodies that are excluded from politics also exclude the dissent that is so crucial for Mouffe's political. The exclusion of the constitutive Other is a source of challenge to the terms of the political, but also keeps the possibility of this dissent alive.

If you accept with Mouffe and Schmitt that antagonism – as an ontological foundation of the political – is both necessary and valuable, then the very attempt to circumvent it risks the loss of the political. For Mouffe, an adversarial model of politics achieves the goal of "taming" violence without actually eliminating its possibility, and thereby retains the political.[111] This is what liberal approaches, in the tradition of John Rawls, fail to do. She argues that, 'in their attempt to ground legitimacy on *rationality*, these theorists have to distinguish between mere agreement and rational consensus. That is why they assert that the process of public deliberation must realize the conditions of ideal discourses'.[112] Therefore, according to Mouffe:

> Consensus in a liberal-democracy is – and always will be – the expression of hegemony and the crystallization of power relations. The frontier that it establishes between what is and what is not legitimate is a political one, and for that reason it should remain contestable. To deny the existence of such a moment of closure, or to present the frontier as dictated by rationality or morality, is to naturalize what should be perceived as a contingent and temporary hegemonic articulation of 'the people' through a particular regime of inclusion-exclusion.[113]

It is against this consensus, and the hegemony it produces, that Mouffe operates.

For children, I suggest that their exclusion in these terms (as constitutive Others) serves a deeply political purpose. That is, as constitutive Others, they occupy the status of *pre*-political, rather than *a*political beings. Bringing children into the political realm through citizenship rights, risks having a depoliticizing effect by requiring advocates to shift the status of children from pre-political, to properly political. As shown, advocates must make claims that emphasize varying degrees of young people's reason, maturity and autonomy. By doing so, these arguments lessen the distinction between children and adults, transforming children into a future political subject with adult-like qualities. In short, emphasising children's adult-like qualities in order to include them in an expanded political realm produces sameness rather than plurality. For Mouffe, this would hold little political value: it is oriented toward the homogeneity and reinforcing the hegemony within. She argues that:

> A key point of Schmitt's approach is that, by showing that every consensus is based on acts of exclusion, it reveals the impossibility of a fully inclusive 'rational' consensus.... Liberalism has to negate antagonism since, by bringing to the fore the inescapable moment of decision – in the strong sense of having to decide in an undecidable terrain – what antagonism reveals is the very limit of any rational consensus.[114]

Mouffe further argues that 'liberalism's central deficiency in the political field [is] its negation of the ineradicable character of antagonism'.[115] That is, in order to circumvent the possibility of violence in the political, liberalism has a tendency to negate any possible antagonism by producing consensus. Liberalism seeks to produce this consensus by rejecting any non-liberal rationality. This goes to the interdependent relationship between the political legitimacy of the liberal state and the very goal of liberalism itself, as premised upon an autonomous citizen, and casts a net of complexity over the question of children's citizenship that is yet to be seriously contemplated. This chapter is an attempt to do so. This relationship informs, shapes and limits how we are able to think and talk about the desirability and possibility of children's right to citizenship. Autonomy rights, and specifically citizenship rights, have emerged in different social movements to transform the political status of an individual from excluded outsider to citizen; to bring women into the public sphere from the private realm of home and family; to reject the place of Indigenous peoples and other marginalized races as too primitive, incapable or less than human and thereby placing them outside of social and political spaces. However, children are the embodiment of concepts of childhood that are integral to the realization of a liberal citizen. It is in this sense that I argue that children are Mouffe's constitutive Other.

By following Mouffe's critique of liberalism in this way, we are able to more fully understand the problematic exclusion of children from the political realm and from citizenship. However, the exclusion of children from the political realm, even from this critical perspective, remains definitive of the included citizenry. Though it is not a perfect characterization, children are a constitutive Other that Mouffe considers crucial to understandings of citizenship and political inclusion. So even while Mouffe seeks a form of citizenship that is broader than that operating in liberal democracies, one broad enough to admit multiple rationalities and legitimize non-hegemonic claims, it cannot possibly be broad enough to admit children who are a necessary, and necessarily excluded, constitutive Other. In the absence of admitting children to the political realm, or realizing a broader political realm as Mouffe seeks to do, questions of the political might best move beyond claims of inclusion to an ethical debate about how those who remain excluded from the political realm might be engaged by those who are included. That is, to move beyond an antagonistic and agonistic friend–enemy relation to a more complex and lived experience of political inclusion and exclusion. One possibility for a more dynamic understanding of the democratic paradox is one that facilitates a more flexible and reflexive political boundary. It is important to remember, for example, that as adults we are free to enter and retreat from the political realm at will. The threshold of the political is not concretely fixed, but constituted by *people* whose experiences of the political both constitute and challenge the very threshold that they occupy.

Reading children's citizenship in this way is intended to highlight the political purpose of their exclusion, and their status as pre-political beings, as constitutive of the political realm. That is not to say that the inclusion of children should not be sought as a means for diversifying citizenship and creating possibilities for better accounting for children's interests in politics. However, it is to say that including children in the political realm carries no promise that these possibilities will be actualized. On the contrary, doing so brings with it the risk that it will depoliticize the status of children even further, by making them the same as their fellow adult citizens.

I have argued that children are pre-political subjects, but political nonetheless. Though they are not political agents, children do make the political possible: not only in their role as ideal, future-citizens that philosophers desire, but as that which separates the political from the non-political realm. Indeed, the exclusion of children is that which makes politics possible.

Conclusion

In these terms, bringing children into the political realm risks having a depoliticizing affect, as pursuing inclusion through citizenship rights presents the need to characterize young people as adult-like – emphasizing the homogeneity of the demos and undermining the plurality (multiple rationalities) of liberalism. By bringing children into the political realm, their inclusion serves no counter-hegemonic purpose, as Mouffe would intend. To bring children into citizenship, whether a liberal or republican citizenship, requires children to demonstrate some qualities of citizenship. Arguably, a republican theory of citizenship, such that Mouffe employs, has a higher standard that is further from the reach of children than the liberal standard. A republican citizen is not one who merely reproduces the political order, but one engaged critically in its operation. A liberal standard of citizenship allows Archard's minimum rationality to be a reasonable standard upon which we might distinguish voting citizens from non-voting citizens. It would have individuals who can grasp the meaning of choice between political leaders, and have the bare capacity to communicate that choice at the ballot box, possessing the most symbolic of citizenship rights, the vote. A republican standard of citizenship calls for a great deal more. Not only should republican citizens grasp the meaning of choice in political debates and contests, but also the ability to critically engage in those debates and to question the choices presented.

An understanding of the exclusion of children from the political realm and citizenship is best understood in political terms. That is, children's place at the frontier of the political does not reduce them to apolitical subjects. Further, extending citizenship rights to children does not necessarily transform their political status to a properly political subject. It is not a reason *not* to do so, that children's political status will necessarily be premised upon their difference – if not their exclusion – rather than their inclusion. Citizenship rights will do nothing to change this.

I have argued that children, insofar as they represent the boundary of inclusion/exclusion in citizenship, occupy Mouffe's constitutive Other at the threshold of the political. As a result, two conclusions must be made: first, that children are integral to our understandings of the concept of the political; and second, that to seek to establish children's citizenship, risks dissolving the meaning of the political. If the political realm is to be truly and wholly inclusive, and to capture everything, it risks collapsing. I argue here that debates about children's citizenship must be conducted with these considerations in mind.

Notes

1 Invernizzi and Milne (2005); Cockburn (2013); Rubenstein and Field (2013); Taylor and Smith (2009); Earls (2011); James Bohman (2011); James (2011).
2 Brian Milne (2013); Invernizzi and Williams (2008).
3 The 1967 referendum removed two references to Aboriginal people in the Australian Constitution, which had the effect of assigning states exclusive responsibility over Indigenous Australians. In practice, these provisions meant that Indigenous Australians could not be legislated for by the Commonwealth Parliament; Indigenous Australians were, in effect, not citizens of the Commonwealth of Australia but subjects of the state or territory in which they lived. The successful referendum effectively recognized Indigenous Australians as citizens of the Commonwealth of Australia.
4 Roche (1999: 479).
5 Young (1990: 54).
6 Cockburn (2013).
7 Ibid., 226.
8 Archard (2004: 98).
9 Ibid.
10 Ibid.
11 Marshall (1950).
12 Samantha Brennan considers how analysis of children's rights has been used to test rights theories more broadly; see Brennan (2002: 58).
13 Roche (1999:476).
14 Ibid.
15 Ibid., 481.
16 Ibid., 482.
17 Cohen (2005); Lister (2007).
18 The exception to this is stateless children, which is considered by Jacqueline Bhabha (2009). See also Bhabha (2011).
19 Lister (2007:695).
20 Ibid.
21 Ibid.
22 Kulynych (2001: 232).
23 Ibid.
24 Ibid., 239–50.
25 Ibid., 247–9. Specifically, Kulynych refers to children's descriptions of their experience of foster care, displacement due to war and race, and culture to argue that children's lives are politically relevant.
26 Ibid., 247.
27 Rehfeld (2011: 143).
28 Cohen (2005).
29 Rehfeld (2011: 142).
30 Ibid., 143.
31 Ibid., 146.
32 Goodin and Gibson (1997: 185–203).
33 Rehfeld (2011:149).
34 Ibid.
35 Ibid., 146
36 Ibid., 152. Rehfeld quotes Harry Brighouse, 'What Rights (if Any) do Children Have?', in Archard and Macleod (2002: 46).
37 Brighouse (2002: 46).
38 Rehfeld (2011: 157).
39 Ibid., 158–61.
40 Roche (1999: 482).

41 Ibid., 484.
42 Archard (2004).
43 Lister (2007: 694).
44 Cohen (2005) has explored this theory in the context of migrants, children and the disabled in her book; see also Cohen (2009). I only attend to her arguments around children which are attended to explicitly in Cohen (2005).
45 Lister (2007: 696). Here Lister points to three separate texts that use these terms.
46 Marshall (1950: 25).
47 Ibid., 697.
48 Ibid.
49 Dobrowolsky (2002: 67).
50 Roche (1999: 483).
51 Lister (2007: 698).
52 Ibid., 710–11.
53 Ibid., 712–14.
54 Ibid., 714–15.
55 Ibid.
56 Daiva Stasiulis (2002: 509).
57 Lister (2007: 716).
58 Roche (1999: 476–78).
59 Ibid., 484.
60 There is no explicit right to vote in Australia. Indeed, a referendum to entrench the right failed in 1974. Instead, the High Court of Australia has found that there is only an "implied" right to vote, established by sections 7, 8, 24 and 30 of the Australian Constitution. These sections refer to the Senate and House of Representatives being 'directly chosen by the people' and the rules regarding the 'qualification of electors' in state parliaments. There is nothing in these constitutional provisions to provide guidance on citizenship or broader citizenship rights in Australia. They are, for the most part, very technical provisions regarding parliamentary process.
61 The question of whether prisoners have a right to vote was considered in the 2005 High Court decision of *Roche* v. *Electoral Commissioner*, 223 CLR 162 (2007).
62 Archard (2004: 101) refers to a notion of "minimum rationality" with respect to voting rights.
63 *King* v. *Jones* (1972) 128 CLR 221, Barwick CJ.
64 *King* v. *Jones* (1972) 128 CLR 221, Barwick CJ, 29.
65 Gribbin (2004: 1).
66 Ibid.
67 Ibid., 2.
68 Ibid.
69 Australia Youth Summit (2008: 8).
70 Department of Prime Minister and Cabinet (2009).
71 Australia Youth Summit (2008) 'Australia 2020 Youth Summit Communique'.
72 Cohen (2005: 224).
73 Ibid.
74 Mouffe (1993: 9–22).
75 Cohen (2009). She also discusses migrants and the disabled as examples of individuals who may hold some, but not all, citizenship rights.
76 Though, she does not present any empirical evidence of this.
77 Cohen (2005: 224).
78 Ibid.
79 Ibid., 229–30.
80 Ibid., 230.
81 Ibid., 235.
82 Ibid.

83 Freeman (1992: 66–67).
84 Archard (2004: 100–2).
85 Young (1989: 250).
86 Ibid.
87 Arendt (1998: 9). Arendt's concept of natality and new beginnings was, interestingly, informed by her doctoral dissertation on a study of St Augustine, see Arendt (1996).
88 Arendt (2006: 173).
89 Ibid., 187.
90 Kulynych (2001: 243). In making this point, Kulynych quotes Hannah Arendt's argument that:

> The more completely modern society discards the distinction between what is private and what is public, between what can thrive only in concealment and what needs to be shown to all in the full light of the public world, the more, that is, it introduces between the private and the public a social sphere in which the private is made public and vice versa, the harder it makes things for its children, who by nature require the security of concealment in order to mature undisturbed.
>
> (Arendt 2006: 185)

91 Arendt (1959).
92 Arendt (2006: 182).
93 Carl Schmitt (1996).
94 Mouffe's characterization of a "constitutive Other" draws broadly from the work of Jacques Derrida and is to be distinguished from Edward Said's conception of Otherness, which lends itself more usefully to discussions of identity rather than an analysis of the concept of the political: see Said (1978).
95 Mouffe (2000: 36–57 especially).
96 Cohen (2005).
97 Prokhovnik (2009).
98 Schmitt (1996: xv).
99 Mouffe (2000: 3).
100 Though, it is possible: for example the conception of the child as sinner, as seen especially in debates about children's criminality.
101 Schmitt (1996: 32).
102 Mouffe (2000: 43).
103 Mouffe (2005).
104 Mouffe writes that '[t]his term has been proposed by Henry Staten to refer to a number of themes developed by Jacques Derrida around notions such as "supplement", "trace" and "difference"', ibid., 15.
105 Ibid.
106 Ibid., 16.
107 Ibid., 30.
108 Ibid., 21.
109 Schmitt (1996).
110 Mouffe (2000).
111 Mouffe (2005: 20).
112 Ibid., 48.
113 Ibid., 49.
114 Ibid., 11–12. Also see, Mouffe (1993: 115), where she writes that 'politics cannot be reduced to rationality precisely because it indicates the limits of rationality'.
115 Ibid., 10.

7   Governmentality

Introduction

According to Nikolas Rose, 'childhood is the most intensively governed sector of personal existence'.[1] The formative years are spent regulating the potential and the risk of a child, with a view towards producing the kind of individual that liberalism both identifies as its end and as its only source of legitimacy. In the previous three chapters, I have argued that debates about childhood and children's rights are both informed by and redeploy broader normative claims about social and political communities. Across these debates about criminality, sexuality and citizenship I have argued that claims of children's reason, maturity and autonomy establish the discursive limits of the children's rights discourse. These discursive limits operate to inform, shape and limit both the possibilities and impossibilities of how children, childhood and their rights can be known, claimed and debated.

I have argued that a paternalistic paradigm underpins this discourse of children's rights. It does so in ways that reflect the paternalistic paradigm evident in the liberal rights movements of women and Indigenous peoples. However, because children are in a literally paternal relationship with the adults around them, this paradigm presents more than a metaphorical device to overcome in the name of autonomy. Indeed, it presents autonomy itself as either an undesirable or impossible goal of children's rights. This paradigm is reinforced by a liberal rationality, which emphasizes reason, maturity and autonomy as requisite capacities for an individual's inclusion in public and political life. This positions a protectionist mode of children's rights against an autonomy mode of children's rights in a seemingly irreconcilable manner. I argue that this tension is underpinned by three main conceptions of childhood: the innocent, the sinner and the blank-slate. These conceptions of childhood are all oriented toward a future subject. While the rights advocated by protectionist and autonomy approaches differ, they share the goal of realizing a good, future-adult, liberal citizen.

In this chapter, I wish to problematize these claims by considering the concept of governmentality. Nikolas Rose first made the connection between childhood and governmentality.[2] The purpose of this chapter is to build on Rose's claim to argue further that governing childhood is fundamental to the rationality of liberal political philosophy. This sits at odds with broader liberal values derived from the Kantian tradition, which emphasizes individual freedom and autonomy. This unease sheds light on how and why the children's rights discourse comes to be caught between protectionist claims and autonomy claims. Indeed, this chapter will argue that liberal political philosophy is not the neutral foundation it is often presumed to be. Liberal political philosophy remains tied to normative claims about reason, maturity and autonomy, which are problematic not only for how we conceptualize childhood and our understanding of children's rights, but also for our understanding of the political itself.

Revisiting the earlier discussion of autonomy, I argue that there is an inherent tension within liberalism between the ideal of free-thinking and free-acting, autonomous individuals and liberalism's need for a rationality that ensures its legitimacy (via the consent of free-thinking and free-acting citizens) without the risk that those autonomous individuals will not provide this consent. It is against this apparent paradox of autonomy that I reconsider debates about children's rights. Using Nikolas Rose's analysis of governmentality and family, I argue that the child is both a potential contribution and source of risk to the liberal state. It becomes necessary to know children in terms of reason, maturity and autonomy so that it is possible to regulate their conduct in a manner that most efficiently maximizes this potential contribution, while minimizing its risk. Rose demonstrates that this occurs through medical and psychological understandings of "development", which identify various norms at different stages, and then govern toward this norm. These biological and psychological development norms, I argue, are not merely scientific artifices, but serve a political function in maintaining the liberal state. This disrupts our understanding of liberal political philosophy as a neutral discourse and children within it as apolitical subjects. I draw upon the work of Jacques Rancière and Judith Butler to question the boundaries of legitimacy in the political. Finally, I revisit my earlier discussion of Chantal Mouffe to consider the implications of this analysis for understandings of the concept of the political.

Revisiting autonomy and liberal political authority

One of the tasks of this book has been to understand the tensions between children's rights claims premised upon protection and those rights claims premised upon autonomy. I have suggested that in the work of Kant, Foucault and Hindess is a strong argument that a truly autonomous being is not possible. For Kant, autonomy is realized in the striving toward a true autonomy, driven by critical reflexivity. However, one never reaches that end and persisting becomes, paradoxically, the end in itself. For Foucault, existing within a complex of power relations means that there is always both freedom and constraint. Our autonomy then, is only a claim to freedom made within certain constraints. This is echoed by Hindess' articulation of liberal unfreedom. In this section, I wish to explore these tensions in the context of liberal political philosophy more broadly for both the state and for individuals. Following this, I will consider what implications this has for the children's rights debates discussed in the previous chapters.

On the one hand, liberal society serves liberty. It serves to facilitate, with as light a hand as possible, private, social and political realms in which individuals can consort and act according to their own free-will, in the pursuit of their liberty and happiness. These are the same individuals who offer the hypothetical consent to the liberal state, thereby providing its only claim to political legitimacy. In this sense, the liberal state exists by the grace of, and for the purpose of, free individuals. On the other hand, these free individuals are also a potential threat to liberal society. They are free to conduct themselves in ways contrary to the interests of the liberal state. It is broadly accepted that the liberal state is empowered to regulate conduct so as to maximize individual freedom, but also minimize the adverse effects of that freedom on society at large. Mitchell Dean describes this relation between security and liberty in the following way: 'security entails the regulation of certain individuals and groups in order to lead them to choose to exercise their liberty in a disciplined and responsible manner'.[3] The tension evident between power and freedom in these ways is not necessarily a critique of liberalism but instead one of its defining features.

There are three points to make about this paradoxical role for individual liberty in liberal societies. First, if free individuals are a source of political legitimacy of states, then it is necessary for a political community to produce those consenting individuals. Second, it is equally necessary for a political community to exclude those who cannot act as those consenting individuals. Third, free individuals also pose a risk to a liberal state, either by failing to consent to the legitimacy of the exercise of power by a state over its citizens or, more likely, by being an undermining influence (by failing to pay taxes, adhere to laws, or loudly occupy a soapbox).[4] Thus, there are two main aspects to the discussion that follows: first, the individual autonomy that defines the freedom of liberal citizens; second, the autonomy of the liberal state that seeks escape the need for an external source of political legitimacy and to diminish the status of the sovereign. I have undertaken this book ever-mindful that it is within this context that debates about children and their rights occur.

Capitalize Liberalism is both the embodiment of, as well as the foundation for, liberty and individualism. However, for Foucault, 'there is nothing more thoroughly harmful to freedom' than liberalism.[5] Some of Foucault's thinking sought to assert an alternative to the liberal rationality of the state, or a variation of its liberalism. Hindess refers to Foucault's attempt to assert a 'politics of ourselves' as an alternative to a politics of state,[6] while Mitchell Dean explores Foucault's critique of liberal political authority.[7] In response to the impact of the Enlightenment, which at once rejected external sources of political authority while continuing to maintain the political authority of the sovereign, Foucault declares that 'In political thought and analysis, we still have not cut off the head of the king.'[8] That is, even upon abandoning a sovereign figure, political theory remains tied to the need for sovereignty: for a locus of authoritative and legitimate power. This sits at odds with the liberty of citizens that liberal political philosophy otherwise emphasizes. For Dean, Foucault's understanding of the rationality of the liberal state is about modern government having its own peculiar and internal rationality. This attempt to theorize a different kind of liberal rationality, which is autonomous insofar as it is no longer required to answer questions about sovereignty and claims to legitimacy, is distinct from the autonomy of individuals and citizens. Hindess observes that the 'practice of what Foucault understands by political reason in fact creates conditions for the emergence of a politics and a political reason of a very different kind'.[9] Even by rejecting the sovereignty of God, it remains that political authority necessarily asserts a sovereign, and relies upon a source of legitimacy: this speaks to the conditions of liberal rationality, not to its autonomy. The idea that autonomous rationality is autonomous not merely in the liberal sense of free individuals engaging in critical thought, but also of no longer being tied to concepts of sovereignty or claims to, and debates about, political legitimacy, is a difficult one.[10] By abandoning references to God, or the strategies of a prince (to reference Machiavelli),[11] the rationality of the state locates its legitimacy in its citizens; in itself.[12] The rationality of the state is designed 'to reinforce the state itself ... by protecting it from other states and its own internal weakness'.[13] This weakness lies in the freedom of liberalism's citizens.

Liberalism, with its dual focus on free individuals and government of those individuals, relies upon each and every individual embodying certain desires and beliefs that serve a liberal society. For those that fail to observe these desires and beliefs, grounds are required to rationalize their exclusion from social and political communities. It is difficult for individuals to act subversively without being rendered invisible and irrelevant to the world. That is, in Rancière's terms, to act subversively is to engage in conduct that cannot be heard, that constitutes noise rather than speech. This is also emphasized by feminist theorist Judith Butler, who draws out the tension involved in being free or autonomous, but in ways that separate and exclude that free individual from social and political communities. She distinguishes between the oppressed, who 'already exist as a subject of some kind', and the 'unreal', who are 'fundamentally unintelligible'.[14] The citizen-child, discussed in Chapter 3, can only be made sense of in terms of reason, maturity and autonomy; that is, as an adult-like subject. The citizen-child is, itself, unintelligible.

Specifically, Butler argues that the language of liberal rights forces some (she is referring to gays, lesbians, transgenders and bisexuals) to 'present ourselves as bounded beings, distinct, recognizable, delineated, subjects before the law, a community defined by sameness'. She goes on to argue that:

> Although this language might well establish our legitimacy within a legal framework ensconced in liberal versions of human ontology, it fails to do justice to passion and grief and rage, all of which tear us from ourselves, bind us to others, transport us, undo us, and implicate us in lives that are not our [*sic*] own, sometimes fatally, irreversibly.[15]

Furthermore, Barry Hindess writes that,

> in Foucault's view while liberalism is certainly concerned to free the actions of individuals from police regulation and other forms of direct state control, it nevertheless aims to ensure that they behave according to the standards of civility, orderliness and reason required for the proper functioning of state agencies, markets, households and other aspects of social life.[16]

Those who adhere to these norms and regulatory conduct are deemed free, while the consequences of failing to act in these ways may be met with more direct and dogmatic regulatory conduct. Liberalism is freedom, so long as you fit within its scope of appropriate behaviour. Liberalism operates as a neutral and benevolent form of government, only if you are intelligible and normal. If you are not these things, liberalism will assert its values, knowledges and rationality in order to govern you toward the norm. If this is not possible, liberalism silences and marginalizes, positioning you out of view, possibly even out of existence.[17] This is evident in how those who are deemed not to possess rationality capacities are marginalized: as madmen or children, as deviants and delinquents. Children are institutionalized in the school and family in order to educate toward an adult, liberal citizenship. Madmen are institutionalized for the purposes of reform, but also to protect society. Deviants and delinquents are incarcerated for the same dual purpose of reform and protection. In this way, liberalism's governmentality is far from neutral, even in the supposedly private realms of family and child-raising. Indeed, these individuals may be governed out of the ability to act politically, not only through a denial of the right to vote, but because any political statement in their conduct is articulated and mediated in terms of their exclusion from the political community. This is what Chantal Mouffe's radical theory of democracy seeks to escape: liberal rationality defines the limits of the political; an ever-expanding constitution of the political (women, gays and lesbians, Indigenous peoples and so on) is only possible if those groups incorporate liberal rationality into their speech and conduct. This is because, as Barry Hindess observes, 'politically oriented action poses a particular problem for rationality of government committed to the illusory ideal of its own autonomy'.[18] If the political legitimacy of the state is the ability of its own rationality to question itself, that politically legitimacy does not serve to reinforce and secure the state, but rather undermines it. Therefore, to minimize this risk, it becomes necessary to exclude those individuals from the political community who embody this risk.

Knowing, normalizing and governing children

Government must, therefore, police liberty in order to preserve itself and maintain its sovereignty. To do this, the individuals that are governed must believe that they are free and that they agree to the limitations imposed upon their freedom. For the most part, these practices of government are rendered invisible. They limit the possibility of our individual autonomy in an effort to assert the autonomy of a liberal rationality government, and secure the state. It becomes necessary, then, to identify those individuals who pose a risk to the state and the liberal rationality of government from those who do not. To do this, the art of government requires knowledge of the state and all that it seeks to govern, including, most importantly, its population.[19] The purpose of modern government becomes the preservation of a reason of state, based on the 'problem of the *security* of the state'.[20] This demands discourses of knowledge that surround the population of a state, as much as any specific individual in it. It requires knowledge of madmen, children, deviants, etc.; this knowledge is required not for the preservation of individual liberty, but for the preservation of the liberal state.

Government is not merely actions of the state intervening in our lives, but a range of practices that "conduct our conduct" to produce normalized modes of being. This allows clear distinctions to be drawn within the population, between the governed and unintelligible, between the citizens and the delinquents and deviants that fall foul not only of the law, but also of the norm. Governmentality refers to the range of practices and relations of power that make this possible.

It is within this context of liberal society that debates about children and their rights occur. And so, it is also within this context that knowledge about who children are (not merely what they do) is produced, and making the truth-claims that inform what children's rights can be claimed as the focus of debate. Earlier, I considered liberal rationality, and the ideal of the free-thinking, free-acting autonomous individual. I argued that this sits at odds with the governmentality of liberal states. Judith Butler has theorized the limits of autonomy through gender and sexuality. She writes that

> where the body is not understood as a static and accomplished fact, but as an aging process, a mode of *becoming* that, in becoming otherwise, exceeds the norm, reworks the norm, and makes us see how realities to which we thought we were confined are not written in stone.[21]

This recognition of the body as a becoming reflects the language of childhood as a stage of becoming. In liberal society, I have argued, much concern around childhood is oriented towards ensuring that children become good, liberal, adult citizens. However, as Butler describes it, this process of becoming also produces the possibility for "becoming otherwise". Herein lies the potential risk of childhood and the need to govern childhood.

Barry Hindess explains that, for Foucault, liberalism requires both government and self-governing actors. These actors must be "autonomous" in the sense that they are both fully developed and free. In the West, 'this developmental view means that many people ... will be seen as not – or not yet – ready for freedom'.[22] Childhood, then, is a period in which liberalism's necessary actors are formed. They are formed by a set of governing practices that serve a specific end: to create the kinds of individuals necessary for a good, liberal social and political community. I argue that this is not necessarily a free and autonomous individual (evident in Butler's characterization of becoming otherwise) but, rather, a normalized individual (one that has "become").

The governing practices that produce this normalized individual and the political purpose it serves produces a tension between the notion of an autonomous individual citizen and a good, liberal citizen. On the one hand, writes Hindess:

> as a subject that knows, man is constituted by the faculties of reason and perception and is therefore capable, at least in principle, of autonomous action in something like the Kantian sense. On the other hand, like all objects of knowledge, many appear to be moulded by the effects of external forces and stimuli.[23]

For Hindess, this produces a tension between a view of the 'qualities of rationality and moral autonomy' as inherent to human beings, or as 'the product of very particular conditions', such as experience and education.[24] If reason and autonomy are inherent in our being, then what is left of a distinction drawn between childhood and adulthood based upon claims to maturity and reason? If an individual's subjectivity is determined as much by external forces as one's own faculties of reason and perception, then the 'very particular conditions' to which Hindess refers must govern individuals in ways that operate against their autonomy. Indeed, the conditions to which Hindess refers are arguably governed from before our birth and continue throughout our lives, irrespective of any reason or maturity or autonomy that we might claim along the way.

There is always the possibility for subversive action, for rebellion, disagreement and refusal to adhere to the norm. Indeed, without this possibility one could not be (in Foucault's terms) the subject of power, but instead would be under physical constraint.[25] However, the freedom and autonomy that are exercised in these forms of conduct are always and necessarily exercised *against* the norm, against government. In this sense, autonomy presents not as an absolute or total freedom, but merely an assertive action made in our relation to things. It cannot be a completely independent act by a completely autonomous being because it is an act that operates against norms and within discourses of knowledge that already determine the possibilities (and impossibilities) of action. Our autonomy, quite simply, is governed. To suggest otherwise is to suggest that we exist beyond society, beyond relations to other individuals and things, including relations of power. Autonomy, therefore, lies not only in the particular exercise of reason in any given scenario, but also in the action that is exercised within a set of existing power relations. Autonomy is not complete and absolute, but conditioned and conditional.

Returning to childhood, the distinction between a risky child and a young potential citizen was made, argues Nikolas Rose, 'not so much by *moralization* as by *normalization*'.[26] That is, the distinction is made not by inherent claims about goodness and badness, but by the discovery of a normal child, which allows the deviant child (and the exceptional child) to be identified (and thus, reformed or punished). The use of intelligence tests and other diagnostic tools relies upon a developmental model of life that regards age as the 'key conceptual device for ranking individuals according to their abilities'.[27] What these tests and other assessments facilitated was a 'degree of adaptation of individual children to the expectations others had of them'.[28] That, and not the realization of any inherent truth, is the product of normalization. It 'codifies, mathematizes and normalizes difference'.[29] It also assigns to that difference a condition of personhood that operates to include or exclude them from the world. What is judged and administered as a result of this process is no longer 'what one *does* but what one *is*'.[30]

Rose describes this as a 'new scientific gaze focused upon the young children from the perspective of evolution. Observation of young children could, it appeared, cast light upon the nature of human evolution and the characteristics distinguishing man from the animals'.[31] Further, in marking out the development of a young person along a spectrum of specific ages, there is not merely an observation being made, but a valuation:

> It contains not only a judgment about what is desirable, but an injunction as to a goal to be achieved. In doing so, the very notion of 'the normal' today awards power to scientific truth and expert authority.[32]

This was evident in the cases discussed in Chapter 4 on criminality. And so it is, Rose argues, that 'the soul of the young citizen has become the object of government through expertise'.[33] This establishes children at the heart of a set of power relations, in which they are known by discourses of science and of politics. This, however, does not necessarily subjugate children into passivity. Rose observes that this expert authority over children is challenged in many forums, usually by parents on behalf of children.[34]

What Rose does not specifically observe in these relations of power is that discourses about children and childhood have been constructed in such a way that it is impossible for children to know themselves. To follow Foucault, to know in a liberal society is to be able to reason in terms consistent with the dominant paradigm. It is not that children reason in terms beyond the dominant paradigm (such as Carol Gilligan's argument regarding girls and an ethic of care)[35] but that children are defined as *not* being able to reason at all; they are defined by their intellectual immaturity. These discourses are premised upon the qualities of maturity and reason and autonomy, along with other qualities such as scientific objectivity. This reduces the possibilities for children's utterances to be heard as speech, rather than mere noise. This, in turn, has implications for the central tension in children's rights debates between a protectionist mode and an autonomy mode. If children's knowledge of themselves and their childhood cannot be heard, if they are silenced not by practices of exclusion but by discourses of knowledge and politics itself, then it is impossible to position autonomy as the foundation for children's rights. The paternalistic paradigm of a children's rights discourse caught between protection and autonomy claims presents as irresolvable and inescapable.

Children's political subjectivity

If childhood is the period of most intensive governing, then it is possible to see that one of the essential tasks of a liberal society is to distinguish the potential contribution from the potential risk in its population, to regulate the conduct of individuals so as to maximize this potential and minimize this risk.[36] To do this, it is necessary to have knowledge of the population. This speaks to the potential and risk dichotomy that underlies the role of individuals and citizens in liberal political communities, and is reflected in the protection versus autonomy claims of children's rights debates. Further, it is important to ensure a population that embodies the values and practices that underpin liberal society. It is not possible to separate children from the rest of the population in this process. On the contrary, children and childhood are crucial to the preservation and progress of liberal society. Hence, Rose's concern that childhood is the most heavily governed part of an individual's life arises from the necessity of governing childhood in liberal society.

Rose's work on governmentality opened up space for discussion of the governing of childhood more specifically.[37] Rose and others have focused on developing understandings of governmentality, and the practices and conduct present in liberal societies that come to be employed upon children and families. However, my interest moves beyond this focus on governmentality to look more closely at its impact on the kinds of claims that are made in debates about children's rights. I argue that the impact of governmentality on childhood is not just a relation of power that diminishes freedom in liberal societies, but one that determines what claims can be made about childhood, children and their rights. Specifically, I argue that children's rights claims are necessarily grounded in a pre-existing ideal of their future-adult life and citizenship, and this in turn determines how we can think about politics in childhood and understand the boundaries of the political itself.

As discussed above, discourses of knowledge are crucial to this project. The work of Michel Foucault has documented extensively the rise of interest in the eighteenth and nineteenth centuries across a breadth of individual and social behaviours. This reflected a concern with population and security of the state. The disciplines of medicine, psychology and psychiatry played just one role in this. However, these 'psy-knowledges', Rose argues, established forms of expertise that reshaped subjectivity by constructing images of what we should become. Rather than merely being cured of illness, psy-knowledges have urged us to 'help fulfil the dream of realigning what we are with what we want to be'.[38] It follows that in a world that governs what we want to be through a range of disciplinary practices, the family and period of childhood are key sites within which these practices are enacted. It is in this sense that the family can be viewed as a highly governed institution. The outcome is the production of particular political subjects. I argue that this is not just the production of a citizen, but also the production of a *child* as that future-adult citizen. It produces the child as a future-adult subject and a becoming. In turn, this status as a future-adult subject necessarily determines that children are not yet present in politics, that their lives are prior to the political and that any claims made on their behalf are not political claims. This neutralizes children's rights debates in ways that preclude the possibility of politics in children's lives and reinforces children's rights as a discourse impossibly caught between claims for protection on the one hand, and claims for autonomy on the other.

Nikolas Rose observed that the late nineteenth century saw childhood emerge 'as a distinct period during which bad habits could be laid down and have a lifelong influence'.[39] This created a need to identify 'feeble-minded children' in order to separate them from 'the rest of the school population and segregated in specialized institutions that would seek to awaken their moral sensibilities and increase their resistance to vice and crime'.[40] This process gave rise to, notably, a juvenile justice system and reformatory schools. However, the rise of the modern, compulsory, public school system itself also played a role in this. Rose observes that two purposes motivated the rise of a compulsory school system, each serving two different kinds of children: a working-class child, who posed a risk to society; and a middle-class child, whose potential had to be maximized.[41] This again reflects the dichotomy that informs the key tension in children's rights debates as between protection claims and autonomy claims. In this way, education served its main purpose not in "teaching", but rather as an emancipatory programme designed to save children from the vices of their lower class, and to save society from the potential risk these children presented. These examples demonstrate the external forces that govern childhood. Both children and society are governed via the institution of the school. However it is conceptualized, childhood presents an opportunity to determine the future of society and politics. To govern society demands the government of childhood, which represents future life. This is not only problematic in its masking of power and the limits on freedom it imposes, as Rose argues, but also because it dramatically shapes how we are able to speak of, and for, children and their childhood. This governmentality of childhood is a political function, and one that limits the claims that can be made in debates about children's rights.

Rose argues that a public education system was only one institution that sought to realize a normalized, liberal individual. He argues that technologies of government expanded into the private sphere of the home, though carefully did so without destroying the autonomy of the family.[42] In this way, governing practices become internalized, not only by children but also by those who parent them. To demonstrate this, Rose highlights the "playgroup" movement in the United Kingdom during the 1960s, in which communities of mothers (they were mostly mothers rather than fathers) organized themselves to meet regularly in each other's homes to engage in early education practices. Together with the rise of games, books, television and other media as sources of information about how to be a good mother who was ensuring the normal development of her children, these resources sought to assist parents rather than to replace them (as Kindergartens and schools do).[43] Where schools and Kindergartens govern childhood in a external manner, the playgroup movement represents the internalization of childhood governmentality: informed by outside relations of power and privileged knowledges, but conducted by parents themselves in their own homes. The governing practices that were formed were not practices of the state, but practices of parents. As Rose argues, this incorporates:

> pedagogic norms within the mother's own desires and fantasies, for them to form an inescapable and pervasive grid for calculating and judging her own behavior and that of her child ... the mother was to operate the regimes in the 'privacy' of her own home, under the direction of her personal wishes and fears.[44]

The individual governed here is the parent, who, in turn, enacts a regime of government upon her child, ostensibly acting in the child's best interest; otherwise articulated as educating toward the norm, and conditioning the autonomy of the future-adult subject. The normalization of the child and childhood repeatedly reiterates the preoccupation with development, of becoming rather than being. The developmental norms of a child become the norms that a child is measured against, as good, bad, right, wrong, culpable or not culpable, mature or immature, rational or irrational, autonomous or dependent. As discussed in Chapters 3, 4 and 5, the debates about what children do and do not have rights to do, come to be oriented around these very terms. The kinds of governing practices that institute and maintain these norms are the same as those that regulate our adult selves as citizens, as autonomous members of our liberal political community.

Nikolas Rose regards the emphasis on protection as a counter-discourse to the autonomy, not of the child, but of the family unit:

> Faced with the complex of legal powers that have come to surround the family, especially those within and around the juvenile court system, a powerful 'counter-discourse' has taken shape, which has sought to limit incursions into the freedom of the family in the name of the protection of children.[45]

The protection of children here is equally about the protection of the autonomy of the family unit. However, in cases where the protection of the child is at odds with the autonomy of the family unit, children's rights debates remain oriented around a protection versus autonomy dichotomy. A protectionist mode advocates greater regulation of the family: for example, legislating against parents' "right" to smack their children as a form of discipline in order to protect children from violence and potential abuse. Or, an autonomy mode that de-emphasizes the regulation of the family in order to give greater voice to the expressed interests and desires of the child. This is rationalized on the ground that one of the great risks to children is their inability to speak and act for themselves on their own behalf and that they are in a relationship of power with adults around them.

Discourses that take children as their subject gravitate to a strong historical literature based around a developmental model. The normalization of individual development has informed how we conceptualize and know young people. Politically, this serves a very specific purpose: not to realize an autonomous individual in a Kantian sense, as many references to political citizenship would have it, but to form a self-regulating member of liberal society; to form, in Rose's terms, a governed soul. Again, there need be no objection to this purpose, since all societies must reproduce themselves and do so on the basis of existing norms. When departures from existing norms do occur, they are likely to be attached to "generational" shifts. For example, in the West, young adults largely drove the social and political movements of the 1960s, marking their difference from their parents' more conservative generation. However, it seems a great misapplication of the term "autonomy" when discussions of liberty in debates about children's rights (both claims for and against) refer to the realization of a normalized individual-like-all-others, rather than a free-thinking and free-acting individual who embodies the possibility of new beginnings.[46]

I argue here that the purpose of children's protection or autonomy is not strictly grounded in empirical claims of their best interest. What these technologies of governance, practices of normalization, and self-governing tools reveal, is that there is no way to separate the child and his or her interests from the broader functions of our liberal society and the role of the family within it. This does not mean that we cannot still *act* in what we regard to be the child's best interests or justify it in empirical terms. The discourse of children's rights is such that advocates do act in these ways and face great difficulties in doing otherwise. My argument is that doing so, unquestioningly, is problematic and that the purpose of children's rights themselves cannot be reduced to this alone. Instead, children's rights claims are also in the service of our liberal society. Whether or not this is a good thing is a normative debate, which occurs within a liberal approach to children's rights. My argument takes a critical position that is at arm's length from this. In the meantime, it is important to be clear within debates about children's rights that we no more seek to protect children than we seek to value children's (potential) autonomy, but only insofar as they are able to offer consent to the liberal state and operate within liberal regimes of governmentality. It is impossible to separate the interests of children from broader social and political agendas. To approach children's rights as a neutral, liberal discourse beyond the reach of political contest and dissensus is to misunderstand children's role in public and political life. This book has not argued that children are political actors in their own right. Indeed, Chapter 6 presented the paradoxical character of children's citizenship. However, while it may be impossible to characterize children in political terms, that does not mean that they are not crucial to our understanding of the political in liberal society. It is this complexity of the relationship between children, childhood and our understanding of the concept of the political that children's rights must be better attuned to in order to escape the fundamental tension between protection and autonomy arguments that characterize its debates.

Through these debates, it is apparent that adults are trying to navigate children toward a social and political community in which they operate as free, liberal citizens. However, our liberal political community is governed in ways that mean that the ideal of autonomy can never, really, be reached. How can we make autonomy the goal of children's rights, if autonomy itself is inherently limited within the governmentality of liberal political communities? And if autonomy were not underpinned by claims to reason and maturity, by what would we distinguish childhood from adulthood? What good is a mode of protectionist rights if it precludes any possibility of young people acting and thinking freely, which liberalism purports to value so greatly? Finally, by problematizing conceptions of childhood, rights and liberalism in these ways, is it satisfactory to remain tied to reason, maturity and autonomy as the key terms of children's rights debates? I argue that there is still some worth in these concepts: reason, particularly critical reason, provides a language and standard for debate through which a political community is able to make decisions about agreed problems; indeed, critical reason is also what makes it possible to enter into debates, while disagreeing with the problem itself; maturity embodies a range of lived experiences that shape how one reasons, and to consider these experiences redundant because they exist in the past is less than helpful; finally, autonomy, despite its impossibility, offers an aspirational and normative ideal that would be difficult to surrender without doing away with political liberalism completely. However, despite my acknowledgment of the worth of these concepts, my greater argument is that we cannot remain tied to these concepts in a satisfied and uncritical manner. It is not satisfactory to remain tied to them in the ways that they are currently employed, because they present insurmountable challenges for those seeking to understand children, childhood and their rights. If, after critical reflection, a paradigm of reason, maturity and autonomy is the most useful framework for conceptualizing children and their rights, then it is much better that we have a strong justification for believing so, rather than simply accepting it by the accident that is the history of a political order still attached to its king's head.[47]

Governing and the concept of the political

This governmentality analysis of childhood furthers ideas raised in the preceding chapter, regarding the boundary of the political in liberal political communities. Whereas much of children's rights discourse positions children as excluded (for protectionists a necessary exclusion, for autonomy advocates a problematic exclusion), governmentality offers a perspective that brings the place of children into the political more explicitly, through an analysis of power relations. My earlier analysis of Chantal Mouffe's concept of the political placed children at its threshold as an excluded, but ever-present challenge to that exclusion. In the final section of this chapter, I argue that children can be both excluded from, and constitutive of, the political. This more complex analysis of children's political subjectivity is one designed to complicate our understandings of the rights claims made about and on behalf of children.

Judith Butler's description of oppression offers a more complicated understanding of political subjectivity. She claims that:

To be oppressed means that you already exist as a subject of some kind, you are there as the visible and oppressed other for the master subject, as a possible or potential subject, but to be unreal is something else again. To be oppressed you must first become intelligible. To find that you are fundamentally unintelligible (indeed, that the laws of culture and of language find you to be an impossibility) is to find that you have not yet achieved access to the human, to find yourself speaking only and always as if you were human, but with the sense that you are not, to find that your language is hollow, that no recognition is forthcoming because the norms by which recognition takes place are not in your favour.[48]

In mainstream liberal thought, acts of political exclusion are considered unjust. This is the implication of paternalistic practices on women and Indigenous peoples addressed in Chapter 1. However, to be oppressed also suggests that you are known and that the way in which you are known is at odds with your knowledge of your self. In order to be known, and therefore oppressed, Butler explains that it is necessary to be intelligible.[49] Jacques Rancière also expresses this sentiment in his claim that:

If there is someone you do not wish to recognise as a political being, you begin by not seeing him as the bearer of the signs of politicity, by not understanding what he says, by not hearing what issues from his mouth as discourse.[50]

That is, what marks the exclusion of children from the political realm is not necessarily tied to their lack of reason, maturity or autonomy, but rather their political unintelligibility. What the alternative conceptions of childhood as innocents, blank-slates or sinners share is that they are not political. Instead, they are apolitical, pre-political or anti-political, and have been constructed as such to preserve the integrity of the ideal, liberal political realm.[51] In the Introduction to this book, I offered examples of three scenarios in which a child entered the public, political realm. These scenarios set up different claims about what rights children should and should not have. They also challenged the exclusion of children from the political realm. They are examples of children being inserted into a political space that cannot make sense of them. To make sense of children as political actors, as criminals or even as sexual beings, does not simply disturb our understandings of childhood but our understandings of the political. It is in this way that I have argued that these issues set up political questions about our understandings of childhood, children and their rights.

It is for this reason that I return to the discussion of the concept of the political raised earlier. I argued that debates about children's citizenship are tied to claims about their reason, maturity and autonomy. This is notwithstanding that the exclusion of children from the political realm is a defining aspect of it. To include children in a theory of citizenship, which Elizabeth Cohen argued was both desirable and possible, can only produce a shift in the age of citizenship and not a rethinking of citizenship itself, which she set out to do. The reason for this, I argued, was because of the place of children in constituting the threshold of the political as a constitutive Other. Those children who are excluded from the political, whether by an arbitrarily determined voting age or a conception of children as apolitical or pre-political, may very well have a claim to be included. Children's rights advocates who make autonomy claims do so on this basis; advocates of protection rights dismiss this claim outright. The tension between these competing positions must be taken seriously to fully understand debates about children's rights.

The governing of childhood helps make sense of this tension by revealing how protection facilitates autonomy in liberal communities. That is, the protection of children and of childhood as a period of becoming, makes it possible to craft individual's autonomy in such a way that maximizes freedom while minimizing the risk inherent within that freedom. Protection and autonomy are not at odds with one another, because the former plays a vital role in making the latter possible. This speaks to the paradox of liberalism. The lack of freedom that might otherwise be construed as illiberal is actually definitive of political liberalism. Uday Mehta makes this argument when she claims that the origins of liberalism are premised on two rather contradictory sets of claims:

first, that human beings are by their nature free, rational, and equal; second, that they are therefore capable of murder, theft, and mayhem and are hence in mortal danger. Liberalism, thus originates in ambivalence – in the need to order, if not limit, what it valorizes to be natural and emancipatory.[52]

Therefore, freedom must be limited for political liberalism, premised upon plurality and equality, to be possible. However, the limits on this freedom must as much as possible be self-governing. If there are too many external limits on individual freedom, liberalism finds itself dangerously compromised.

Chantal Mouffe's description of the democratic paradox further positions the tension between a democratic politics and individual human rights and liberties:

democratic logics always entail drawing a frontier between 'us' and 'them', those who belong to the 'demos' and those who are outside it. This is the condition for the very exercise of democratic rights. It necessarily creates a tension with the liberal emphasis on the respect of 'human rights', since there is no guarantee that a decision made through democratic procedures will not jeopardize some existing rights. In a liberal democracy limits are always put on the exercise of the sovereignty of the people. Those limits are usually presented as providing the very framework for the respect of human rights and as being non-negotiable. In fact, since they depend on the way 'human rights' are defined and interpreted at a given moment, they are the expression of the prevailing hegemony and thereby contestable. What cannot be contestable in a liberal democracy is the idea that it is legitimate to establish limits to popular sovereignty in the name of liberty. Hence its paradoxical nature.[53]

The paradox here is the tension between democratic decision-making, that is premised upon consensus and 'prevailing hegemony', and liberal freedom. While ideas and claims are contestable within the *demos*, the limitation of freedoms in order to preserve the *demos* is not. To extend Chantal Mouffe's paradox, political exclusion can be justified in defence of the political realm, just as restrictions on freedom can be justified in the defence of liberty.

I am not arguing for a fully inclusive politics, or suggesting that the exclusion of children from the political realm is necessarily unjustified. On the contrary, I share Hannah Arendt's concern that a fully inclusive political realm risks collapsing into a social realm.[54] Instead, what this democratic paradox helps illuminate is that how the *demos* determines its limits, and therefore, the limits of the political are not a neutral or natural function of liberalism but an uncomfortable, paradoxical function of liberalism; one which is fully encompassing and also limiting. Children play a central role in this liberal function and debates about their rights can no longer be understood in isolation from this politics.

Whereas Chantal Mouffe seems to argue that the legitimacy of limiting the political in the name of liberty is not contestable, my argument – as it relates to children – claims that it is. While those beyond the threshold of politics find themselves unable to enter the realm of political discourse in which decisions are contested and made, those at the threshold (such as children) represent a persistent reminder of liberalism's political exclusion. To argue for the lowering of the voting age from 21 to 18, or from 18 to 16, is the agitation of this threshold. In the decision-making process of determining an age of entry into this aspect of political life, one expands the political realm by moving its boundary, not removing it. The boundary is ever-present and its place, while always determined by those within the political realm, is constantly subject to challenge from those beyond it. It is subjected to challenge, not only by those agitating at the threshold by making claims and representations of their own that demand to be recognized as political, but by the very presence of exclusion.

Children offer an important insight into the operation of private and political realms because they occupy a unique status in that their exclusion from the political realm is only a temporary one. Despite debate about the capacities of children for reason, maturity and autonomy, it remains notable that children have to do very little in order to be admitted into the political realm. Indeed, all they have to do is 'grow up'.[55] There are few tests for admittance, few initiations; all that is required is the passing of time, during which an individual's age ticks over from 17 years and so many days, to 18 years. It is an arbitrary threshold, one that is problematic for those who debate what rights children should or should not have. However, it is also an unusual threshold in that its existence can be rationalized on the basis that this exclusion is what makes politics possible. Even for those who might view the exclusion of children as unjust, it is an injustice that remedies itself so long as children live into adulthood.

However, this does not speak to the fixed nature of the political realm, but to its fluidity. Without having to demonstrate any particular capacity for admittance, the boundary reveals itself as porous and not cemented. This is also evident in how we understand adults in the political realm. An individual does not move into the political realm, only to have iron gates lock behind them. Rather, adults, having been recognized as a legitimate actor in the political realm, are free to move across the boundary at will. In this way, the political realm can be viewed as dynamic and fluid. The political autonomy of adulthood lies not in particular capacities or forms of action, but instead in the freedom to move across the threshold of private and political life. Sometimes, this even means asserting private experiences as political. Adults continue to avail themselves of the privacy and protection of the private realm of home and family life without making themselves less legitimate in the political realm. On the contrary, the private realm becomes a space that allows the political actor to rest, regenerate and re-emerge into the political realm refreshed.[56] For children, this movement is denied. That children require the care and protection of their private family life makes them ineligible for autonomy in the political realm. For adults, protection and autonomy are not mutually exclusive; for children, they are. The denial of children's political autonomy is, in this sense, not premised upon a lack of capacity for political action but upon the arbitrary determination by the *demos* that the political realm is better served by the exclusion of children, rather than their inclusion.

Conclusion

In Chapter 1, I referred to a particularly Kantian view of autonomy that characterizes the liberal political subject. Immanuel Kant described Enlightenment as 'man's emergence from his self-incurred immaturity'.[57] Here, Enlightenment is both an historical moment and an individual quest. The two are entwined. Enlightenment, in the individuated sense, is the process by which one ceases to be immature. By exercising one's own reason, you justify (and realize) your own freedom and sovereignty, and find yourself closer to his ideal of autonomy. Kant's maturity is the realization and exercise of an individual's capacity to reason. At the same time, the Enlightenment as a historical moment saw the birth of the liberal state arising from a rejection of unquestioned, divine authority tied to this belief that an individual was sovereign over himself and no other.

Furthermore, the legitimate political authority of the liberal state is premised upon a social contract between the governed and those that govern. Liberalism is a political theory that, at least hypothetically, creates a consensual relationship of power between the governed and those that govern, requiring a political subject that can provide the necessary consent. To provide this consent, you must engage in a rational act that leads you to accept this relationship, trading off degrees of your own freedoms in exchange for protection of your rights. Arising from the Enlightenment, this has never been considered a natural process. Instead, it is one that demands reason, maturity and experience. An individual born with the natural capacity to develop this reason, maturity and experience requires the appropriate education and care to become this adult citizen: the 'subject child, becomes the adult citizen'.[58] As a consequence, the child exists as both a pre- and future- citizen figure.

The work of this book has been to problematize children's rights debates. In doing so, I have sought to reveal the future-adult subject as a political configuration of childhood. This is evident in alternative conceptions of childhood that each, in their own way, reflect a political ideal of future citizenship while also denying children's political subjectivity. However, to realize the ideal of liberal citizenship, it is necessary that childhood exists as a period of development that is separate from, and exists prior to, adulthood. This adulthood encompasses not only political citizenship, but also the individual's role as a law-abiding member of the social community, and a healthy and responsible member in the private realm of sex and family. For all this to be possible, without instituting authoritarian forms of rule and conduct that undermine the liberal state, it is necessary that childhood becomes a time of government. Governing childhood produces good liberal individuals in the realms of political, public, social and private life. This is a political project. Claims about what rights children should and should not have cannot be separated from this political project. Children, are, at once, both outside of, and constitutive of, the political. This, I argue, is the politics of becoming adult.

Notes

1 Rose (1999: 121).
2 Rose (1991).
3 Dean (2010: 139).
4 On the significance of the soapbox in Australian free speech laws, see Chesterman (2001).
5 Hindess (1997: 276).
6 Ibid., 258.
7 Dean (2010: 156–63, especially).
8 Foucault (1978: 88–9).
9 Hindess (1997: 257).
10 Ibid.
11 *The Prince [1532]* (1984).
12 Dean (2010: 104).
13 Ibid.
14 Butler (2004: 30).
15 Ibid., 20.
16 Hindess (1997: 268).
17 Butler (2004).
18 Hindess (1997: 269).
19 Dean (2010: 104–5).
20 Ibid., 105.
21 Butler (2004: 29).
22 Hindess (2001: 95).
23 Ibid., 98.
24 Ibid.
25 Foucault writes that 'slavery is not a power relationship when a man is in chains, only when he has some possible mobility, even a chance of escape': Foucault (1994d: 342).
26 Rose (1999: 128).
27 Ibid., 139.

28 Ibid.
29 Ibid., 140.
30 Ibid.
31 Ibid., 141; Also see, generally, Morss (1995).
32 Rose (1999: 131).
33 Ibid., 131.
34 Ibid., 131–3.
35 Gilligan (1982).
36 Ibid., 121.
37 Discussions of childhood and governmentality include McGillivray (1997); Brownlie (2001); Nadesan (2010; Freeman (1997b).
38 Rose (1999: xiii).
39 Ibid., 151.
40 Ibid., 137.
41 Ibid., 178–9.
42 Ibid., 196.
43 Ibid.
44 Ibid.
45 Ibid., 203.
46 This references Hannah Arendt's concept of natality as discussed earlier in this book (pp. 145).
47 Foucault and Rabinow (1984: 63).
48 Butler (2004: 218). As above, Butler refers specifically to intelligibility of the oppressed subject.
49 The importance of recognition as a form of justice arises from the work of Axel Honneth; see Honneth (1995).
50 Rancière (2010: 38).
51 The sinner can be characterized as anti-political in the sense that they refuse to adhere to the rules of shared discourse.
52 Mehta (1992: 1).
53 Mouffe (2000).
54 Hannah Arendt (1998).
55 Onora O'Neill (1988: 463).
56 This adopts Hannah Arendt's characterization of the private realm, though I acknowledge the breadth of feminist literature that criticizes this private/public divide in politics.
57 Kant [1784].
58 Arneil (2002).

8   The politics of becoming adult

This project set out to consider the distinctly political problems of how we understand, discuss and debate childhood, children and their rights. This is informed, in part, by a broader consideration of liberal rights. For adult groups, the paternalistic paradigm through which reason, maturity and autonomy was denied can be redressed through claims to those very qualities. However, in debates about children's rights, this tension is presented as irreconcilable. Therefore, the intent is to offer a further contribution that might allow us to better understand the tensions between protection and autonomy claims that characterize children's rights debates. Rather than engage in debates about what rights I believe children should or should not have, this book offers an analysis of how we understand childhood, children and their rights. To do this, I have used Foucault's method of problematization as a way to cleave open some space in which to ask unconventional questions about children's rights. By doing so, this book has shifted how we make sense of children's political subjectivity. It has sought to make the politics of children's lives intelligible, by revealing the conceptual limitations that make this politics unintelligible. By revealing reason, maturity and autonomy as the discursive limits of children's rights debates, I have argued through an analysis of governmentality that children's rights debates cannot be separated from broader social and political ideals. Specifically, I have argued that these debates are not exclusively child-centered, but rather come to focus upon a future-adult subject. As a result, this analysis allows controversies of childhood to be considered in new and different terms. The purpose of re-reading these controversies is no longer tied to normative objectives of children's rights, and instead seeks to complicate our understandings of the political.

When Elizabeth Eckford sought to enter the newly desegregated Little Rock High School, a photographer captured a public and deeply political moment. Yet, despite photos of her being splashed across newspapers, Elizabeth Eckford disappeared almost entirely from view. Instead, what emerged from this moment was a heated debate between political philosopher, Hannah Arendt, and African American author, Ralph Ellison.[1] This debate centred on whether or not schools were a proper site for politics. Arendt and Ellison disagreed with one another about where the adults in this moment were. For Arendt, adults were neglectfully absent. For Ellison, despite their physical absence, African American adults were ever-present in that moment, as part of a broader political claim for the right to equal education as a necessary part of securing lasting social and political change.

The image of Elizabeth Eckford was confronting, not for its violence or its outright racism but for its ordinariness: a 15-year-old girl walking to school. Every day, then and now, schoolgirls and schoolboys leave home, often alone, making their way to school via public footpaths, trams, buses and trains and almost always arrive safely at the school gates. By doing so, these schoolchildren transition from the protection of the private realm of home and family life, through a public domain from which they are otherwise sheltered, and finally reach school, where they are ushered back into the care and guidance of authoritative adults. The presence of children in the public domain is a brief, yet frequent, interlude between private and social realms. Elizabeth Eckford's interlude was notable, not because she appeared in the public realm, but because she got stuck there. She found herself in the middle of a public space, a space where politics is possible *because* of the exclusion of children. As a result, her place in that moment was rendered unintelligible. For Arendt to make sense of this unintelligible moment, she viewed Eckford as a victim, unjustly thrust into a political fight that a child should not have to fight. For Ellison, Eckford was the victim of a broader and social injustice attached to the segregation and racism that characterized African American's lives. For Ellison, the lives of all African American children were political. It was unfortunate that the schoolgirl found herself in this position, but it was a fight all African Americans had to fight.[2] To make Eckford intelligible, Ellison refocused discussion of her identity from her child status to her racial status. As a child, Elizabeth Eckford's experience was unjust and unwarranted; as an African American child, it was unjust but necessary. What informs our discomfort with a child entering public and political space? It is the knowledge that these public and political spaces are fraught with complexities and difficulties that take a toll on those who enter; the belief that the private realm is one where these complexities and difficulties do not exist;[3] and the necessity of childhood as being a protected time of life in order to properly prepare individuals for public life and political fights.

Following the 1993 murder of James Bulger, the British public were not just coming to grips with how to ensure justice for a young boy murdered by two other young boys, but with the very understanding of childhood. Childhood innocence was both startlingly evident in the trust James Bulger showed when he took the hands of his would-be murderers and startlingly absent in the violence that his two murderers inflicted upon him. The crime was grave because of the innocence of the victim. It was graver still because of the age of the murderers. The murder of a two-year-old elicits and reinforces conceptions of childhood innocence. The age of the murderers ruptured this conception. To be able to reconcile childhood innocence with childhood sinfulness requires the ability to hold two competing, contradictory conceptions alongside one another. To be able to do so requires letting go of any absolute truth claims about what childhood is. It requires a rejection, or at least a scepticism, of the use of psy-knowledges that seek to discover and employ these claims in debates about children's rights.

What makes children less culpable than adults for their crimes? Arguments about cognitive development aside, the lesser culpability lies in the profound faith that children offer possibilities for new beginnings and to deny this by sentencing them to death or to life in prison is to close off those possibilities. That children are held less culpable for crimes than adults is premised not only upon their lesser capacities for reason, maturity and autonomy, but also upon broader social and moral principles. As blank-slates, childhood is a period in which they can be educated and governed toward a good, adult life. A child's mistakes should not be fatal or defining, or preclude the possibilities of their future potential. In this sense, it is argued that children have a greater capacity for redemption. This argument can be sustained theoretically, or, with the right kind of evidence, empirically. However, it is not simply that children's minds are malleable in ways that adults' minds are not; it is also that society places a faith in the future of the next generation. We have faith that, irrespective of mistakes are made in childhood, children embody the promise of a new beginning.

To conceive of children's sinfulness, indeed of their supposed evil, is to also surrender their potential as good, future-adult citizens. The sinful child embodies the risk of liberalism's ever-possible failure. This is a possibility that is inherent in the freedom of liberal citizens. For example, a child who commits a crime produces a public interest in enacting forms of justice that go beyond redressing the wrong, to mitigating the risk that this liberal freedom presents. A child, in the process of becoming, has within them the possibility for great good and great evil. Hence, the governing of childhood serves to direct children toward their capacity for good. William Connolly describes this as the 'tragic possibility' of becoming.[4] In a world of becoming, Connolly is not explicitly interested in children. Rather, Connolly's world of becoming speaks to competing temporal experiences that shape the human estate. He argues that, 'These two dictates, engendering each other while remaining in tension, constitute the problematic of political action in a world of becoming.'[5] In processes of becoming, competing forces operate to create possibilities for good and bad, possibilities that hegemonic discourses consider valuable or troubling. In debates about children's rights, this complexity is sidestepped in favour of arguing about whether children are innocent, or evil, or blank-slates of our own making (whose successes and failures are, therefore, our own). The James Bulger murder ruptured established conceptions of childhood because it presented society with this tragic possibility of becoming. No longer could childhood be understood in simple and absolute terms.

In 2008, Australian artist Bill Henson's photographic exhibition depicted undressed girls and boys on the cusp of adolescence. On the one hand, this controversy dealt with children in the public realm: photographic images of children presented in an art exhibition. On the other hand, the debate focused on the most private of domains, that of sex and sexuality. In both public and private domains, the intelligibility of the child subjects was complicated. The dark mood of these images, coupled with the subjects in various states of undress and nakedness, elicited concerns from some about child pornography, exploitation and possible criminal acts. This public outcry was concisely expressed by then Prime Minister Kevin Rudd's assertion that the photographs were 'absolutely revolting'.[6] This sentiment was rationalized with arguments about the inability of these subjects to consent to the photographs being taken, and the argument that no parent or guardian could offer this consent on their behalf. Those who defended Bill Henson emphasized the "art" over the "pornography" of the images. In this debate, the child was positioned out of view and rendered unintelligible. As a result, the adult community was able to conduct a public debate about consent and a debate about art versus pornography that was removed from the experiences of the young people in the photographs. Debates about consent and about art versus pornography are informed by privileged knowledges of law, culture and sexuality that only adults are fully privy to. In debates about children's sexuality, what does consent have to do with the alleged sexual exploitation of the child? I have argued that it is not very much; and instead demonstrated that these debates focus more strongly upon adult anxieties about the loss of innocence and riskiness of sex.

The controversy of this debate was not simply about childhood innocence being threatened by premature sexualization. In Bill Henson's exhibition, innocence was complicated due to the subject's emerging sexuality. That is, rather than innocence being clearly tied to the supposed *asexuality* of childhood, in this exhibition this innocence had to be tied to "budding breasts". The subjects of his exhibition were no longer young children, but nor had they become adults. The physicality and sexuality depicted in the exhibition was literally one of becoming and they were, as a result, unintelligible beings. Subjects that are no longer young children, but not yet full mature adults, complicate our conceptions of childhood once again by revealing a moment of vulnerability and risk. These images were not sexual, but nor were they asexual. They were confronting because the images represented something between these two states, between the sexuality of adulthood that can be understood and known as normal, and the asexuality of childhood that cannot be challenged without giving rise to claims of abuse and exploitation. Bill Henson's photographs were unintelligible. Notwithstanding that the state of in-betweenness that characterizes adolescence is familiar to every pubescent young person, the Australian public failed to make sense of the emerging sexualities and competing conceptions of childhood that these images revealed.

Through debates about citizenship, sexuality and criminality, this book has attempted to stress how the focus of debates so easily shifts from children as present-beings, to children as future-adult subjects. This has otherwise been described as beings versus becomings. Children are a pre-cursor to the good, liberal, adult citizen. However, so long as they are this pre-cursor, they embody within them the possibility of failure. This, I argued in Chapter 2, is reflective of a liberal paradox: one that requires freedom to sustain its own legitimacy, but one that is placed at risk by that very freedom. In accounts of criminality, conceptions of childhood are revealed as simplistic and unhelpful in navigating the full possibilities of becoming. Children are innocents, but they are also sinners. Children are blank-slates, formed in our own making, but they can also do unspeakable, arguably evil, acts of violence. As much as any concern for sexual harm done to children weighs into debates about children's sexuality, I have argued that there is also a concern about what harm this does in adulthood. Children's experiences of sexuality have the potential to inhibit a healthy and rational sexuality in adulthood. In debates about children's rights, the child cannot be separated from the future-adult subject; efforts to do so fail to address the complexity of not only children's lives, but the complexity of our own adult world.

Childhood is both an age of perfection and imperfection. As an age of perfect innocence, any risk to this innocence or evidence of contrary behaviour disrupts how we can think and talk about childhood, children and their rights. As an age of imperfection, the discourses of children's rights are oriented toward ensuring that children develop into the good, if not perfect, liberal, adult citizens they are required to be. Whether as innocents, sinners or blank-slates, or in debates about voting, citizenship or political subjectivity more broadly, even in debates about criminality and sexuality, the ways in which we speak for, and about, children and childhood are necessarily tied to the politics of the adult world.

As mentioned, a key tension exists within political liberalism between the freedom and equality of individuals, and the risk inherent in this freedom. In Chapter 1, I argued that the liberal rights discourse presents a paternalistic paradigm, which answers grievances regarding a lack of freedom with claims to autonomy. This autonomy, when premised upon claims to reason and maturity, offers an insurance against the risk that freedom presents. In children's rights debates, this paradigm emerges as a debate between protection and autonomy claims.

Thus, the politics of these controversies is evident not in children as political beings, but in how these controversies reveal politics. Specifically, children are a constitutive Other of the political realm. This makes the political realm contingent upon the ever-changing, yet permanent, population of children but also constantly subject to its challenge. Indeed, a key problematic for Joanne Faulkner in her analysis of childhood innocence lies in the very impossibility of children's movement between the private and public realms; impossible, not due to physical limits, but conceptual limits. Once again, unaccompanied children in public spaces are unintelligible. This is the case, notwithstanding that children do enter public spaces unaccompanied, and that this can produce political encounters, as happened with Elizabeth Eckford. This book has argued that debates about what rights children should or should not have cannot fully grapple with this complexity so long as debates are tied to empirical and normative claims about children's reason, maturity and autonomy. For adults, autonomy does not preclude the ability and freedom to retreat to the private realm at will, a space in which they can be protected from the rigours of public and political life. However, for children, it does exactly that. To argue for children's autonomy risks casting children out into the public and political realm completely, surrendering any particular protections that might otherwise have been afforded to them. It is in this way that children's rights debates demand that children be *either* private subjects of home and family life, *or* public citizens of a political community. Where adults are free to do both, children can only be one or the other. For adults to desire and demand the respite afforded to them in the privacy of their own homes, to have relations of dependency and co-dependency, to be cared for and protected, does not make them ineligible for the rights that facilitate their movement into and legitimacy within public and political life. In children's rights debates, caught between protection and autonomy claims, it does.

To grapple with why children are understood differently from adults in these ways, I offered – in Chapter 2 – a deconstruction of social meanings of childhood. By raising three alternative meanings of childhood that are related to liberal political philosophy, these social meanings have been revealed as contingent upon broader political ideals and claims. The process of deconstruction presents a post-structuralist void of meaning. It is always tempting to fill such a void with new or alternative meanings of childhood. However, if I were to do so, I would be offering an alternative empirical account of who children are and what childhood is, or a normative account of who children should be and what childhood should mean. This would be inconsistent with the methodological framework of this book. Further, the risk of doing this would be the closure of this void as a space in which further interrogations and problematizations can be made about how these meanings and claims inform, shape and limit our understandings of childhood, children and children's rights. Having deconstructed social meanings of childhood, only to replace them with an empirical or normative account would, as I argued in my Introduction, undermine the very purpose of my methodological framework. It is for this reason that I have endeavoured not to fill this void.

The paternalistic paradigm remains in place, with a lack of reason, maturity and autonomy employed in various ways to make certain claims about children's rights: that children have no political interests separate from their parents and hence no claim to vote; that children are not rational enough to be held fully responsible for their crimes; and that children are not mature enough to make decisions over their bodies and sexual lives. I have not argued this paradigm out of relevance, but instead sought to reveal its effect on children's rights debates. Claims made within this paradigm are grounded in both empirical and normative assertions about who children are, what childhood is and who children and what childhood *should* be. I have argued that any such assertions can be difficult to sustain. This was concisely expressed by United States Supreme Court Justice Scalia's argument that to present evidence of the cognitive capacity of a child as mature enough to make a decision about an unwanted pregnancy is inconsistent with that same evidence being used to argue that the capacity of a child of the same age is too immature to be held responsible for murder. It could be argued, of course, that different kinds of decisions demand different cognitive capacities and that claims for rights have to be made in the context of specific problems that must be addressed. However, this overlooks the political function of rights: that rights are claimed and ascribed not only for the good of the individual, but also for the good of society.

This was explored more fully through the analysis of debates in Chapters 4, 5 and 6. In Chapter 7, I departed from the terms of children's rights debates bound, as they are, to claims of reason, maturity and autonomy in this paternalistic paradigm. I did so by exploring the governmentality of childhood. I did so not to argue that the governing of childhood is a necessarily good or bad thing. Instead, I argued that it is a political function that ensures children are governed toward their adulthood. This is what allows the re-reading of the three controversies first raised in my Introduction. In liberal societies, adulthood is fully autonomous and characterized by individual freedom. It is consistent, then, that children are governed until they can be self-governing. Their freedom and autonomy is restricted until such time that they can be deemed as able to conduct their freedom and autonomy in a way that is safe – for themselves, for others and for society as a whole. It is at this point that they are ushered into adulthood and gain admittance to the political realm.

It was in Chapter 6 that I first raised the idea that children's exclusion from the political realm makes politics possible. They are, in Mouffe's terms, a constitutive Other. In Arendt's terms, children offer natality. However, unlike other groups, the exclusion of children from the political realm is both temporary and permanent. That is, for children, so long as they grow into adulthood, it is a temporary exclusion. However, children as a group are also a permanent feature of our world, and so, in this sense, children are always part of the politically excluded. I have argued in this book that this exclusion makes politics possible through governmentality. Children's exclusion from the political realm allows external governing practices to operate without challenge, until children come to embody these practices within themselves. This maintains the freedom of the individual that is so crucial to political liberalism, while also ensuring against the risk inherent in this freedom. It is in this way that admittance to the political realm is not strictly premised upon reason, maturity and autonomy in any demonstrable sense. Instead, this admittance is granted on the assumption that the governing practices enacted during childhood are effective in producing good, liberal, adult citizens.

It is in this way that debates about children's rights come to be debates about these governing practices. Normative claims about what rights children should and should not have are not made independent of this governmentality. Normative claims both produce this governmentality, and are produced by it. Further, empirical evidence is not just a set of truth claims about the facts of childhood and the facts of who a child (generally, or specifically) is, but is a privileged form of knowledge that is complicit in governing practices. It is evidence that compels an analysis of whether children need protection, or whether children are better served by greater autonomy. It is evidence that circumvents the political, reiterating childhood as an apolitical, knowable fact. This book has sought to reveal this effect of governmentality in order to claim a politics of childhood that is not premised upon the reason, maturity or autonomy of the child, but upon the function the child plays in our liberal political community.

By undertaking an explicitly political analysis of children's rights debates, this book has revealed that claims to reason, maturity and autonomy operate discursively to inform what rights children should or should not have. It has also revealed that these discursive limits are tied to the ideal of a future-adult, liberal citizen. Thus, through protection rights claims, while the exclusion of children from the political is rationalized in the interests of children, it is also tied to broader concerns from the social and political community. Hence, the governing of childhood ensures that children do not pose a risk to themselves or society either now or in the future.

All this is not to say that I do not find some empirical claims about childhood more persuasive than others, or that I do not have normative positions of my own. However, it is important to acknowledge that whatever meaning of childhood I might be tempted to fill this void with (and tempted, I have been), will be one that necessarily reflects a set of power relations that determine the discourses of knowledge around childhood. It would only serve to further my own normative positions about what childhood should be, and in doing so would only reproduce my own positions about social and political life. To do so, is not necessarily bad or unproductive. It is, however, always limiting. In pursuing normative goals around children's rights, we will be limited in how we are able think of and talk about children. This book has offered an analysis of these limitations. For normative projects, this research should serve to signpost those limitations so that those projects can be conducted in a more critical and reflexive manner. For others, it should offer a point of departure that provides a new path of critique and challenge, not only for understandings of childhood but for understandings of the political also. Irrespective of the goals or nature of the research project, this book offers a radical critique of the children's rights discourse that must not be ignored.

Hannah Arendt's description of a child as both 'a new human being' and a 'becoming human being' articulates the inherent contradiction of our child and adult lives.[7] We are always here, and always still becoming. Upon adulthood, we have permission to enter the realm of public and political life. Our adulthood, however, does not cast us out into this realm without support or relationships. Rather, we are free to retreat to the private realm of our childhoods at will. And, in every return back to our private retreats of home and family life, we seek out new possibilities. Our autonomy is conducted in the freedom of our movement between these spaces. Our adulthood is not determined by our arrival at a final destination, but by the ever-present possibility of new beginnings. In debates about children's rights, the politics of becoming adult is a politics that is not tied to our childishness, but to the potential of our adult lives: one that is always becoming.

In debates about children's criminality, sexuality and citizenship, adults seeking to better advocate children's interests and rights use claims about their reason, maturity and autonomy. This book has argued that these kinds of claims are problematic because children are defined against reason, maturity and autonomy. That these key terms operate so powerfully upon debates about children's rights is attributed to their discursive function in liberal rights discourse more broadly. No doubt this has implications for children's rights claims. However, this book has argued that there are also important implications for how we understand the political. By problematizing the relationship between autonomy and adulthood, and the political realm as the end destination that marks our adulthood, this book has revealed children's place at the threshold of the political. Here, children serve to both constitute the political realm through their exclusion and remain as an ever-present challenge to its limits. This politics of becoming adult is the politics of children's lives. It is a politics that informs, shapes and limits how we are able to think about and debate childhood, children and their rights. The most important contribution this book has made is to open up the theoretical and conceptual space where this politics can be revealed, and new questions and interrogations made. These questions will no longer be about who children are or what childhood is. Instead, explicitly political questions will be posed: questions that are tied to how we know who children are, why we desire childhood to be a certain way, and the discursive limits that make such knowledge and desire possible.

Notes

1 I have written about this debate elsewhere: Nakata (2008). Also see Arendt (1959); Allen (2001).
2 Ibid.
3 My use of Hannah Arendt's distinction between the private and public realm is problematic from a feminist perspective. The faith that the private realm is one where political fights do not take place, or where there is a genuine possibility for rest and restoration has been highly and persuasively criticized by a range of scholars, particularly feminists. My continued use of Arendt's description of the private realm is not employed due a belief that the private realm is, in fact, always a place of respite but rather that the private realm conceived in this way informs our understanding of the political.
4 Connolly (2011: 6).
5 Ibid., 7.
6 Kevin Rudd, televised comment, reported in Westwood (2008).
7 Arendt (2006: 182).

Bibliography

Alderson, Priscilla (2007) 'Competent Children? Minors' Consent to Health Care Treatment and Research'. *Social Science & Medicine* 65: 2272–83.

Alderson, Priscilla, K. Sutcliffe and K. Curtis (2006) 'Children's Competence to Consent to Medical Treatment'. *Hastings Center Report* 36 (6): 25–34.

Allen, Danielle (2001) 'Law's Necessary Forcefulness: Ralph Ellison vs. Hannah Arendt on the Battle of Little Rock'. *Oklahoma City University Law Review* 26: 857–95.

Allen, Louisa (2005) *Sexual Subjects: Young People, Seuality and Education*. Basingstoke: Palgrave Macmillan.

Amnesty International (1990) 'Executions of Juveniles since 1990'. www.amnesty.org/en/death-penalty/executions-of-child-offenders-since-1990 (last accessed 16 Decmber 2014).

Amnesty International (2002) 'Children and the Death Penalty: Executions Worldwide since 1990'. 31, www.amnesty.org/en/library/info/ACT50/007/2002 (last accessed 16 Decmber 2014).

Archard, David (1998a) *Sexual Consent*. Oxford: Westview Press.

Archard, David (1998b) 'John Locke's Children'. In *The Philosopher's Child*, edited by Susan M. Turner and Gareth B. Matthews, 85–104. Rochester, NY: University of Rochester Press.

Archard, David (2004) *Children: Rights and Childhood*. 2nd edn. Abingdon, Oxon: Routledge.

Archard, David (2006) 'The Moral and Political Status of Children'. *Public Policy Research* 13 (1).

Archard, David and Colin M. Macleod (eds) (2002) *The Moral and Political Status of Children*. Oxford: Oxford University Press.

Archard, David and Marit Skivenes (2009) 'Balancing a Child's "Best Interests" and a Child's Views'. *International Journal of Children's Rights* 17: 1–12.

Arendt, Hannah (1951) *The Origins of Totalitarianism*. Orlando: Harcourt.

Arendt, Hannah (1959) 'Reflections on Little Rock'. *Dissent* 6 (1): 45–56.

Arendt, Hannah (1996) *Love and Saint Augustine*, eds. Joanna Vecchiarelli Scott and Judith Chelius Stark, Chicago: University of Chicago.

Arendt, Hannah (1998) *The Human Condition*. Chicago: University of Chicago.

Arendt, Hannah (2006) 'The Crisis in Education'. In *Between Past and Future*, 170–93. London: Penguin.

Ariès, Phillipe (1962) *Centuries of Childhood: A Social History of Family Life*. Translated by Robert Baldick. London: Jonathon Cape.

Arneil, Barbara (2002) 'Becoming Versus Being: A Critical Analysis of the Child in

Liberal Theory'. In *The Moral and Political Status of Children*, edited by David Archard and Colin M. Macleod. Oxford: Oxford University Press.

Australian Institute of Criminology (2005) 'Crime Facts Info: The age of criminal responsibility', edited by Australian Institute of Criminology. Canberra: AIC Press.

Australian Law Reform Commission (2010) 'Family Violence – a National Legal Reponse'.

Australia 2020 Youth Summit (2008) 'Australia 2020 Youth Summit Communique'. Canberra.

Baumeister, Andrea T. (2000) *Liberalism and the Politics of Difference*. Edinburgh: Edinburgh University Press.

Bedell, Geraldine (1993) 'James Bulger: The Death of Innocence'. *Independent*, 28 November.

Benhabib, Seyla (1992) *Situating the Self: Gender, Community and Postmodernism in Contemporary Ethics*. New York: Routledge.

Bevir, Mark (1999) 'Foucault and Critique: Deploying Agency against Autonomy'. *Political Theory* 27 (1): 65–84.

Bhabha, Jacqueline (2009) 'Arendt's Children: Do Today's Migrant Children Have a Right to Have Rights?' *Human Rights Quarterly* 31 (2): 410–51.

Bhabha, Jacqueline (ed.) (2011) *Children without a State: A Global Human Rights Challenge*. Cambridge, MA: The MIT Press.

Bignell, Jonathon (2002) 'Children's Media Culture as Postmodern Culture'. In *Postmodern Media Culture*, 114–38. Edinburgh: Edinburgh University Press.

Blackstone, William (2001) 'Book IV, Chapter 2, of the Persons Capable of Committing Crimes'. In *Blackstone's Commentaries on the Laws of England* [1765], edited by Wayne Morrison. London: Cavendish.

Bohman, James (2011) 'Children and the Rights of Citizens: Non-Domination and Intergenerational Justice'. *Annals of the American Academy of Political and Social Science* 633: 128–40.

Bradley, Lisa (2003) 'The Age of Criminal Responsibility Revisited'. *Deakin Law Review* 8 (1).

Brennan, Samantha (2002) 'Children's Choices or Children's Interests: Which Do Their Rights Protect?' In *The Moral and Political Status of Children*, edited by David Archard and Colin M. Macleod. Oxford: Oxford University Press.

Brennan, Samantha and Robert Noggle (1998) 'John Rawls's Children'. In *The Philosopher's Child: Critical Perspectives in the Western Tradition*, edited by Gareth B. Matthews and Susan M. Turner, 203–32. Rochester: University of Rochester Press.

Brighouse, Harry (2002) 'What Rights (If Any) Do Children Have?'. In *The Moral and Political Status of Children*, edited by David Archard and Colin M. Macleod, 31–52. Oxford: Oxford University Press.

Brownlie, Julie (2001) 'The "Being-Risky" Child: Governing Childhood and Sexual Risk'. *Sociology* 35 (2): 519–37.

Buckingham, David and Sara Bragg (2004) *Young People, Sex and the Media*. London: Palgrave Macmillan.

Burman, Erica (1994) *Deconstructing Developmental Psychology*. 1st edn. London: Routledge.

Butler, Judith (2004) *Undoing Gender*. New York: Routledge.

Cauffman, Elizabeth, Jennifer Woolard and N. Dickon Reppucci (1999) 'Justice for Juveniles: New Perspectives on Adolescents' Competence and Culpability'. *Quinnipiac Law Review* 18.

Chesterman, John (2001) 'Sellars V Coleman: The Limits of Free Speech'. *Australian Journal of Political Science* 36 (2): 373–5.

Chesterman, John (2005) *Civil Rights: How Indigenous Australians Won Formal Equality*. St Lucia: University of Queensland Press.

Chesterman, John and Brian Galligan (1997) *Citizens without Rights: Aborigines and Australian Citizenship*. Cambridge: Cambridge University Press.

Christiano, Tom (2004) 'Authority'. *Stanford Encyclopedia of Philosophy Online*, http://plato.stanford.edu/entries/authority (last accessed 30 July 2014).

Christman, John (2003) 'Autonomy in Moral and Political Philosophy'. *Stanford Encyclopedia of Philosophy Online*, http://plato.stanford.edu/entries/autonomy-moral (last accessed 30 July 2014).

Cockburn, Tom (2013) *Rethinking Children's Citizenship*. Basingtoke: Palgrave Macmillan.

Cohen, Elizabeth F. (2005) 'Neither Seen nor Heard: Children's Citizenship in Contemporary Democracies'. *Citizenship Studies* 9 (2): 221–40.

Cohen, Elizabeth F. (2009) *Semi-Citizenship in Democratic Politics*. Cambridge: Cambridge University Press.

Cohen, Howard (1980) *Equal Rights for Children*. Totowa, Canada: Littlefield, Adams & Co.

Cohen, Stanley (1972) *Folk Devils and Moral Panics: The Creation of the Mods and Rockers*. 1st edn. London: Macgibbon and Kee.

Cohen, Stanley (2002) *Folk Devils and Moral Panics: The Creation of the Mods and Rockers*. 3rd edn. London: Routledge.

Connolly, William (2011) *A World of Becoming*. Durham, NC: Duke University Press.

Cooney, William, Barry Trunk and Charles Cross (1993) *From Plato to Piaget: The Greatest Educational Theorists from across the Centuries and around the World*. Lanham, MD: University Press of America.

Cowden, Mhairi (2011) 'What's Love Got to Do with It? Why a Child Does Not Have a Right to Be Loved'. *Critical Review of International Social and Political Philosophy*: 1–21.

Crimes Act 1958 (Victoria, Australia).

Criminology, Australian Institute of (2005) 'Crime Facts Info: The Age of Criminal Responsibility', edited by Australian Institute of Criminology. Canberra: AIC Press.

Critchley, Cheryl (2009) 'Mums Outraged over Saucy Messages on Infant Clothes'. *Herald Sun*, 22 July.

Dean, Mitchell (2010) *Governmentality*. London: SAGE Publications.

Department of Prime Minister and Cabinet (Australia) (2009) 'Electoral Reform Green Paper: Strengthening Australia's Democracy'. Canberra, September.

Dewey, John (1966) *Democracy and Education: An Introduction to the Philosophy of Education*. 1st edn. New York: Free Press.

Dewey, John (1998) 'The Moral Training Given by the School Community [1909]'. In *The Essential Dewey, Vol. 1: Pragmatism, Education, Democracy*, edited by Larry A. Hickman and Thomas M. Alexander. Bloomington: Indiana University Press.

Dewey, John (1998a) 'My Pedagogic Creed [1897] '. In *The Essential Dewey, Vol. 1: Pragmatism, Education, Democracy*, edited by Larry A. Hickman and Thomas M. Alexander. Bloomington: Indiana University Press.

Dewey, John (1998b) 'The Need for a Recovery of Philosophy [1917]'. In *The Essential Dewey, Vol. 1: Pragmatism, Education, Democracy*, edited by Larry A. Hickman and Thomas M. Alexander, 46–70. Bloomington: Indiana University Press.

Dewey, John (2011) *The Child and the Curriculum, Including the School and Society*. New York: Cosimo.

Dobrowolsky, Alexandra (2002) 'Rhetoric Versus Reality: The Figure of the Child and New Labour's Strategic 'Social Investment State''. *Studies in Political Economy* 69: 43–73.

Doherty, Elissa (2010) 'Kids' Fashion Trends Concern Child Advocates'. *Herald Sun*, 5 October.

Dolgin, Janet L. (1999) 'The Age of Autonomy: Legal Reconceputalisations of Childhood'. *Quinnipiac Law Review* 18: 421–50.

Douzinas, Costas (2000) *The End of Human Rights: Critical Legal Thought at the Turn of the Century*. Portland: Hart Publishing.

Durham, M. Gigi (2009) *The Lolita Effect: The Media Sexualisation of Young Girls and What We Can Do About It*. New York: Overlook Press.

Dworkin, Gerald (2005) 'Paternalism'. *Stanford Encyclopedia of Philosophy Online*, http://plato.stanford.edu/entries/paternalism (last accessed 30 July 2014).

Earls, Felton J. (2011) 'Special Issue: The Child as a Citizen'. *Annals of the American Academy of Political and Social Science* 633.

Edney, Richard and Mirko Bagaric (2007) *Australian Sentencing*. Cambridge: Cambridge University Press.

Eekelaar, John (1986) 'The Emergence of Children's Rights'. *Oxford Journal of Legal Studies* 6 (2): 161–82.

Eekelaar, John (1994) 'The Interests of the Child and the Child's Wishes: The Role of Dynamic Self-Determinism'. *International Journal of Law and the Family* 8: 42–61.

English, Jane (1977) 'Justice between Generations'. *Philosophical Studies*: 91–104.

Ennew, Judith (2008) 'Children as "Citizens" of the United Nations'. In *Children and Citizenship*, edited by Antonella Invernizzi and Jane Williams, 66–78. London: SAGE.

Farson, Richard (1974) *Birthrights*. New York: Macmillan.

Faulkner, Joanne (2008) 'The "Innocence of Victimhood" Versus the "Innocence of Becoming": Nietszche, 9/11 and the "Falling Man"'. *Journal of Nietszche Studies* 35/36: 67–85.

Faulkner, Joanne (2011) *The Importance of Being Innocent: Why We Worry About Children*. Cambridge: Cambridge University Press.

Feinberg, Joel (1980) 'A Child's Right to an Open Future'. In *Whose Child? Parental Rights, Parental Authority and State Power*, edited by Hugh LaFollette William Aiken, 124–53. Totowa, NJ: Littlefield, Adams, & Co.

Firestone, Shulamith (1970) *The Dialectic of Sex: The Case for Feminist Revolution*. London: Jonathon Cape.

Flynn, Thomas (2003) 'Foucault's Mapping of History'. In *The Cambridge Companion to Foucault*, edited by Gary Gutting, 29–48. Cambridge: Cambridge University Press.

Fortin, Jane (1998) *Children's Rights and the Developing Law*. London: Butterworths.

Foster, Jonathon (1993) 'James Bulger Suffered Multiple Fractures'. *Independent*, 10 November.

Foucault, Michel (ed.) (1975) *I, Pierre Rivière, Having Slaughtered My Mother, My Sister, and My Brother ...: A Case of Parricide in the 19th Century*. Lincoln: University of Nebraska Press.

Foucault, Michel (1978) *History of Sexuality, Vol. 1: The Will to Knowledge*. London: Penguin.

Foucault, Michel (1980) *Power/Knowledge: Selected Interviews and Other Writings 1972–1977*. Edited by Colin Gordon. Brighton, Sussex: Harvester.

Focault, Michel (1984) 'Right of Death and Power over Life'. In *The Foucault Reader*, edited by Paul Rabinow, 258–72. New York: Pantheon Books.

Foucault, Michel (1985) *The History of Sexuality, Vol. 2: The Use of Pleasure*. London: Penguin.

Foucault, Michel (1986) *History of Sexuality, Vol. 3: The Care of the Self*. London: Penguin.

Foucault, Michel (1991) *Discipline and Punish: The Birth of the Prison*. Translated by Alan Sheridan. London: Penguin.

Foucault, Michel (1994a) *The Birth of the Clinic: An Archaeology of Medical Perception*. New York: Vintage Books.

Foucault, Michel (1994b) 'Governmentality'. In *Power: Essential Works of Foucault 1954–1984*, edited by James D. Faubion, 201–22. London: Penguin Books.

Foucault, Michel (1994c) 'The Subject and Power'. In *Power: Essential Works of Foucault 1954–1984*, edited by James D. Faubion, 326–48. London: Penguin Books.

Foucault, Michel (1994d) 'Truth and Power'. In *Power: Essential Works of Foucault 1954–1984*, edited by James Faubion, 111–33. London: Penguin Books.

Foucault, Michel (1994e) 'What is an Author?' In *The Foucault Reader*, edited by Paul Rabinow, 101–20. London: Penguin Books.

Foucault, Michel (2002a) *The Archaeology of Knowledge*. Translated by A. M. Sheridan Smith. London: Routledge Classics.

Foucault, Michel (2002b) *The Order of Things: An Archaeology of the Human Sciences*. London: Routledge Classics.

Foucault, Michel (2006) *History of Madness*. Edited by Jean Khalfa. London: Routledge.

Foucault, Michel (2007) 'What Is Enlightenment?' In *The Politics of Truth: Michel Foucault*, edited by Sylvère Lotringer. Los Angeles: Semiotext(e).

Foucault, Michel and Paul Rabinow (1984) *The Foucault Reader*. 1st edn. New York: Pantheon Books.

Fraser, Nancy (1989) *Unruly Practices: Power, Discourse and Gender in Contemporary Social Theory*. Minneapolis: University of Minnesota Press.

Freedan, Michael (2005) 'What Should the "Political" in Political Theory Explore?' *The Journal of Political Philosophy* 13 (2): 113–134.

Freeman, Michael (1997a) *Taking Children's Rights More Seriously*. The Hague: Kluwer.

Freeman, Michael (1997b) 'The James Bulger Tragedy: Childish Innocence and the Construction of Guilt'. In *Governing Childhood*, edited by Anne McGillivray, 115–34. Aldershot, England: Ashgate.

Freeman, Michael (1992) 'Taking Children's Rights More Seriously'. *International Journal of Law and the Family* 6: 52–71.

Gale, Julie (n.d.) 'Kids Free 2b Kids – Home'. Website: www.kf2bk.com (last accessed 16 December 2014).

Getis, Victoria (2000) *The Juvenile Court and the Progressives*. Urbana, Illinois: University of Illinois Press.

Gillick v. *West Norfolk and Wisbech Area Health Authority* (1985) 3 All ER 402.

Gilligan, Carol (1982) *In a Different Voice: Psychological Theory and Women's Development*. Cambridge, MA: Harvard University Press.

Golder, Ben and Peter Fitzpatrick (2009) *Foucault's Law*. Abingdon, Oxon: Routledge.

Goode, Erich, and Ben-Yehuda Nachman (1994) *Moral Panics: The Social Construction of Deviance*. Maldern, MA: Blackwell.

Goodin, Robert E. and Diane Gibson (1997) 'Rights, Young and Old'. *Oxford Journal of Legal Studies* 17 (2): 185–203.

Graham v. *Florida* (2010) 560 United States Reports unbound.

Gribbin, Christoper (2004) 'Lowering the Voting Age'. Edited by Victorian Electoral Commission. Melbourne.

Guggenheim, Martin (2005) *What's Wrong with Children's Rights*. Cambridge, MA: Harvard University Press.

Haag, Pamela (1999) *Consent: Sexual Rights and the Transformation of American Liberalism*. Ithaca, NY: Cornell University Press.

Hall, Stuart (1978) *Policing the Crisis: Mugging, the State, and Law and Order*. London: Palgrave Macmillan.

Hartman, Saidaya V. (1996) *Scenes of Subjection: Terror, Slavery, and Self-Making in Nineteenth-Century America*. New York: Oxford University Press.

Hartsock, Nancy (1990) 'Foucault on Power: A Theory for Women?' In *Feminism/Postmodernism*, edited by Linda J. Nicholson. New York: Routledge.

Hathaway, Oona (2002) 'Do Human Rights Treaties Make a Difference?' *Yale Law Journal* 111: 1935.

Hawes, Joseph M. (1991) *The Children's Rights Movement: A History of Advocacy and Protection*. Boston: Twayne.

Haydon, Deena and Phil Scraton (2000) 'Condemn a Little More, Understand a Little Less: The Political Context and Rights' Implications of the Domestic and European Rulings in the Venables–Thompson Case'. *Journal of Law and Society* 27 (3): 416–48.

Hekman, Susan J. (ed.) (1996) *Feminist Interpretations of Michel Foucault*. Philadelphia, PA: The Pennsylvania State University Press.

Held, David (1987) *Models of Democracy*. Stanford, CA: Stanford University Press.

Hindess, Barry (1997) 'Politics and Governmentality'. *Economy and Society* 26 (2): 257–72.

Hindess, Barry (2001) 'The Liberal Government of Unfreedom'. *Alternatives* 26: 93–111.

Hirschel, J. David and William Wakefield (1995) *Criminal Justice in England and the United* States. Westport, CT: Praeger.

Honneth, Axel (1995) *The Struggle for Recognition: The Moral Grammar of Social Conflicts*. Translated by Joel Anderson. Cambridge, MA: Polity Press.

House of Represenatatives Parliament of Australia (1902) 'Hansard'. 11937. Canberra: Government Printer.

Hymowitz, Kay (1998) 'Kids Today Are Growing up Way Too Fast'. *Wall St Journal*, 28 October.

In Re A (1996) 16 Family Law Report 715.

In Re Gault (1967) 387 United States Reports 1.

Invernizzi, Antonella and Brian Milne (2005) *Children's Citizenship: An Emergent Discourse on the Rights of the Child*. Delhi: Kamla-Raj.

Invernizzi, Antonella and Jane Williams (2008) *Children and Citizenship*. London: SAGE.

JDB v. *North Carolina* (2011) 564 United States Reports unbound.

James, Allison (2011) 'To Be (Come) or Not to Be (Come): Understanding Children's Citizenship'. *Annals of the American Academy of Political and Social Science* 633: 167–79.

James, Allison and Chris Jenks (1996) 'Public Perceptions of Childhood Criminality'. *The British Journal of Sociology* 47 (2): 315–31.

Jeffreys, Sheila (1997) 'Sexual Violence, Feminist Human Rights and the Omission of Prostitution'. In *The Idea of Prostitution*, 275–305. Melbourne: Spinifex.

Jeffreys, Sheila (2000) 'Challenging the Child/Adult Distinction in Theory and Practice on Prostitution'. *International Feminist Journal of Politics* 2 (3): 359–79.

Jeffreys, Sheila (2005) *Beauty and Misogyny: Harmful Cultural Practices in the West.* London: Routledge.

Jeffreys, Sheila (2006) 'Judicial Child Abuse: The Family Court of Australia, Gender Identity Disorder, and the "Alex" Case'. *Women's Studies International Forum* 29: 1–12.

Jenks, Chris (2005) *Childhood.* London: Routledge.

Kant, Immanuel (1990) 'Enlightenment as Autonomy'. In *The Enlightenment and Its Shadows*, edited by Peter Hulme and Ludmilla Jordanova. London: Routledge.

Kant, Immanuel (1996) 'An Answer to the Question: What Is Enlightenment? [1684]' In *Practical Philosophy: Immanuel Kant*, edited by Mary J. Gregor. Cambridge: Cambridge University Press.

Kant, Immanuel (1998) 'Critique of Pure Reason'. Edited by Paul Guyer and Allen W. Wood. Cambridge: Cambridge University Press.

Kant, Immanuel (2004) 'Was Ist Aufklärung? [1784]'. In *The Politics of Truth: Michel Foucault*, edited by Sylvère Lotringer. Los Angeles: Semiotext(e).

King, Michael and Christine Piper (1995) *How the Law Thinks about Children*, 2nd edn. Aldershot: Arena.

Kociumbas, Jan (1997) *Australian Childhood: A History.* St Leonards, NSW: Allen & Unwin.

Krinsky, Charles (ed.) (2008) *Moral Panics over Contemporary Children and Youth.* Surrey: Ashgate.

Kulynych, Jessica (2001) 'No Playing in the Public Sphere: Democratic Theory and the Exclusion of Children'. *Social Theory and Practice* 27 (2): 231–64.

Lacey, Nicola (1998) *Unspeakable Subjects: Feminist Essays in Legal and Social Theory.* Oxford: Hart.

Lavaque-Manty, Mika (2006) 'Kant's Children'. *Social Theory and Practice* 32 (3): 365–88.

Lee, Nick (2001) *Childhood and Society: Growing up in an Age of Uncertainty.* Buckingham: Open University Press.

Levy, K. S (1998) 'The Australian Juvenile Justice System: Legal and Social Science Dimensions'. *Queensland Law Review* 18.

Liao, Matthew (2006) 'The Right of Children to Be Loved'. *Journal of Political Philosophy* 4: 420–40.

Linde, Robyn (2014) 'The Globalization of Childhood: The International Diffusion of Norms and Law against the Child Death Penalty'. *European Journal of International Relations* 20 (2).

Lister, Ruth (2007) 'Why Citizenship: Where, When and How Children?' *Theoretical Inquiries in Law* 8: 693–718.

Little, Adrian (2012) 'Political Action, Error and Failure: The Epistemological Limits of Complexity'. *Political Studies* (forthcoming).

Locke, John (1993) *Two Treatises of Government.* London: Everyman.

Locke, John (1996) *Some Thoughts Concerning Education.* Edited by Ruth W. Grant and Nathan Tarcov. Indianapolis: Hackett.

Machiavelli, Niccolo (1984) *The Prince.* Translated by Peter Bondanella and Mark Musa. Oxford: Oxford University Press.

Maguire, Emily (2010) 'Naomi Wolf on the Porn Myth'. *The Age.* 3 May.

Manson, Neil C. and Onora O'Neill (2007) *Rethinking Informed Consent in Bioethics.* Cambridge: Cambridge University Press.

Marshall, Dominique (1999) 'The Construction of Children as an Object of International

Relations: The Declaration of Children's Rights and the Child Welfare Committee of the League of Nations'. *International Journal of Children's Rights* 7.

Marshall, T. H. (1950) *Citizenship and Social Class, and Other Essays*. Cambridge: Cambridge University Press.

McGillivray, Anne (ed.) (1997) *Governing Childhood*. Aldershot: Dartmouth.

Mehta, Uday (1992) *The Anxiety of Freedom*. Ithaca, NY: Cornell University Press.

Melton, Gary B. (1983) 'Decision Making by Children: Psychological Risks and Benefits'. In *Children's Competence to Consent*, edited by G. P. Koocher, Gary B. Melton and M. J. Saks, 21–37. New York: Plenum Press.

Melton, Gary B., G. P. Koocher and M. J. Saks (eds) (1983) *Children's Competence to Consent*. New York: Plenum Press.

Miranda v. *Arizona* (1996) 384 United States Reports 436.

Milne, Brian (2013) *The History and Theory of Children's Citizenship in Contemporary Societies*. Dordrecht, The Netherlands: Springer.

Morss, John (1995) *The Biologising of Childhood: Developmental Psychology and the Darwinian Myth*. Hove: Erlbaum.

Mouffe, Chantal (1993) *The Return of the Political*. New York: Verso.

Mouffe, Chantal (2000) *The Democratic Paradox*. London: Verso.

Mouffe, Chantal (2005) *On the Political*. Abingdon: Routledge.

Muncie, John (2009) *Youth and Crime*. 3rd edn. London: SAGE Publications.

Musgrove, Frank (1964) *Youth and Social Order*. Bloomington: Indiana University Press.

Nadesan, Majia Holmer (2010) 'Governing Childhood into the 21st Century: Biopolitical Technologies of Childhood Management and Education'. E-book: Palgrave Macmillan.

Nakata, Martin (2007) *Disciplining the Savages, Savaging the Disciplines*. Canberra: Aboriginal Studies Press.

Nakata, Sana (2008) 'Elizabeth Eckford's Appearance at Little Rock: The Possibility of Children's Political Agency'. *Politics* 28 (1): 19–25.

NSW Law Reform Commission (2008) 'Young People and Consent to Health Care', 83–7. Sydney: New South Wales Law Reform Commission.

Nussbaum, Martha (2007) *Frontiers of Justice: Disability, Nationality, Species Membership*. Cambridge, MA: Harvard University Press.

O'Neill, Onora (1988) 'Children's Rights and Children's Lives'. *Ethics* 98: 445–63.

O'Neill, Onora (1989) *Constructions of Reason: Explorations of Kant's Practical Philosophy*. New York: Cambridge University Press.

O'Neill, Onora (1990) 'Enlightenment as Autonomy'. In *The Enlightenment and Its Shadows*, edited by Peter Hulme and Ludmilla Jordanova, 186–99. London: Routledge.

O'Neill, Onora (1992) "Children's Rights and Children's Lives'. *International Journal of Law and the Family* 6: 24–42.

Okin, Susan Moller (1979) 'Rousseau's Natural Woman'. *The Journal of Politics* 41: 393–416.

Okin, Susan Moller (1989) 'Reason and Feeling in Thinking About Justice'. *Ethics* 99: 229–49.

Okin, Susan Moller (1994) 'Political Liberalism, Justice and Gender'. *Ethics* 105: 23–43.

Oswell, David (2013) *The Agency of Children: From Family to Global Human Rights*, 38–42. Cambridge: Cambridge University Press.

Paras, Eric (2006) *Foucault 2.0: Beyond Power and Knowledge*. New York: Other Press.

Parker, Graham (1976) 'The Juvenile Court Movement'. *University of Toronto Law Journal* 26: 140–72.

Parlett, Kate and Kylie-Maree Weston-Scheuber (2004) 'Consent to Treatment for Transgender and Intersex Children'. *Deakin Law Review* 9 (2): 376–97.

Parliament of Australia, House of Representatives (1902) *Hansard*, p. 11937. Canberra: Government Printer.

Piaget, Jean (2001) *The Psychology of Intelligence*. London: Routledge Classics.

Piaget, Jean (2002) *The Language and Thought of the Child*. 3rd edn. London: Routledge Classics.

Pilcher, Jane and Stephen Wagg (1996) *Thatcher's Children? Politics, Childhood and Society in the 1980s and 1990s*. London: Falmer Press.

Powell, Anastasia (2007) 'Youth "at Risk" '. *Youth Studies Australia* 26 (4): 21–7.

Powell, Anastasia (2008) 'Amor Fati? Gender Habitus and Young People's Negotiation of (Hetero)Sexual Consent'. *Journal of Sociology* 44 (2): 167–84.

Powell, Anastasia (2010) *Sex, Power and Consent*. Cambridge: Cambridge University Press.

Prokhovnik, Raia (2009) ' "Men Are Not Born Fit for Citizenship, but Must Be Made So": Spinoza and Citizenship'. *Citizenship Studies* 4: 413–29.

Purdy, Laura (1998) 'Shulamith Firestone's Children'. In *The Philosopher's Child: Critical Perspectives in the Western Tradition*, edited by Gareth B. Matthews and Susan M. Turner, 189–202. Rochester, NY: University of Rochester Press.

R v. *Brown* (1994) 1 AC 212.

Rabinow, Paul (ed.) (1984) *The Foucault Reader*. London: Penguin.

Rancière, Jacques (2004) 'Who Is the Subject of the Rights of Man?' *South Atlantic Quarterly* 103 (2/3): 298–310.

Rancière, Jacques (2010) *Dissensus: On Politics and Aesthetics*. Translated by Steven Corcoran. Edited by Steven Corcoran. London: Continuum.

Rawls, John (1971) *A Theory of Justice*. Cambridge, MA: Belknap Press of Harvard University Press.

Rawls, John (1993) *Political Liberalism*. New York: Columbia University Press.

Rawls, John (2005) *Political Liberalism*. Expanded ed. Columbia Classics in Philosophy. New York: Columbia University Press.

Re Alex (2004) 180 Federal Law Review 89.

Reath, Andrews (2006) *Agency and Autonomy in Kant's Moral Theory*. Oxford: Oxford University Press.

Rehfeld, Andrew (2011) 'The Child as Democratic Citizen'. *The Annals of the American Academy of Political and Social Science* 633: 141–66.

Roche, Jeremy (1999) 'Children: Rights, Participation and Citizenship'. *Childhood* 6 (4): 475–93.

Roche v. *Electoral Commissioner* (2007) 223 Commonwealth Law Reports 162.

Rodham, Hilary (1973) 'Children under the Law'. *Harvard Educational Review* 43 (4): 487–514.

Roper v. *Simmons* (2005) 543 United States Reports 551.

Rose, Nikolas (1989) *Governing the Soul: The Shaping of the Private Self*. London: Routledge.

Rose, Nikolas (1999) *Governing the Soul: The Shaping of the Private Self*. 2nd edn. London: Free Association Press.

Rousseau, Jean-Jacques (1986) *The Social Contract, and, Discourses*. Edited by John C. Hall, G. D. H. Cole and J. H. Brumfitt. Everyman Classics. London: Dent.

Rousseau, Jean-Jacques (1993) *Émile*. Translated by Barbara Foxley. London: Everyman.

Rubenstein, Kim, and Jacqueline Field (2013) 'Conceptualising Australian Citizenship for Children: A Human Rights Perspective'. *Australian International Law Journal* 20: 77.

Rush, Emma and Andrea LaNauze (2006) 'Corporate Paedophilia: Sexualisation of Children in Australia'. Australia: The Australia Institute.

Said, Edward W. (1978) *Orientalism*. London: Penguin.

Sawicki, Jana (1994) 'Foucault, Feminism and Questions of Identity'. In *The Cambridge Companion to Focault*, edited by Gary Gutting, 286–310. Cambridge: Cambridge University Press.

Schaeffer, Denise (1998) 'Reconsidering the Role of Sophie in Rousseau's "Emile"'. *Polity* 30 (4): 607–26.

Schmitt, Carl (1996) *The Concept of the Political*, edited by George Schwab. Chicago: University of Chicago Press.

Secretary, Department of Health and Community Services v JWB and SMB ('Marion's Case') (1992) 175 Commonwealth Law Reports 218.

Sereny, Gitta (1995) *The Case of Mary Bell: A Portrait of a Child Who Murdered*. London: Random House.

Shaw, Karena (2008) *Indigeneity and Political Theory: Sovereignty and the Limits of the Political*. Oxon: Routledge.

Simon, Jonathon (2004) '"A Situation So Unique That It Will Probably Never Repeat Itself": Madness, Youth and Homicide in Twentieth-Century Criminal Jurisprudence'. In *Law's Madness*, edited by L. Douglas, A. Sarat and M. M. Umphrey, 79–118. Ann Arbor: The University of Michigan.

Spencer, John R. and Rohna H. Flin (1993) *The Evidence of Children: The Law and Psychology*. 2nd edn. London: Blackstone.

Springhall, John (2008) 'The Monsters Next Door: What Made Them Do It? Moral Panics over the Causes of High School Multiple Shootings (Notably Columbine)." In *Moral Panics over Contemporary Children and Youth*, edited by Charles Krinsky. Surrey: Ashgate.

Stasiulis, Daiva (2002) 'The Active Child Citizen: Lessons from Canadian Policy and the Children's Movement'. *Citizenship Studies* 6 (4): 507–38.

Stortz, Mary Ellen (2001) '"Where or When was your servant innocent?": Augustine on childhood'. In Marcia J. Bunge (ed.) *The Child in Christian Thought*, edited by Marcia J. Bunge, 78–102, Grand Rapids: W. B. Eerdmans.

Tadros, Victor (2006) 'Rape without Consent'. *Oxford Journal of Legal Studies*. 26 (3): 515–43.

Taylor, Affrica (2010) 'Troubling Childhood Innocence: Reframing the Debate over the Media Sexualisation of Children'. *Australiasian Journal of Early Childhood* 35 (1): 48–57.

Taylor, Nicola and Anne B. Smith (2009) *Children as Citizens?: International Voices*. Dunedin, New Zealand: Otago University Press.

The Senate Standing Committee on Environment, Communications and the Arts ('SCECA') (2008) 'Australian Senate Inquiry into the Sexualisation of Childhood in the Media'. Canberra.

Tobin, John (2004) 'Partners Worth Courting: The Relationship between the Media and the Convention on the Rights of the Child'. *International Journal of Children's Rights* 12: 139–67.

Tyler, Meagan (2010) 'The Politics of Pornography and Pornographication in Australia'. In *Australian Political Studies Association*. The University of Melbourne.

United Nations (1989) 'Convention on the Rights of the Child'. United Nations General Assembly.

Weale, Albert (1999) *Democracy*. London: Macmillan Press.

Weiss, Penny A. (1990) 'Sex, Freedom and Equality in Rousseau's "Emile"'. *Polity* 22 (4): 603–25.

Weithman, Paul J. (1992) 'Augustine and Aquinas on Original Sin and the Function of Political Authority'. *Journal of the History of Philosophy* 30 (3): 353–76.

Westwood, Matthew (2008) 'PM Says Henson Photos Have No Artistic Merit'. *The Australian*, 23 May.

Wollstonecraft, Mary and Ulrich H. Hardt (1982) *A Critical Edition of Mary Wollstonecraft's a Vindication of the Rights of Woman, with Strictures on Political and Moral Subjects*. Troy, NY: Whitston Publishing Co.

Wyness, Michael (2006) *Childhood and Society: An Introduction to the Sociology of Childhood*. Hampshire, UK: Palgrave Macmillan.

Young, Iris Marion (1989) 'Polity and Group Difference: A Critique of the Ideal of Citizenship'. *Ethics* 99: 250–74.

Young, Iris Marion (1990) *Justice and the Politics of Difference*. Princeton: Princeton University Press.

Zweig, Arnulf (1998) 'Immanuel Kant's Children'. In *The Philosopher's Child: Critical Perspectives in the Western Tradition*, edited by Susan M. Turner and Gareth B. Matthews, 121–36. Rochester, NY: University of Rochester Press.

Index

For Product Safety Concerns and Information please contact our EU
representative GPSR@taylorandfrancis.com
Taylor & Francis Verlag GmbH, Kaufingerstraße 24, 80331 München, Germany